AF333754

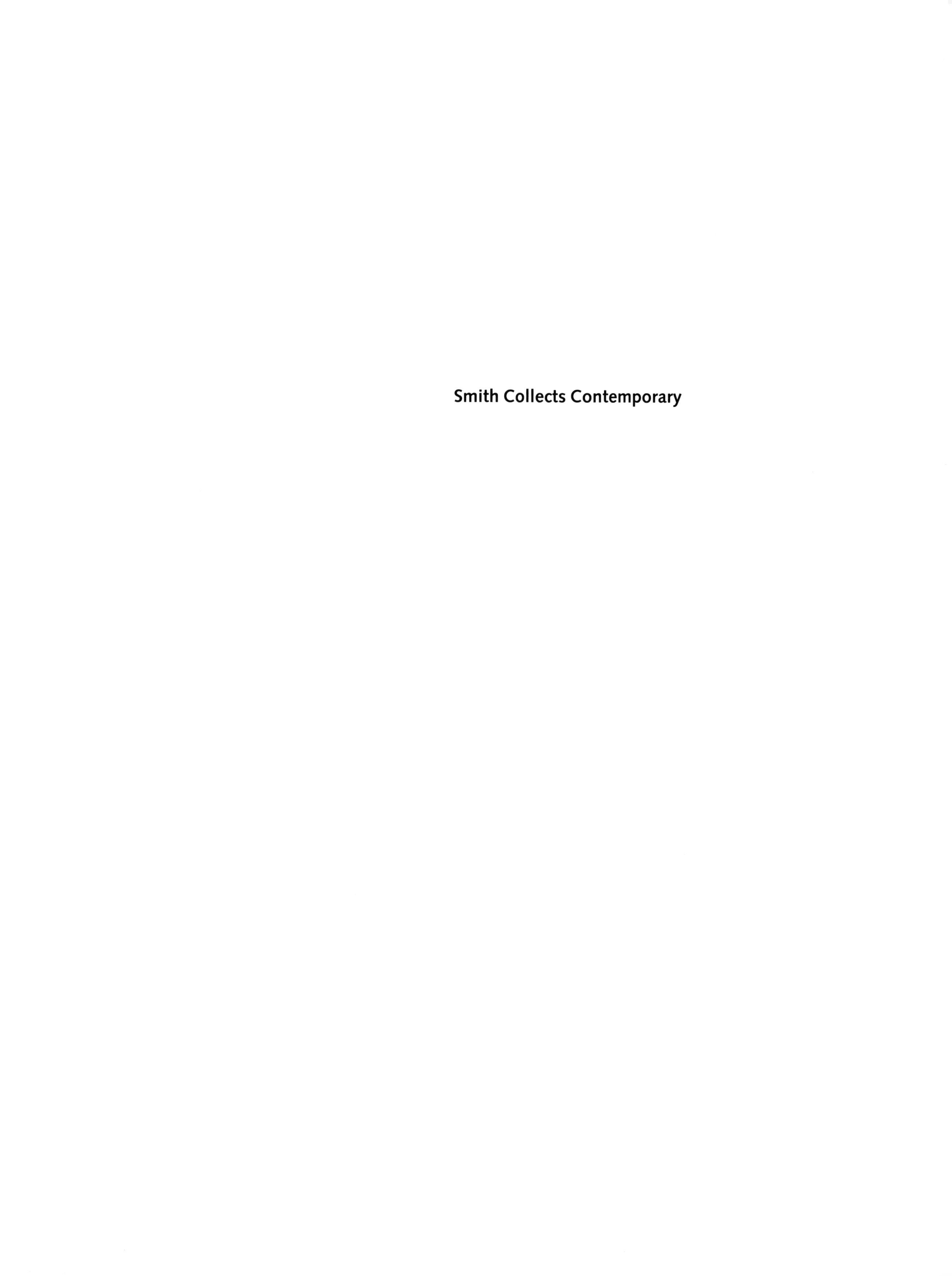

Smith Collects Contemporary

SMITH COLLECTS CONTEMPORARY

Smith College Museum of Art

Northampton, Massachusetts

May 3 through September 15, 1991

This exhibition was made possible in part through the contributions of the
Tryon Associates, founded in 1990 to provide annual support for the Smith
College Museum of Art.

Support for the catalogue came from the Maxine Weil Kunstadter ('24) Fund.

Copy editing, keyboarding, and coding for electronic typesetting by
Elizabeth P. Richardson ('43).

Library of Congress number 91-60788
ISBN 0-87391-044-3

One of the joys of being director of a college museum is that there is an enthusi-
astic built-in support group, the alumnae. Many Smith graduates have gone on to
careers in the visual arts; others serve as trustees and volunteers in museums across
the country; still others are collectors in various fields. Perhaps there is something
in Smith's air that fosters the growth of artistic interests in its students. I like to
think that the museum has played a role in this development.

Exhibitions like *Smith Collects Contemporary* bring the college, students, and
alumnae together in a venture that acknowledges the importance of the visual arts
in our lives. This is not, of course, the first show organized by the museum to tap
the extraordinarily rich resources of alumnae collections, but it is the largest since
One Hundred, mounted in 1975 to honor Smith's centennial. It is also one of the
most focused, concentrating as it does on post-1950 painting and sculpture.

I wish to thank those alumnae who have been so forthcoming with their loans.
There are undoubtedly collectors whom I have not met (I leave that pleasure to my
successor), but those represented here have been unfailing in their generosity—in
their loan of works of art as well as in their financial support for this undertaking.
The names of lenders are listed elsewhere in the catalogue.

Smith Collects Contemporary was the focus of a museum seminar I gave in the
fall of 1990. Nine women—five from Smith, two from Mount Holyoke, one from
Hampshire College, and one from the University of Massachusetts—helped make
this exhibition a reality: Wendy Bolger, Christina Clark, Lisa Gallo, Betzy Hainley,
Valerie Kohn, Gabriela Lobo, Jobie Summer, Wendy Vanasselt, and Melissa Zipser.
Each wrote five entries for the catalogue. Two student interns, Sarah Scheffel and
Audrey Tanner, also contributed. I would especially like to thank Audrey for serv-
ing as my assistant.

Exhibitions obviously do not just appear without staff help. In this case, Linda
Muehlig, Associate Curator of Painting and Sculpture, and Michael Goodison,
Program Coordinator, both wrote entries. I am also indebted to Michael for over-
seeing the production of the catalogue. His student assistant, Christine Fall ('91),
spent many hours in the library checking bibliographic citations. Special acknowl-
edgment is due to Louise Laplante, for arranging the shipment of art; to David
Dempsey, for installing the works; and to Ann Johnson, for handling a myriad of
administrative details.

EDWARD J. NYGREN
The Robert and Ryda H. Levi Director
of the Smith College Museum of Art

The Smith College Museum and Contemporary Art

Since 1879, when Smith's first president, L. Clark Seelye, announced his intention
of forming a collection of contemporary American art, the college has been com-
mitted to acquiring and presenting original works by living artists.[1] *Smith Collects
Contemporary* renews that commitment. This exhibition of over seventy paintings
and sculptures by some of the leading artists of the second half of this century is a
testament to the college, to its students and alumnae, and to the museum.

Among its sister institutions Smith was unique in its early dedication to contemporary art. Like many other colleges and universities with art programs, Smith
purchased casts and reproductions of the masterpieces of western art for teaching
purposes, but President Seelye was also convinced of the importance of acquiring
original works so that students could study art of quality at first hand. The decision
to purchase only contemporary American art may have been due in part to the fact
that Smith had an affiliated art school for the training of aspiring women artists,[2]
but the decision was still unusual. Established to collect and preserve the finest
examples of human creativity, museums in this country, like their European counter-
parts, focused on historical art. Although American and contemporary art were
exhibited in a variety of institutions, to my knowledge no other museum founded in
the nineteenth century made the commitment to collect works in either or both of
these fields exclusively. It was a radical departure.

In one respect Seelye's decision was understandable, coming as it did in the wake
of the centennial celebration of American independence. Following the Civil War,
Americans became increasingly confident of their future and proud of their past.
American art expressed that growing self-confidence. 1876 was a watershed; it saw
a burst of national optimism. Like the country itself, the art of the United States,
built on European traditions, had enormous potential. By concentrating on American art Seelye added his voice to the expression of national confidence.

Financially speaking, Seelye's decision also made good sense. The college had
only a pittance to spend on art. Small objects of high quality could be obtained

1.
A detailed chronol-
ogy of the museum
is given in Charles
Chetham et al., *A
Guide to the Collec-
tions: Smith College
Museum of Art,*
Northampton,
Mass., 1986,
pp. 15–22.

2.
Charles Chetham,
"Why the College
'Should Have Its
Gallery of Art,'"
*Smith Alumnae
Quarterly,* Feb-
ruary 1980, p. 3.
The art school was
closed in 1902.

3.
Alfred Vance
Churchill, "College
Museum Policy,"
*Bulletin of Smith
College Hillyer Art
Gallery,* March 30,
1923, pp. [6–8];
"Our Concentration
Plan," *Bulletin of
Smith College
Museum of Art,*
May 1932, pp. 2–
22; and "Concentration within
Concentration,"
pp. 26–28; an
abstract of the concentration plan
appears in Chetham,
Guide, pp. 23–24.

at modest prices from artists convinced of the worth of Smith's cause. Persuasive at a time when there was no tax incentive, Seelye would have made a successful museum director.

But the decision was interesting from a philosophical point of view as well. Having opened its doors in 1875 on the eve of America's centennial, Smith was a brand new institution, without a past, only a present and future. It was, in essence, a living experiment, tied by date to the celebration of another American experiment. Building a collection of contemporary American art reinforced that connection by bringing the young women of both the college and the art school in touch with ideas that were relevant to their time and place. What was clear from Seelye's radical vision was that Smith's president viewed art not only as something integral to a liberal education but as a force whose full vitality could be realized only by exposure to the contemporary.

Contemporary art has the habit of becoming historical almost overnight; and as art history established itself as an academic discipline, the museum became severely limited in its teaching capabilities through its restriction to American art. In 1920, after more than forty years of collecting, the museum adopted a new policy, formulated by Alfred Vance Churchill, the first person to hold the title Director of the Smith College Museum of Art. The policy, which became known as the "concentration plan," focused on the development of modern art, particularly French and American. By this time a few contemporary European works, such as a small bronze by Rodin, had entered the collection, and the number of Smith students interested in the study of art history was growing. It was argued that the collection of American art, while certainly justifiable on the basis of nationality, needed to be placed in a historical context.[3]

Although the decision reflected Churchill's personal taste, the focus on the development of modern art was another move without precedent. It has given the Smith collection its particular character. Today the Smith College Museum of Art is known internationally for its outstanding collection of late nineteenth- and early twentieth-century French and American art. Churchill's "concentration plan" did not limit future acquisitions, however. His successors, from Jere Abbott to Charles Chetham, all placed their individual stamp on the museum.

Among the monuments of twentieth-century art acquired in the fifty-six years between the arrival of Abbott in 1932 from the Museum of Modern Art and the retirement of Chetham in 1988 are Picasso's *La Table,* Kirchner's *Dodo and Her Brother,* Sheeler's *Rolling Power,* Calder's *Mobile,* Arp's *Torso,* Stella's *Damascus*

Gate, Oldenburg's *Soft Fan,* and Nevelson's *Distant Column.* Although a number
of these were purchased, alumnae have been extraordinarily generous, giving not
only art but also money for acquisitions. Nor have additions in the contemporary
field been limited to painting and sculpture. In fact acquisitions of prints, drawings, and photographs have been much more numerous, thanks in large measure
to the relatively modest prices of works in these media.

Museums, of course, never have enough money to buy all the art they want. The
Smith College Museum is no exception. Exhibitions therefore became critical to the
institution's educational mission. At Smith, shows have reinforced and redefined
the commitment to the contemporary. Under Abbott, Smith mounted exhibitions
of works by Rouault, Rivera, and Schmidt-Rottluff. During Chetham's administration shows were devoted to Albers, de Kooning, Motherwell, and Neel. There
were many others, including important exhibitions of contemporary photography,
sculpture, drawing, printmaking, and architecture.

As part of an academic institution, the museum plays an educational role: its
collection is constantly used by students and faculty of the Five College consortium.
Members of Smith's Art Department have organized exhibitions, some on contemporary art, and participated in programming. Students have been involved since
1964, when Chetham launched a museum seminar, one of the first at any undergraduate college.[4] *Smith Collects Contemporary* is a continuation of that tradition.

In the last two years the museum has paid increased attention to contemporary
art. The collection has been rehung to place more emphasis on work of the past few
decades. Site-specific installations have become an integral part of the museum's
schedule; students have participated in these efforts, working side by side with
visiting artists, and faculty have served as guest curators.

From this brief history it is clear that the museum's involvement with contemporary art is not a new development. The Smith College Museum of Art has always
been concerned with current artistic expression. In a college that began life with
a strong commitment to the visual arts and has a thriving art department this is
hardly surprising. The works acquired, the programs launched, the exhibitions
mounted, the courses taught—all build on the original vision of President Seelye.
Smith Collects Contemporary celebrates that vision.

The idea for the exhibition grew out of my travels during The Campaign for
Smith in 1988–1989. As the new director I had an opportunity to visit different
parts of the country and meet many alumnae. I was not surprised to find collectors
among Smith graduates, but I was astounded by the quality and range of their

holdings. It was then that I decided to tap this resource. Although many different shows could have been selected, I chose contemporary art, one of the strongest collecting interests of Smith alumnae.

After *Smith Collects Contemporary* was conceived over two years ago, the selection of works followed. The guiding principle, of course, was quality, but other considerations could not be neglected. For example, I had to define what I meant by "contemporary." Given the wealth of material to draw from, I could easily have limited my choices to works produced in the last two decades, but I decided to broaden the chronological and aesthetic range by including works produced since 1950. So much of postwar art is an outgrowth of abstract expressionism or a reaction to it that I felt I could not ignore this pivotal development so closely associated with America. Although I sought important examples by key figures in major movements, I also wanted to include works by lesser known artists or those outside the New York mainstream. The final selection is admittedly idiosyncratic, as any show must be that draws on a variety of collections.

Although *Smith Collects Contemporary* attempts to cover forty years of contemporary art history with over seventy objects, this is not a thesis show. It presents neither one view of contemporary art nor one aesthetic. In fact, I was determined to include a wide range of artistic expressions to underscore the extraordinary diversity in today's art. I also wanted to include as many women artists as possible. Important artists are missing from this assemblage, of course; to some extent this is due to the limitations of the collections or the understandable reluctance of owners to lend fragile objects.

In my selection I was guided by another principle: the show was to be international in scope. While the majority of works are American, as one would expect, given the nationality and interests of the collectors, whenever possible I have included pieces that place the American experience within a broader framework. Perhaps this desire reveals a latter-day concurrence with the reasoning behind Churchill's "concentration plan," but it also reflects the international flavor of so much contemporary art, encouraged by ease of travel and the pressures of the marketplace.

From the outset I intended the exhibition to be a student project. Although selection had to be made in advance of the museum seminar I taught last fall, I wanted the students to learn something about the development of an exhibition at the same time that they channeled their academic energies into writing entries for the catalogue. Student involvement was, I am sure, an important factor in getting the full support of lenders. Such projects offer valuable learning experiences, as the alumnae recognize. In fact several lenders remarked to me and to the students that they wished they had had a similar opportunity when they were at Smith. Although the students were not able to examine all the objects in the exhibition, they did see most of them, usually in the context of collections that contained many more works than those included in the show. This exposure provided us with an opportunity to discuss how the final selection had been made.

Thus *Smith Collects Contemporary* gave the students a chance to work with paintings and sculptures of high quality and to place them within the context of contemporary art. It also enabled them to see how exhibitions are developed and why compromises are frequently necessary; to learn that putting on a show, even with the unfailing support of interested people, is not an easy matter. But preparing the entries provided another and perhaps even more rewarding experience. As the students wrote, rewrote, and then rewrote again their comments on the individual works, they learned, I hope, the importance of being able to present ideas clearly and succinctly.

In a project like *Smith Collects Contemporary* with many contributors to the catalogue the end results vary from student to student and from object to object. The results presented here speak for themselves. But as director of the museum and curator of the exhibition, I want to express my pleasure with the process and satisfaction with the product. It has been for me as well a learning experience, for which I am grateful to the alumnae and especially to my students.

EJN

This catalogue is arranged alphabetically by artist within the two categories of painting and sculpture. All dimensions are in inches and listed with height before width or as height, width, and depth. In the text an asterisk indicates that the artist mentioned is also represented in this exhibition. Contributors are identified by their initials.

AT	Audrey Tanner
BH	Betzy Hainley
CLC	Christina L. Clark
EJN	Edward J. Nygren
GL	Gabriela Lobo
LHG	Lisa H. Gallo
LM	Linda Muehlig
MG	Michael Goodison
MYZ	Melissa Y. Zipser
NJS	Naanine Jobie Summer
SS	Sarah Scheffel
VCK	Valerie C. Kohn
WEB	Wendy E. Bolger
WGV	Wendy G. Vanasselt

Paintings

Homage to the Square, Orange Air, 1963
Oil on Masonite, 48 × 48
Lent by Emily Rauh Pulitzer, daughter of
Harriet Frank Rauh

Josef Albers emigrated from Germany to the
United States in 1933, the year the Nazis closed
the Bauhaus. He taught at Black Mountain College in North Carolina and after 1950 at Yale,
always exploring the problems of harmony and
proportion in abstract painting.

The question "Why did the artist choose to do
this?" is especially relevant to Albers's Homage
to the Square series. Perhaps the most succinct
answer is that

> Albers' work has had one undeviating purpose: to
> clarify and help us make sense of visual phenomena
> and to develop our skills at comparative seeing.[1]

Albers has pursued this aim in his theoretical
writings as well as in his work.

Homage to the Square, Orange Air is one of
over a thousand paintings in this series done
between 1949 and the artist's death in 1976. To
appreciate his ideas it is important to see more
than one of these works, for only then does his
interest in the relativity of color become evident.
A color may advance in the picture plane when
juxtaposed with one color and recede when
placed next to another. Even within one composition the colors appear to change if the lighting
is altered.

How does Albers go about exploring the
interaction of colors? The Homage series was
executed in four sizes ranging from 12 × 12 to
48 × 48, *Orange Air* being among the largest.
Three schemes have three squares each, and one
has four — a nest of squares positioned with

vertical but not horizontal symmetry. In all cases
the space on each side of the central square is
twice as large as that beneath it and the space
above is three times as large. As a result the
image is not static; there is a feeling of weight
and movement. The squares seem to move back
and forth in space, inviting different concurrent
readings. The image appears to be in a state of
perpetual motion.

Within a simple format the Homage series
varies only in color. Collectively the works
demonstrate Albers's belief in "the discrepancy
between physical fact and psychic effect."[2] Since
the colors were applied evenly straight from the
tube over six base coats of white, they vary little
in intensity and the color is as inexpressive as
possible.

Although the presentation stresses control
and logic, Albers draws no single conclusion.

> An element plus an element must yield at least one
> interesting relationship over and above the sum of
> those elements. The more different relationships
> are formed, and the more connected they are, the
> more the elements intensify each other and the more
> valuable is the result and the more rewarding is the
> work. This leads to a major factor in the instruction:
> economy. Economy in the sense of being sparing of
> expenditure in material and labor and optimal utili-
> zation for the effect aimed at.[3]

This fundamental dictated the way Albers
worked and taught. As a teacher, he told his students at Yale to work with materials that mini-
mize the personal handwriting. The goal in art
is not self-expression.[4] This principle lies behind
such paintings as *Orange Air,* whose detached
calm encourages thoughtful meditation.
VCK

Josef Albers

1888 – 1976

1.
Alan Shestack, in
Alan Shestack and
Nicholas Fox
Weber, *Josef Albers,
His Art and Influ-
ence,* Montclair Art
Museum,
Montclair, N.J.,
1981, p. 7.
2.
David Piper, in
Mitchell Beazley,
Looking at Art,
Random House,
New York, 1984,
p. 236.
3.
Eugen Gomringer,
Josef Albers,
George Wittenborn,
Inc., New York,
1967, p. 48.
4.
Werner Spies, *Josef
Albers,* Thames
and Hudson Ltd.,
London, 1971, p. 9.

*Additional
Reference*
Wade, Marcia J.:
"Homage to a
Square Man,"
Horizon, April
1988, pp. 36–40.

Gregory Amenoff

Born 1948

The Surrender, 1981
Oil on canvas, 70½ × 80½
Lent by Suzanne and Maurice Vanderwoude

Gregory Amenoff was born in St. Charles, Illinois. After receiving a degree in history from Beloit College in 1970, he moved to Boston, where he worked in both painting and video, producing monochromatic geometric paintings and planar abstractions that may have been influenced by the work of Boston painter Katherine Porter.[1] Though abstract and formally conceived, without visual references to the natural world, these paintings were given the titles of actual cities, mountains, or lakes. In 1977 Amenoff's work began to incorporate biomorphic forms and to involve greater animation of space and surface. According to the artist, "The geometry came untied."[2]

The Surrender dates from the year after Amenoff moved to New York and began to develop his densely painted organic abstractions. Although it reveals the influence of the early moderns Arthur Dove, Georgia O'Keeffe, and Marsden Hartley, whose work is most often cited in connection with Amenoff along with the nineteenth-century visionary artist Albert Pinkham Ryder, *The Surrender*'s emotionally ambiguous charge may owe its source to the dream world of the surrealists. Painted in a high color key, with strong contrasts of ochre, purple, blacks, and blood red, it suggests both defeat and invitation as the torso-like form at the upper right stretches to display its wounds or opens instead to the viewer. The drama, which appears to be played out in a microcosm of cells, becomes a primordial confrontation enlarged to heroic scale. When the painting was first shown in 1981,[3] its expressive use of color prompted one critic to write:

> . . . in *The Surrender,* red evokes red. Seeing red, stirring things up with red: sense associations yield to emotional stirrings . . . melancholy and passion. . . . Form harnesses painterly energy.[4]

The processes of birth, death, and decay activate these paintings from the 1980s. References made to natural forms are sometimes identifiable and sometimes imaginary. Amenoff describes his paintings in terms of corporal landscapes: "They are about the body. Chest, diaphragm, gut, stomach. . . . Leaf forms, chest, veins, the center point of energy and light and life."[5] Paint applied with narrow brushes in a thick and contoured impasto creates its own terrain on the surface of the canvas. The physicality of the process—painting "pulled back to [the] hand"[6]—increases the physical and emotive power of Amenoff's work.

LM

1.
Susan Krane, *The Painting and Sculpture Collection: Acquisitions since 1972,* Albright-Knox Art Gallery, Buffalo, 1987, p. 46.
2.
Robert Pincus-Witten, "Gregory Amenoff: Untied Geometries," in *Gregory Amenoff,* Hirschl & Adler Modern, New York, 1987, n.p.
3.
Robert Miller Gallery, New York, September 15–October 3, 1981.
4.
Stephen Pentak, "Gregory Amenoff's New Pictures: Feeling Given Form," *Arts Magazine,* November 1981, pp. 156–157.
5.
Pincus-Witten, n.p.
6.
Ibid.

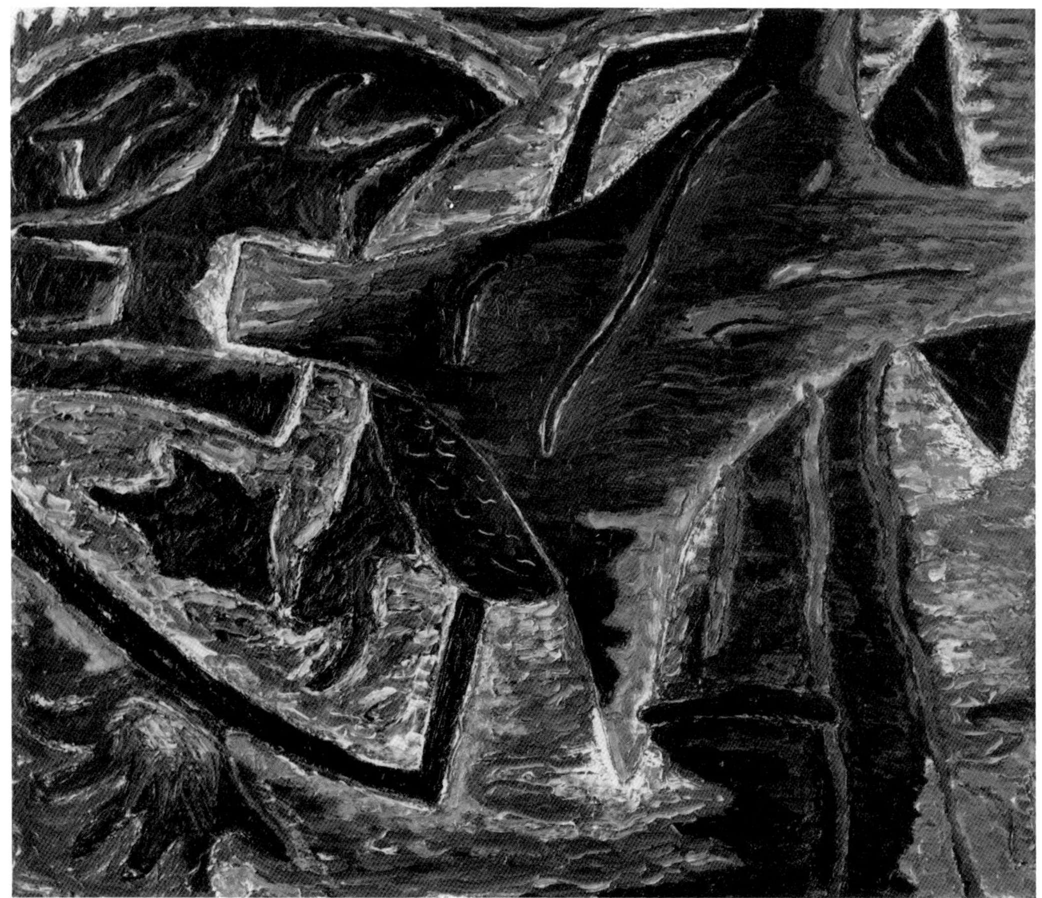

Pisces Dark Star, 1979
Oil, mixed media, and steel plates, 52 × 130
(four pieces)
Lent by Loretta and Robert K. Lifton

Jennifer Bartlett has known since the age of five
that she wanted to be an artist. She grew up in
Long Beach, California, and attended Mills
College in 1960. Since the faculty of its prestig-
ious art department had included at one time
or another such artists as Fernand Léger and
Clyfford Still, the abstract expressionism of the
New York school was a pervasive influence. At
Mills in the early 1960s Bartlett began painting
in a loose, abstract style similar to that of Arshile
Gorky. After graduation she entered the Yale
School of Art and Architecture, where she met
such other well-known artists as Elizabeth
Murray* and Jonathan Borofsky. She moved to
New York after receiving her Master of Fine Arts
degree in 1965.

Although aware of current movements such as
pop art and minimalism, Bartlett was searching
for her own style. In 1968 she stopped using canvas as the support for her painting and began to
use steel plates. "I thought that if I could just
eliminate everything I hated doing, like stretching
canvases, then I'd be able to do a lot more work."[1]
The steel plates, which have since become one
of her trademarks, were inspired by New York
subway signs. After coating the plates with
white enamel, she superimposed a silk-screened
grid of light gray lines, upon which she painted
the image.

Bartlett's works from the late 1960s show the
diversity of influences on her development. With
their colored dots of unmixed enamel paints
these compositions look like computer printouts,
but they also recall the pointillism of Georges
Seurat. On the other hand, her reliance on industrial materials and her interest in concept rather
than object reveals her ties with minimalism.
Pisces Dark Star is representative of the artist's
work of the late 1970s, when Bartlett started
combining steel plates and stretched canvas in a
single composition. She tried this technique first
in 1977 in a commission for a federal courthouse
in Atlanta.

With their references to nature, Bartlett's
images are universal, but they also have autobiographical connotations. The sea, for example, is
important in her oeuvre, perhaps because the
ocean figured so largely in her childhood. As
Pisces Dark Star demonstrates, her seascapes are
extremely expressive and charged with swirling
motion. The transient properties of the sea, its
continual ebb and flow, are reinforced in this
painting by the repetition of motifs and contrasting size of compositional elements. Bartlett is
concerned with the fundamentals of nature: the
weather, the seasons, the passage of time and
how these phenomena register in the sky, land,
and sea. The changing colors and reflecting light
as well as the short, active brushstrokes may
well be indebted to the impressionists, especially
Monet, whose work she greatly admires. In her
attention to the art of the past she carries on a
dialogue with the history of modern painting as
she expresses her own ideas.

MYZ

Jennifer Bartlett

Born 1941

1.
Marge Goldwater,
Jennifer Bartlett,
Abbeville Press,
New York, 1985,
p. 115.

*Additional
References*
Bartlett, Jennifer:
In the Garden,
Harry N. Abrams,
New York, 1982.
*Jennifer Bartlett,
Selected Works,*
November 22–
December 31,
1980, Hallwalls,
Buffalo, N.Y.,
November 23,
1980–January 4,
1981, Albright-
Knox Gallery,
Buffalo, Buffalo
Fine Arts
Academy,
Buffalo, c. 1980.

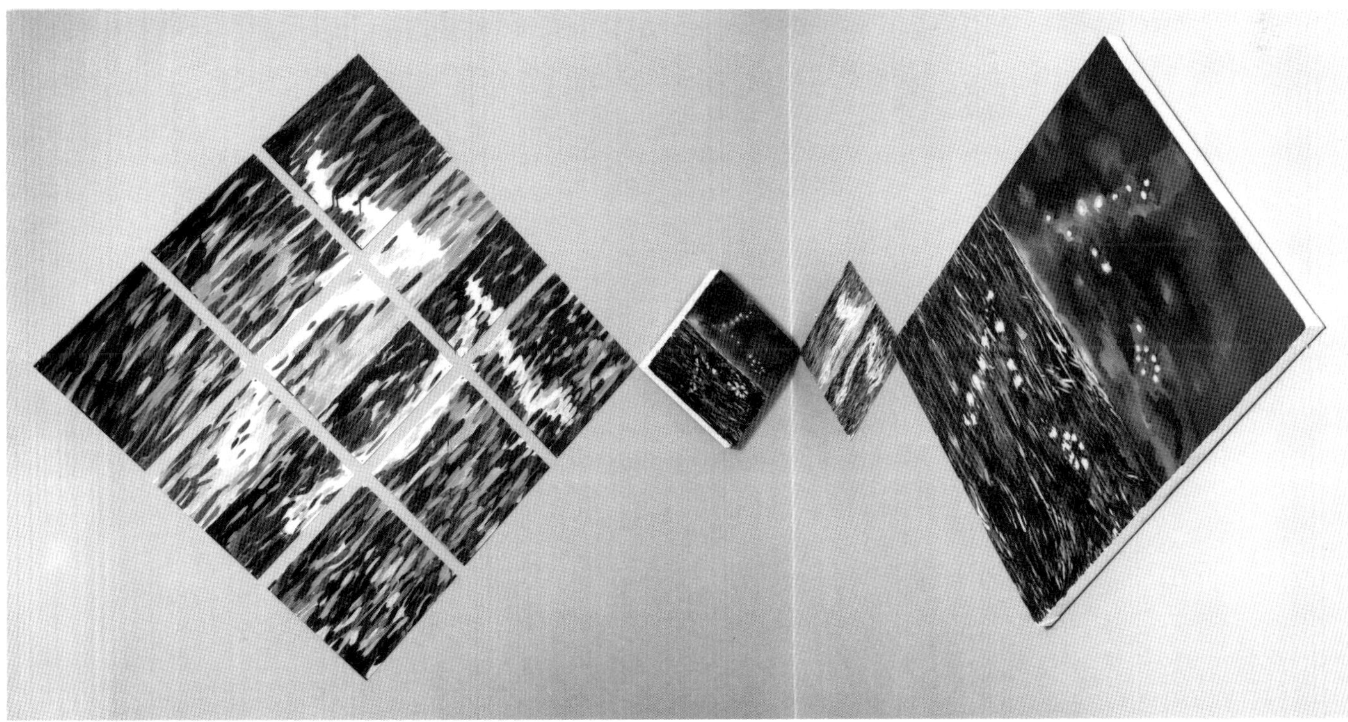

Richard Bosman

Born 1944

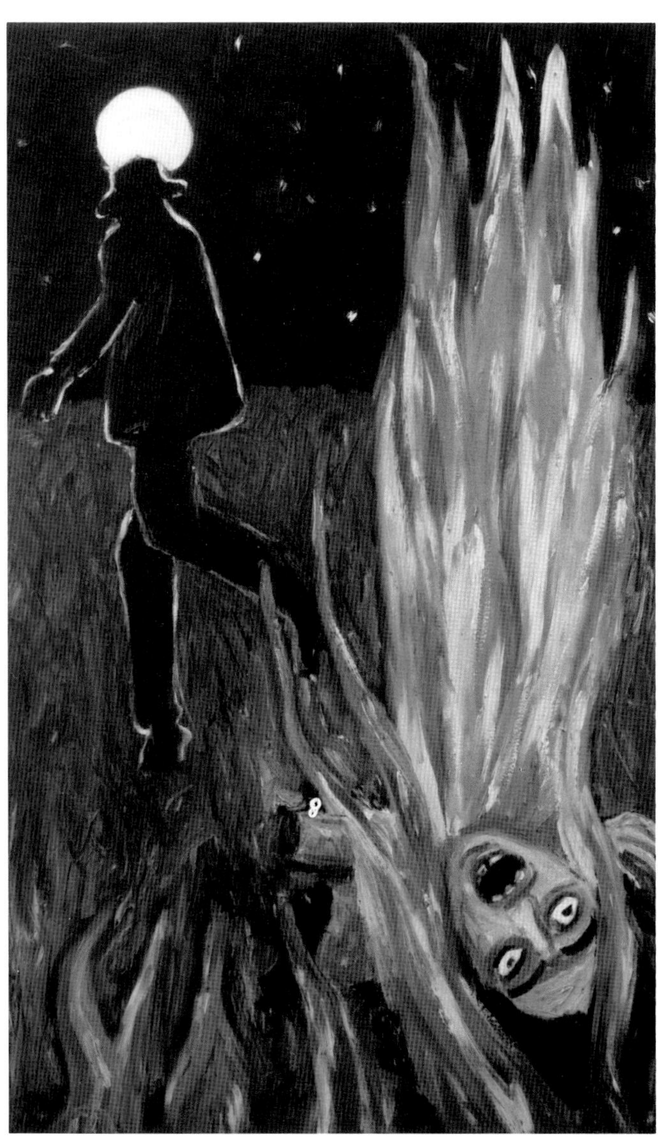

The Pyre, 1981
Oil on canvas, 72 × 42
Lent by Eliot and Wilson Nolen

Like Rainer Fetting* and other artists of the late
1970s, Richard Bosman was attracted to the
emotional content and vivid colors of German
expressionism of the early twentieth century.
Bosman seeks to unsettle and shock, just as his
predecessors did. His paintings are both psycho-
logically charged and coloristically intense.
What sets this artist apart from his contempo-
raries, however, is his grotesque subject matter,[1]
forcing on the viewer horrifying images like this
one of a person immersed in flames. Bosman's
creativity transforms these intensely violent
scenes into fictional dramas.

Bosman was born in India; his father was a cap-
tain in the British Navy. Seascapes dominate his
art of the late 1980s. The early neo-expressionist
style of *The Pyre,* which relied primarily on
shocking subjects, later gave way to a more subtle
approach to visual anxiety.

When Bosman first exhibited in 1980, he had
to struggle to be taken seriously. This effort may
well be reflected in the recurring themes of life
and death in his work.[2] Other influences on his
output at this time were two artists with whom
he studied at the New York Studio School, Philip
Guston* and Alex Katz.*

> Alex taught me that you didn't have to be a Bohe-
> mian. Artists could be just as middle class as the
> next person. . . . Guston was the opposite. He would
> come into class with a bottle of vodka and a pack
> of cigarettes. They both had a quick eye.[3]

Bosman acquired his thick, controlled brushstrokes from Guston and learned succinctness
from Katz.[4]

The Pyre is one of Bosman's earliest compositions. The title refers to the flammable heap on
which a corpse is ritualistically burned. The
screaming bodiless head thrust into the foreground immediately unsettles the viewer. The
person is not dead but dying, a victim perhaps
of the figure lurking in the background. The
violence is so bizarre that it suggests a horror
story.

Bosman's energetic yet controlled brushstrokes
invest the flames with frantic movement. The
orange-red colors graphically convey the destructive heat of the fire as the dynamic painting style
and intense colors add fuel to the unsettling subject. The threat that something bad is about to
happen or the eerie feeling that something horrible has just happened lies at the core of Bosman's
work. His ability to treat the grotesque matter-
of-factly is characteristic of his neo-expressionist
style.

LHG

1.
Jeanne Siegel,
"Richard Bosman:
Stories of Vio-
lence," *Arts
Magazine,* April
1983, p. 126.
2.
Robert L. Pincus,
"Bosman's Sea
Images Also
Examine Self," *The
San Diego Union,*
June 1, 1989, p. C6.
3.
Marsha Miro,
"Expressionistic
Seascapes Show
Contrasts Time
Brings," *Detroit
Free Press,* May 1,
1988, p. C3.
4.
Ibid.

French Top, 1986
Oil on canvas, 87 × 72
Lent by Rima Ayas and Ronald W. Moore

A native of North Carolina, Christopher Brown earned his Master of Fine Arts degree at the University of California, Davis, in 1976. Now living in California, he is associated with other figurative artists of the Bay Area.

Brown works slowly on large canvases. After he has applied the pigment he often sands it down. His earliest paintings feature such images as a fishing box, baseball glove, or other object of personal interest that lend an autobiographical note to the compositions.

Early in the 1980s elliptical forms from everyday things like hats or cups began to appear regularly in Brown's work. In *French Top* although the bottom rim of a sailor's hat in the center of the canvas is an ellipse, the form is not treated realistically. The hat, outlined in red, is a spectral image, almost an illusion, that seems to float above the water and in front of the surface of the painting.

Brown uses luminous strips of color to give his free-floating objects spatial definition. Poking up through blue rippling bands in *French Top* are five heads of people who appear to be wading through water. The artist has worked with similar images of silhouetted heads in other paintings, for example, *The Phases of the Moon,* also from 1986.[1]

In the bottom left of *French Top* the image of an inner tube, in conjunction with the sailor's hat and people bobbing in wave-like bands, establishes it as a beach scene. The artist combines different spatial planes and images to create a collage of maritime impressions.
CLC

1.
Howard Junker, "Christopher Brown," *Second Newport Biennial: The Bay Area,* Newport Harbor Art Museum, Newport Beach, Calif., 1986, p. 12.

Additional References
Berkson, Bill: "Five Bay Area Artists," *Art International,* Autumn 1989, pp. 45–46.
Fischer, Hal: "Christopher Brown," *Artforum,* February 1980, pp. 105–106.

Christopher Brown

Born 1951

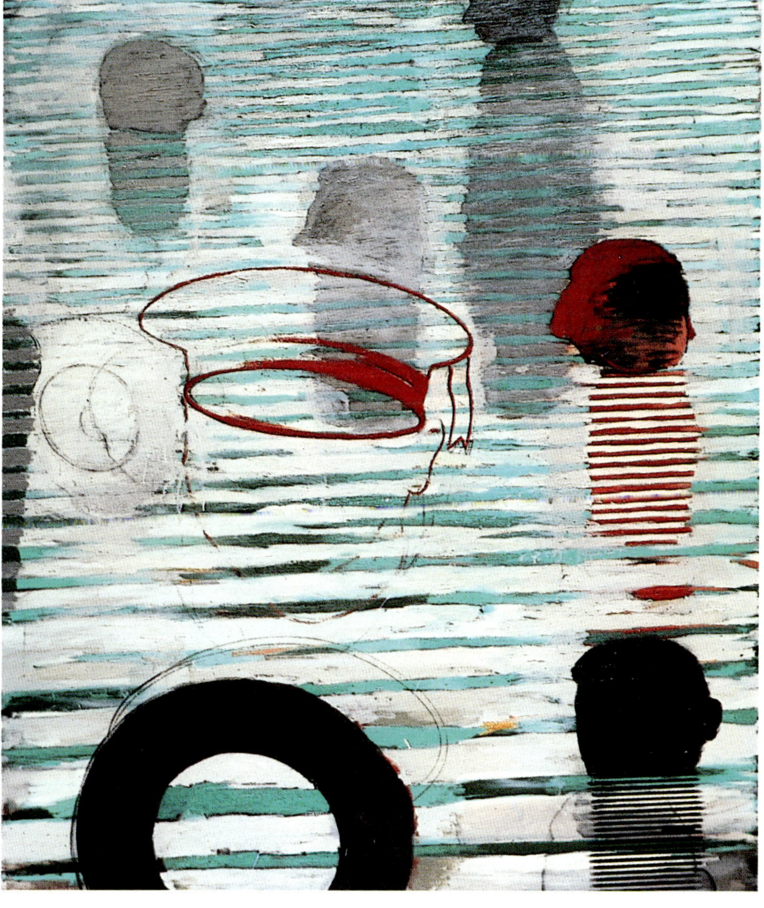

Walkmans and Ghetto Blasters, 1984
Oil on canvas, 48 × 72
Lent by Joan and Irving Harris

In 1961 Roger Brown moved from Alabama,
where he was born, to Chicago, where he still
lives. After brief study at the American Academy
of Art he received both his Bachelor and Master
of Fine Arts degrees from the School of the Art
Institute of Chicago.

Brown uses repetition of forms (architecture,
clouds, and silhouetted figures) to comment
upon current events and attitudes. His themes
derive from contemporary history, religious
mythology, world social and environmental
issues, and everyday urban life. Many of his subjects are drawn directly from the media or from
events and places seen during his travels.

The drama in his paintings comes from
Brown's use of backlighting, complicated shadows, and variable perspectives. Some paintings
are comedic in tone, reflecting the artist's dry wit
and ironic observation of the world we inhabit.
Others are dead serious and convey a sense
of foreboding. All bear witness to the state of
humanity in visual terms that are at once dramatic and simple, overt and complex.

Walkmans and Ghetto Blasters speaks in an
immediately readable urban vernacular. Charac-
teristically, Brown has tipped the ground plane
forward so that the foreground, middle ground,
and distance are established as bands of surface

pattern rather than deep recessions into space.
The strips of cloud emphasizing the horizontality
of the composition are a common feature of his
work.

The figures are typical of Brown's visual
vocabulary. Little more than cartoon images,
they are not meant to be specific people or portraits but agents of identification to make the
painting more immediately accessible to the
viewer. Nevertheless the picture is also inherently
complex. The repetitions of form, crisscrossing
of shadows, alternations in direction and view-
point, and modulations and punctuations of
color all create a rhythm visually suggestive of
rap music, each layer similar but not entirely the
same.

Brown gives us an active and lively cross section of a city where people walk, each tuned into
a different wavelength. Silhouetted figures in lit
windows gesture, some theatrically, and seem to
look out at the passers-by on the street. Each
walking figure strides with radio apparatus
attached, becoming in effect either a "walkman"
or a "ghetto blaster," a wry duality of opposites:
music listened to privately or shared, people
tuning in or tuning out.

Brown does not choose between them, presenting them as equal modern phenomena and
leaving us, like the central figure with her arms
up, to choose for ourselves.

AT

Roger Brown

Born 1941

References
Bowman, Russell:
 "An Interview
 with Roger
 Brown." *Art in
 America,* Janu-
 ary–February
 1978,
 pp. 106–111.
Kahan, Mitchell
 Douglas, Dennis
 Adrian, and
 Russell Bowman:
 Roger Brown,
 Montgomery
 Museum of Fine
 Arts, Montgom-
 ery, Ala., 1980.
Lawrence, Sidney:
 Roger Brown,
 George Braziller,
 Inc., New York,
 in conjunction
 with the
 Hirshhorn
 Museum and
 Sculpture Gar-
 den, 1987.

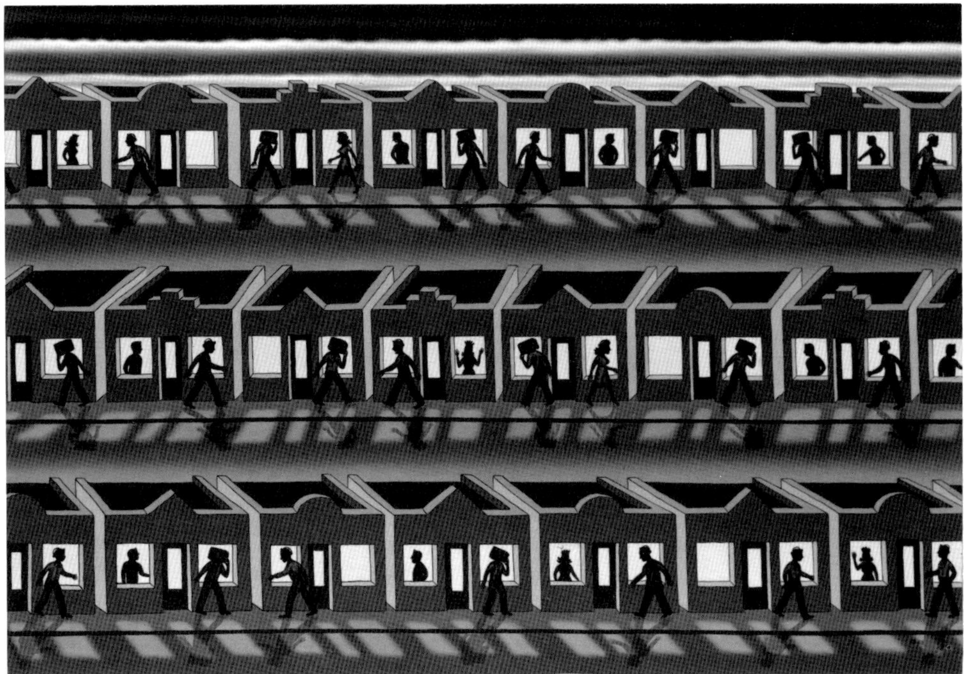

1.
Alessandra Mammì,
"The Archipelago
of the Present," in
Susan Sollins (ed.),
*Eternal Metaphors:
New Art from Italy,*
Independent
Curators Incorpo-
rated, New York,
1991, p. 14.
2.
Susan Sollins, "Eter-
nal Metaphors," in
Sollins, p. 23;
Claudio Verna,
"Bruno Ceccobelli,"
Flash Art, Summer
1985, p. 68.
3.
Bruno Ceccobelli,
"Manifesta,"
*Artscribe Interna-
tional,* February–
March 1986,
pp. 39–41.
4.
Quoted in Sollins,
p. 30.

Con Qual Mezzo, 1988
Mixed media on wood panel, 27 × 36½
Lent by Rima Ayas and Ronald W. Moore

Born in Todi, Italy, Bruno Ceccobelli lives and
works in Rome. During the last decade he
has been closely associated with a group of
young Italian painters including Gianni Dessì,
Domenico Bianchi, and Giuseppe Gallo, whose
use of nontraditional materials was influenced
by the *arte povera* movement of the 1970s. The
1980s marked a break from conceptualism and
radical change in Italian art as many artists
returned to traditional canvas painting, reappro-
priating the figure and the past as subject matter.
In this new artistic climate Ceccobelli and his
group explored the spiritual possibilities of their
art. Choosing materials and colors for their symbolic references, they revived the ancient idea
of the artist as alchemist who has the power to
transform base materials into a higher form.[1]

Bruno Ceccobelli cites a wide range of historical and contemporary influences on his work—
from Caravaggio, Goya, the Russian construc-
tivists, Marcel Duchamp, and the American
abstract expressionists to Joseph Beuys, Anselm
Kiefer, Jannis Kounellis, and Mario Merz.[2]
Many of Ceccobelli's paintings take the form of
altarpieces, icons, or reliquaries; pigments are
combined with a variety of materials—wax,
lead, and sulfur, for example—and found or
manipulated objects. For Ceccobelli these constructions have a ritualistic content in both their

making and meaning. In his "Manifesta" he
writes of the artist's life as a "journey of purifica-
tion." The act of painting becomes a consecra-
tion staged upon the "holy place" of the blank
surface, where the artist "struggles and injures
himself for the final image."[3]

Ceccobelli's references to religion, specifically
to the Catholicism of his Mediterranean heritage,
are unmistakable. *Con Qual Mezzo* (literally,
"with what means") adopts the format of a trip-
tych altarpiece. The side panels contain figural
forms, evoking images of saints or black-robed
monks whose faces are ochre-stained and anonymous. The central panel arrays a trinity of ovoid
shapes. Surmounting the panels are pediments,
each incomplete, broken at the base, and painted
or scratched with signs: the numeral 3 and its
mirror image are incised on the central pediment.

Con Qual Mezzo is not literally an altarpiece
and despite its conscious borrowing of that form
should not be narrowly interpreted as a devo-
tional object, at least in the traditional sense.
The material substance of the painting works in
engaging the immaterial, the spiritual, rather than
in the veneration of a godhead. For Ceccobelli,
"True art is thaumaturgic."[4] Redemptive or
curative power for artist and viewer alike is vested
in both the object and its creation, accomplishing
miraculous transformations as dross is turned
into gold.

LM

Bruno Ceccobelli

Born 1952

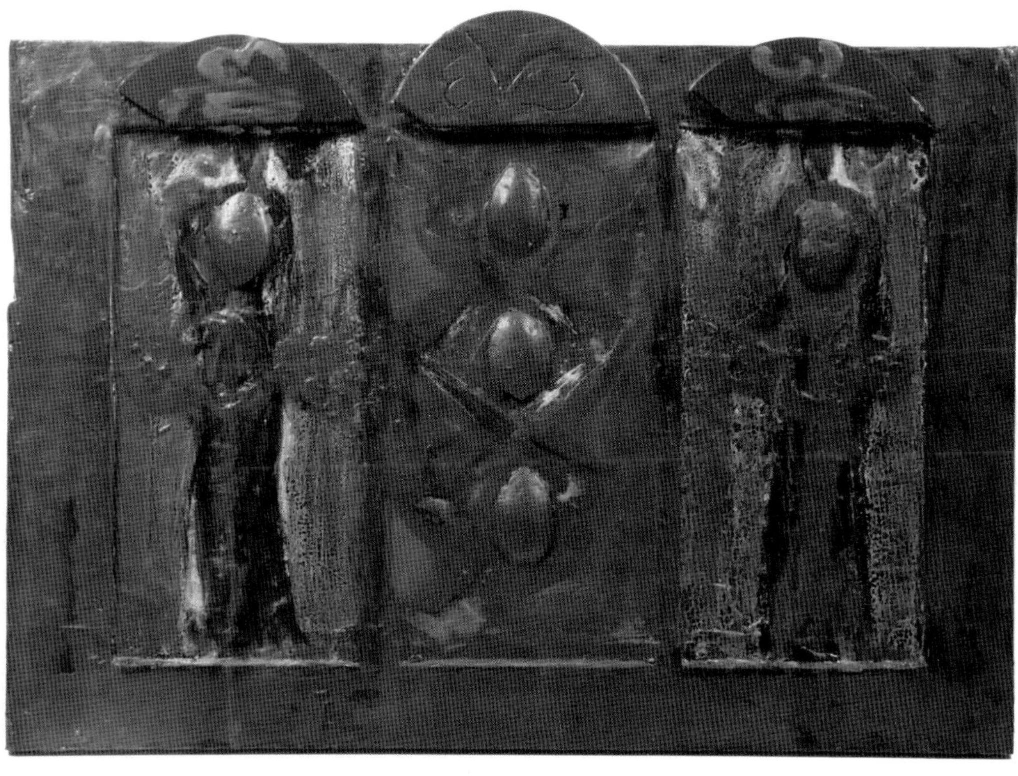

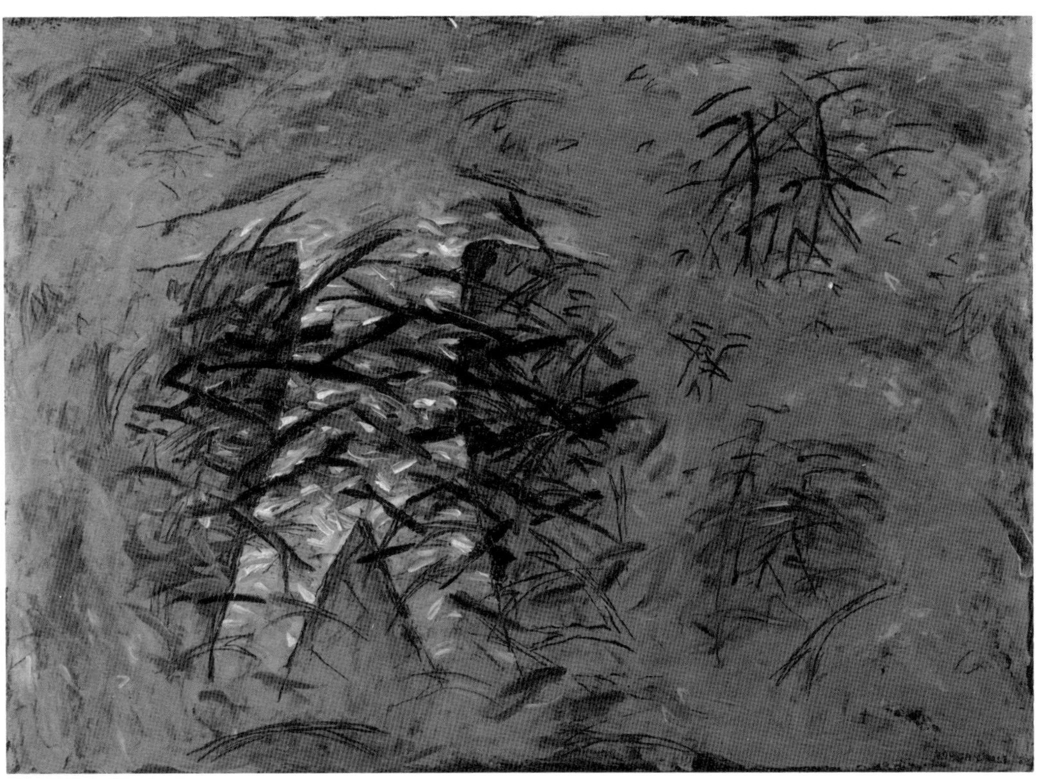

Louisa Chase

Born 1951

Untitled, 1983
Oil on canvas, 48 × 66
Lent by Eliot and Wilson Nolen

The paintings of Louisa Chase, who was born in Panama City, fall into two distinct periods. When she graduated from the Yale School of Art and Architecture in 1975, she painted symbolic landscapes, but by the mid-1980s she moved from figuration to abstraction, changing many elements of her style. *Untitled* is representative of her early work.

The headless torsos that appear in this painting recur repeatedly in Chase's compositions of the late 1970s and early 1980s. According to the artist, the image represents unconsciousness and evokes a sensory state of being.[1] In this painting torsos of varying size, entangled in grass or branches, seem to float on the painted surface and blend with it like dream images.

Such landscapes of Chase's imagination depict no actual occurrences or settings but reflect her feelings about nature and life. "Each painting feels very specific—not only concerning a different phenomenon but having an emotional charge that is contained in color and direction of the mark."[2] In *Untitled* anxiety arising from the fear of being trapped or restrained is mollified by the warm, soft peach and brown tones that support the mindless bodies. The painting's emotional charge is heightened by the way the pigment is applied and scarred or scratched, techniques especially evident here in the strokes that look like branches.

Chase's naive graffiti-like forms are reminiscent of prehistoric cave paintings. Through the simplification of the visual elements the artist has stripped away from the human figure all its senses except touch, exploring emotions and sensory perceptions without the interference of consciousness.

CLC

1.
Telephone interview by CLC with Louisa Chase, November 13, 1990.
2.
Louisa Chase, in *Louisa Chase,* Robert Miller Gallery, New York, March 27–April 21, 1984, p. [6].

Additional References
Karmel, Pepe: "Louisa Chase at Robert Miller," *Art in America,* October 1984, p. 191.
Peters, Lisa N.: "Louisa Chase," *Arts Magazine,* November 1982, p. 8.
Woodville, Louisa: "Louisa Chase," *Arts Magazine,* Summer 1984, p. 11.

Stanley, 1980
Acrylic on canvas, 54½ × 42½
Lent by Valerie and Charles Diker

Close was born in Monroe, Washington; after graduating from the University of Washington School of Art, he received both his Bachelor and Master of Fine Arts degrees from the Yale School of Art and Architecture. With his first major paintings in the later 1960s, he gave new meaning to the tradition of portraiture. In *Self-Portrait* (1967) he established the methodology that dominated his large-scale works until he painted *Stanley* in 1980. On a Polaroid photograph he laid a grid and then transferred the image to a corresponding grid on a 7- by 9-foot canvas. By fusing the grid with the optical distortions inherent in a photograph Close pioneered a new pictorial space that follows neither the conventions of traditional representational painting, in which the canvas mimics a three-dimensional volumetric reality, nor those of modern abstraction, which bans three-dimensional form from the two-dimensional realm of the canvas. The artist then airbrushed on black acrylic to ensure the smoothest possible surface, on which no brushstrokes would be visible.

Close restricted his earliest portraits to black and white to retain a truly photographic quality. The paintings are exhaustive yet neutral studies of features from which nothing is omitted. Even the most minute mole or out-of-place hair becomes an inescapable imperfection. Despite such meticulous attention to detail, the subjects are painted with a jarring indifference to personality.

Over the next several years Close continued to paint portraits in this manner. In 1970 he reintroduced color into his work. Using a complicated technique similar to a photomechanical process, he overlapped primary hues in sequence to produce a single color. Two years later, when Close began experimenting with the print medium, a mistake at the printing studio allowed the grid to become visible and the creative process to show through. The grid remained an integral part of Close's compositions into the 1980s.

Stanley represents Close's return to the medium of oil, which he had abandoned in the late 1960s. Heavily influenced by his Dot drawings of 1973, *Stanley* is composed of densely impastoed dots within the grid format. These dots break up the surface of the painting into hundreds of smaller units, each with its own abstract character. The dots are built up through a series of applications, just as Close's earlier color paintings were, but now both color and texture are of expressive importance. The gestural energy of *Stanley* is unprecedented in this artist's work. Although the painting embodies many of the technical elements of the "classic" Close portrait, its abstract and highly expressive surface is the antithesis of the earlier form.
MYZ

References
Close, Chuck: *Chuck Close,* Kunstraum, Munich, 1979.
———: *Close Portraits,* Walker Art Museum, The Walker Art Center, Minneapolis, 1980.
———, Lisa Lyons, and Robert Storr: *Chuck Close,* Rizzoli International Publications, Inc., New York, 1987.

Chuck Close

Born 1940

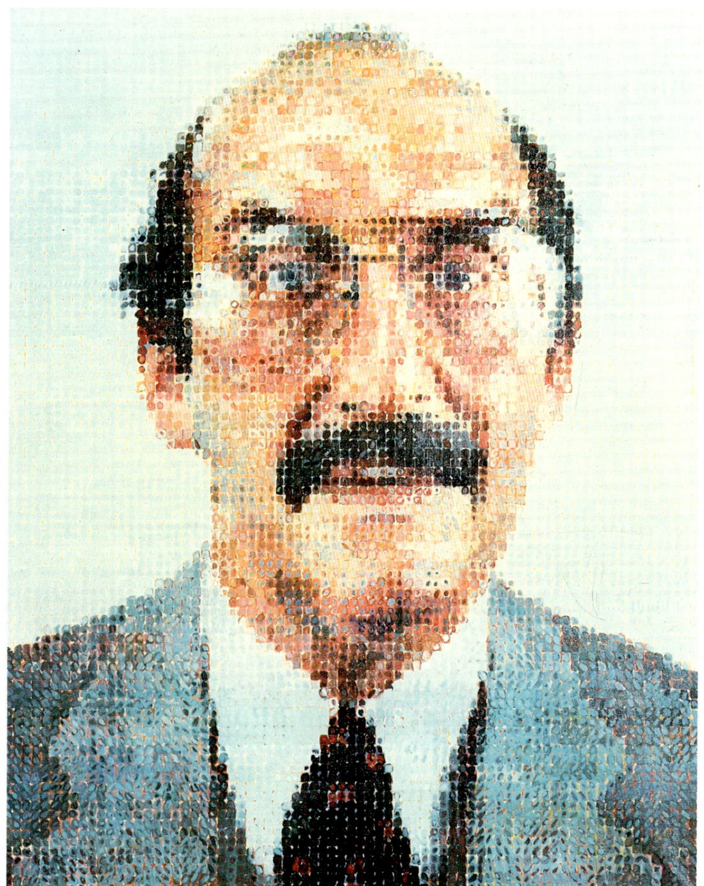

Ralston Crawford

1906–1978

New Orleans #10, 1958
Oil on canvas, 40 × 32
Lent by Margaret Frank Crawford

Born in St. Catherines, Ontario, Ralston Crawford spent his childhood in Buffalo. As a young man he became a sailor and traveled to the Caribbean, Central America, and California. He enrolled in the Otis Art Institute, Los Angeles, and worked in Walt Disney's studio. After two terms at the Institute he returned East to attend the Pennsylvania Academy of the Fine Arts in Philadelphia. A frequent visitor to New Orleans, he completely immersed himself in the culture of that city in the 1950s.

On his visits Crawford photographed the black musicians and the life around their music. His photographs and paintings of New Orleans life became interdependent. Although Crawford frequently transformed his photographs into paintings, these compositions did not necessarily depict actual people and places but represented his response to visual experiences.

New Orleans #10, a work from this series, is composed of fractured planes, perhaps reminiscent of the streets and architecture of the city.

The varied shapes and sizes of colored areas may be a visual response to the jazz heard there. To heighten his feeling for the rhythm Crawford learned as much as he could about life in New Orleans in order to respond to the music emotionally. Just as music has a bass and harmony, his pictures have many recurring themes and elements.

In combining the syncopated rhythm of jazz with geometric abstraction Crawford may have been influenced by Piet Mondrian's Boogie Woogie series, shown at the Museum of Modern Art during the 1940s.[1] Crawford also spent many hours listening to jazz recordings with Stuart Davis[2] and like him translated rhythm into brilliant colors and forms. In *New Orleans #10* the rich primary colors, applied smoothly in crisp geometric shapes, are set against stark white to intensify the rhythm of the composition.

Since Crawford's paintings reflect emotions, his work conveys a depth of feeling combined with a mastery of form, color, and rhythm. Although he strove for this balance throughout his life, the artist felt that he had realized it only a few years before his death in 1978.[3]

NJS

1.
Barbara Rose, *American Art since 1900,* Holt, Rinehart and Winston, Inc., New York, 1975, p. 133.
2.
Barbara Haskell, *Ralston Crawford,* Whitney Museum of American Art, New York, 1985, p. 89.
3.
Bonnie Barrett Stretch, "Reticent Romantic," *ArtNews,* April 1986, p. 121.

Additional References
Freeman, Richard B.: *Ralston Crawford,* University of Alabama Press, Birmingham, 1953.
———: *Ralston Crawford,* University of Kentucky Press, Lexington, 1973.

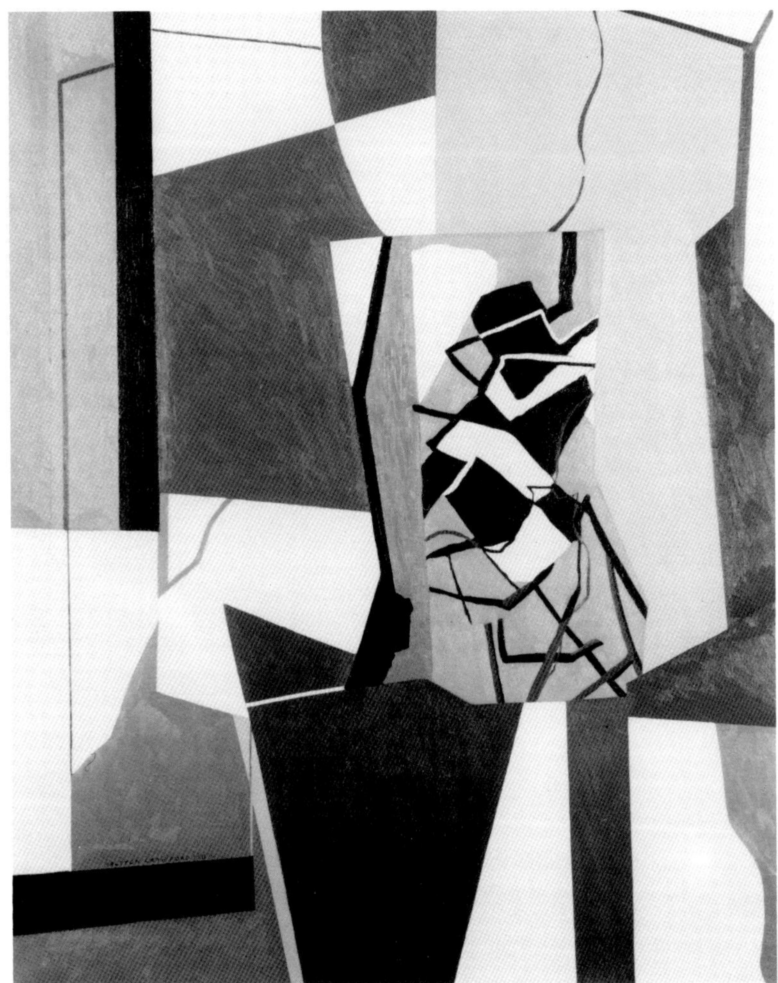

1.
Kay Larson, "Painting the Public Lands," *ArtNews,* January 1976, p. 35.

Additional References
Downes, Rackstraw: "A Landscape Where Dynasties Have Passed," *ArtNews,* October 1981, pp. 184–187.
Goodyear, Frank H., Jr.: *Contemporary American Realism since 1960,* New York Graphic Society, Boston, 1981.
Storr, Robert: "Rackstraw Downes: Painter as Geographer," *Art in America,* October 1984, pp. 154–161.

The Dam at Fairfield, 1974
Oil on canvas, 12¼ × 46½
Lent by Jane and Robert Carroll

Born in England, Rackstraw Downes received a degree in English literature from Cambridge University. He later changed direction when he came to the United States to attend the Yale School of Art and Architecture, where he studied with Al Held, among others. Soon discovering that abstraction was not his true style, Downes was drawn to realistic landscape painting. His initial essays in the genre were painted with thick brushstrokes, but he progressed quickly to the precision of detail seen in *The Dam at Fairfield.*

Whether working in Central Park or the woods of Maine, Downes's practice is the same: he begins a drawing on one sheet of paper and adds successive sheets in either direction as the composition expands until he is satisfied with the result. Downes uses these drawings from nature as the basis for paintings executed in his studio. *The Dam at Fairfield,* with its elongated horizontal axis, is a good example of the panoramic composition achieved by this method.

Avoiding the kinds of dramatic scenes in nature favored by the Hudson River School, Downes intentionally chooses ordinary subjects like *The Dam at Fairfield.* Although no people appear in his paintings, human existence is acknowledged by the artifacts of society like the dam.

Downes's landscapes are recognized for their faithfulness to nature. This accuracy was a factor in his being chosen by the Department of the Interior to be one of forty-five artists to take a new look at America through painting.[1] The result was *The Coke Works at Clairton* (1975), frequently compared with Thomas Cole's *View from Mount Holyoke, Northampton, Massachusetts, after a Thunderstorm (The Oxbow)* (1836) in the Metropolitan Museum.

Although Cole and Downes both depict landscapes with a realistic emphasis on light and spatial relationships, Downes eschews a transcendental view of nature, taking instead a documentary approach to contemporary life. His work makes no comment on man's relation to nature or his destruction of it, simply recording their coexistence.

NJS

Rackstraw Downes

Born 1939

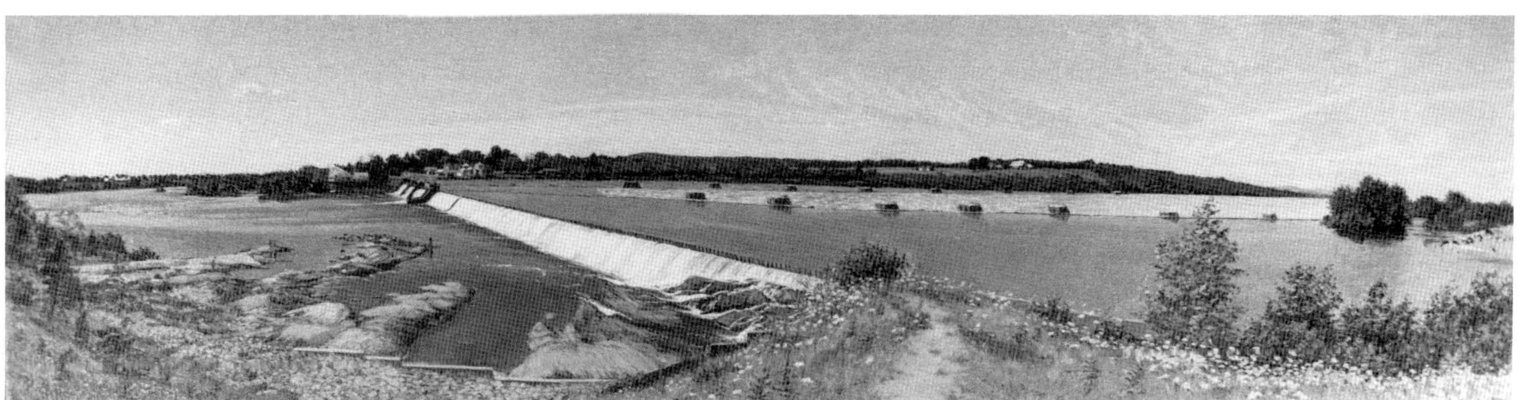

Jean Dubuffet

Born 1901

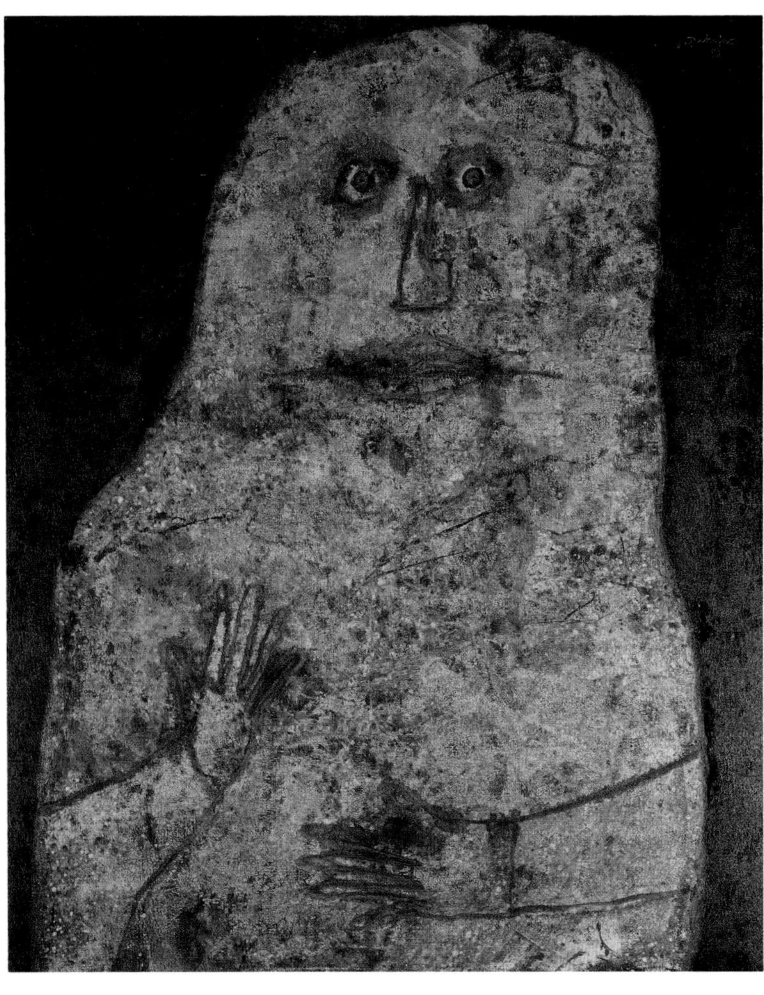

Le Sentencieux, 1958
Oil on canvas, 36¼ × 30
Lent by Elizabeth and Maurice Pinto

Jean Dubuffet's abundant inventiveness has made him one of the pivotal artists of the twentieth century. His accomplishments cannot be measured by his productivity alone; the variety of his media and the range of his themes are equally astonishing.

Dubuffet grew up in Le Havre and when he was seventeen went to Paris to study at the Académie Julian. Nonacademic in style and subject, his work reflects a rejection of the bourgeois concepts of classical beauty. The common man is central to Dubuffet's artistic vision, and his figures, depicted on Parisian streets or in the Métro, are frequently drawn in a child-like fashion.

Le Sentencieux (The Sententious One) belongs to the series called *Figures Augures* (Soothsayers), comprising about twenty paintings and one drawing done between April and October 1958. Finished on April 16, *Le Sentencieux* is one of the earliest pieces in the group. *L'Attentif* (The Attentive One) and *Hauts Lieux de Mariage* (Heights of Marriage) are other canvases in the series. All but two of the works are like *Le Sentencieux* in presenting large, single, bust-length figures frontally in an axial composition. The undulating forms, some of which were created with thick blobs of paint, are silhouetted against an ambiguous background. The fluidity of outline, which makes the shape look as if it would change at any moment, gives a phantasmal quality to these ghostly humanoids. The result is a feeling of uneasiness.

Unlike some of the other figures, *Le Sentencieux* is not frightening; but it is equally inscrutable. The moralizing attitude implied by the title is not in fact apparent in the facial expression of this gray monolithic mass. *Le Sentencieux* resembles many of the other paintings in the Soothsayer series by looking defiantly at the viewer, as if contesting rules set by society. In so doing Dubuffet's *Figures Augures* present a satirical commentary on conventional values.

GL

References
Franzke, Andreas: *Dubuffet,* trans. Robert Erich Wolf, Harry N. Abrams, Inc., New York, 1981.
Jean Dubuffet: A Retrospective, Solomon R. Guggenheim Museum, New York, April 28 – July 29, 1973.
Loreau, Max: *Catalogue des Travaux de Jean Dubuffet,* vol. XIV, *Celebration du Sol,* II: *Texturologies, Topographies,* Weber, [Paris], 1969.
Selz, Peter: *The Work of Jean Dubuffet,* The Museum of Modern Art, New York, 1962.

Arroyo del Oso & Rancho Chonito Orchards
1986
Oil on linen, 26 × 72
Lent by Barbara W. and Steven Grossman

Joellyn Duesberry was born in Richmond, Virginia, in 1944. After graduating from Smith College in 1966 and studying at Dartmouth, she earned a Master's degree from the Institute of Fine Arts of New York University. Since then she has studied at the Art Students League, the National Academy of Design, and the New York Academy. She now lives in Colorado.

Duesberry recently remarked, "I have discovered that personal expression through landscape painting is far more necessary to me than the 'scene' painting as a realist."[1] Her approach to plein air painting is described as complete immersion in which the artist "confronts this landscape directly, painting within it surrounded by its sounds, smells, textures, moisture, heat and cold."[2] Yearly painting trips to favorite places like Mt. Desert, Maine, and Millbrook, New York, allow Duesberry to develop the physical and spiritual presence of a location. In the past five years she has widened her itinerary and prowess with Alaskan and Western landscapes, of which *Arroyo del Oso & Rancho Chonito Orchards* is a fine example.

"Duesberry's landscapes, intensely felt and burgeoning with life, present a constantly changing synthesis of the artist's vision and of the earth itself as an independent reality, boundlessly alive."[3] The palpable vivacity of *Arroyo del Oso & Rancho Chonito Orchards* gives us the feeling of a February landscape about to burst into spring. A horizontal panoramic view, the painting has a deep recession into space which the viewer's eye can traverse through converging triangular planes. These planes lead from a hazy foreground to a middle ground that is clear and on to the background range of mountains. Thus "the viewer's eye is fixed on the middle and background— the parts of the canvas in which the painter's mark best approximates what we would see were we actually looking at nature."[4]

Arroyo del Oso & Rancho Chonito Orchards reflects a dichotomy of imposed and natural order. Although there are no people in the picture, a human presence is asserted by the road, the fenced-off fields, architecture, and the carefully orchestrated rows of the orchard. The landscape is not idealized; human disorder is suggested by the debris left at the side of the road. Even the signs of imposed order—the road, fence posts, and rows of trees—are not tightly regimented, appearing instead much as they would in reality.

The natural order of the landscape asserts itself in the uneven contour of the land and mountains and in the clumpy growth of bushes and trees that divide the road and orchard. Clouds in the background sky are drawn out as if across an immense distance and add to the sense of a natural order beyond human control. The passage of time is suggested by the uplift and flux of the clouds and by the shadows that wind across the road. Rather than a scene frozen in time, *Arroyo del Oso & Rancho Chonito Orchards* suggests a place in continual change.
AT

1.
Joellyn Duesberry, quoted in *Recent Western Paintings,* Gerald Peters Gallery, Santa Fe, 1990, p. [1].
2.
May Brawley Hill, "Joellyn Duesberry," *Arts Magazine,* October 1985, p. 127.
3.
Ibid.
4.
Blair T. Birmelin, "Joellyn Duesberry at Tatistcheff," *Art in America,* February 1986, p. 132.

Additional Reference
Bolt, Thomas: "Joellyn Duesberry," *American Artist,* October 1986, pp. 48–53 et seq.

Joellyn Duesberry

Born 1944

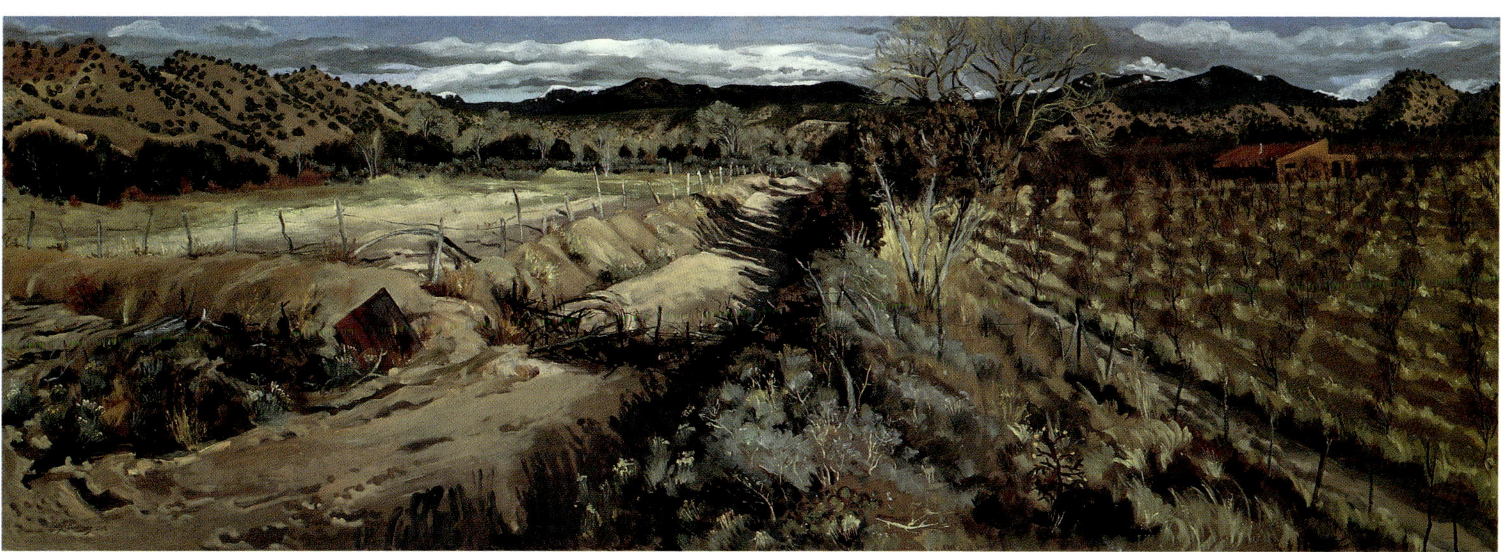

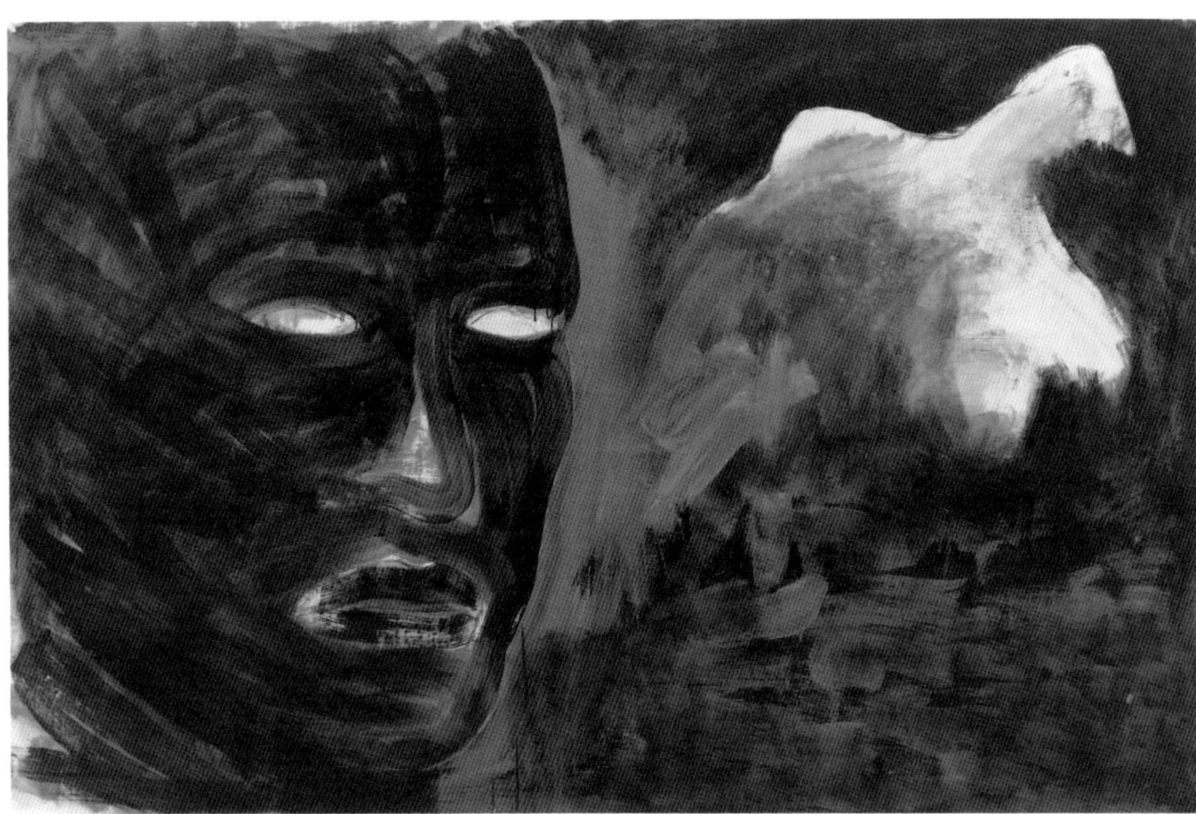

Claes Eklundh

Born 1944

Portrait, 1987
Oil on canvas, 54 × 80
Lent by Rima Ayas and Ronald W. Moore

Claes Eklundh was born in 1944 in Malmö, Sweden. After attending the Royal Academy of Fine Arts in Stockholm, he continued his studies in Copenhagen. The artist painted in Paris and Malmö before coming to New York, where he currently has a studio. *Portrait* was included in his first one-man exhibition in the United States, held at the Dolan/Maxwell Gallery in Philadelphia in 1987.

Although at that time Eklundh was concentrating on portraiture, this work is not a traditional example of the genre. The title is generic rather than specific, simply suggesting a way of looking at the work. The artist believes that painting is a language of its own that can seldom be translated into words.[1] Eklundh prefers to let his art express itself on a nonverbal level.

The painting contains two images. The dark head in the left foreground may be said to represent a strong supernatural power contained in a generalized human form. The ominous mask-like face, lit from within, stares menacingly out at the viewer through blank eyes. The other image, a bird-like form on the right, suggests the spirit, which has just left the body in a blaze. Perhaps the theme is transformation. Confronted with the shell of a man burning with inner light, we feel in the presence of an eternal force.

The powerful imagery is intensified by the use of strong colors. The paint is applied with broad, feathery strokes. Set against the expressionist brushwork are the sharply defined lines of the head. Through his use of color, form, and brushstroke, Eklundh has intensified the image's emotional content to increase the impact of the painting as whole.

CLC

1.
Telephone interview by CLC with Claes Eklundh, January 8, 1991.

Additional References
Mats, B.: "New Paintings in Sweden," *Flash Art,* January 1983, pp. 52–55.
Nilsson, Bo: "Northern Positions," *Flash Art,* February–March 1987, pp. 92–95.
———: *Claes Eklundh,* Dolan/Maxwell Gallery, Philadelphia, September 12–October 10, 1987.

Nedick's, 1968–1969
Oil on Masonite, 48 × 36
Lent by Beatrice Oenslager Chace

Although urban life is usually characterized by
people, noise, and high-speed activity, Richard
Estes depicts an uninhabited city, captured for a
moment in complete quiet, all motion arrested.
His subjects are familiar scenes of human life—
streets, automobiles, storefronts, movie theaters,
restaurants—easily overlooked in the bustle of
the city. Estes brings out the details of this man-
made world with the sharp focus and vivid realism of a photograph.

Estes was born in Kewanee, Illinois, and
studied at the School of the Art Institute of
Chicago before working as an illustrator and
layout artist. In 1966 he began painting full time
and soon turned to the urban landscapes which
have remained his primary subject. "I live in the
city," Estes remarks. "If I lived somewhere else,
that is what I would paint."[1]

Although some of his compositions are panoramic views of a street and others, like *Nedick's,*
a single building or details, there is little variation
in style or theme. In defense, Estes asks, "What's
wrong with doing the same thing over and over
again? I think the most—the silliest thing is
to try to come up with some new gimmick every
year."[2]

Estes works from photographs. After selecting
a scene from hundreds of images shot at random
throughout the city, he decides which elements
he will include in the composition and which he
will either alter or eliminate. Parking meters and
cars are carefully arranged, and the angle of a
street or placement of the horizon may be shifted
after Estes has examined additional photographs
of the chosen site. The end result is a composite
image, rich with a myriad of visual details taken
from the photographs.

"Painting is trickery, because you can make
people respond by guiding their eyes around the
picture," says Estes.[3] For this artist the "trickery" stems from the clarity of each element in
the composition. His use of complex reflections
in plate-glass windows, as in *Nedick's,* demands
a close reading. In other paintings of the restaur-
ant Estes has set the building at a distance, but
in this version the window fills the canvas. Viewed
through the glass and reflected upon its surface,
layer upon layer of images, all in focus, create
visual and spatial ambiguities.

Estes's paintings project none of his feelings
about urban America and elicit no emotional
response from the viewer. He eliminates the
human form from his compositions to avoid any
narrative quality although evidence of human
activity persists. Nevertheless, landscapes like
Nedick's seem dehumanized and sterile, portray-
ing empty streets washed with timeless, ethereal
light.

WGV

1.
Louis K. Meisel,
PhotoRealism,
Harry N. Abrams,
Inc., New York,
1980, p. 209.
2.
John Arthur, "A
Conversation," in
John Canaday,
*Richard Estes: The
Urban Landscape,*
Museum of Fine
Arts and New York
Graphic Society,
Boston, 1979, p. 22.
3.
Ibid., p. 27.

*Additional
References*
Gaugh, Harry:
"The Urban Vis-
ion of Estes," *Art
in America,*
November–
December 1978,
pp. 134–137.
"The Photo-
Realists; 12 Inter-
views," *Art in
America,*
November–
December 1972,
pp. 78–80.

Richard Estes

Born 1936

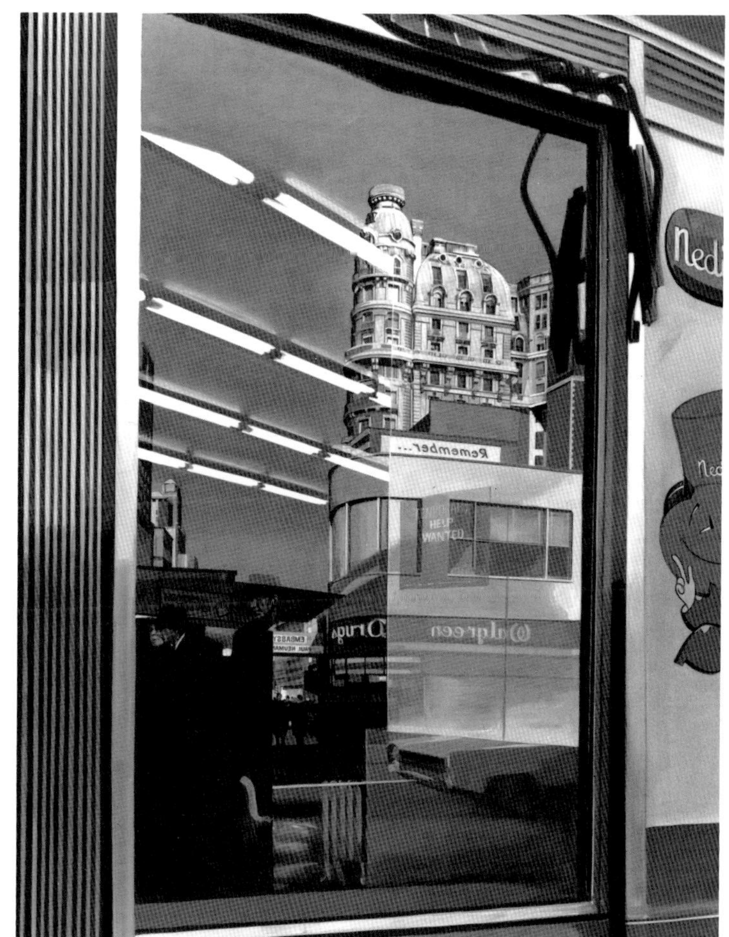

Rainer Fetting

Born 1949

Manhattan Acrobat, 1983
Oil on canvas, 91½ × 73½
Lent by Rena Bransten

A renewed interest in German expressionism of the 1920s led to the contemporary movement of neo-expressionism. Rainer Fetting, together with fellow Berlin artists Salome and Helmut Middendorf, was in the forefront of this stylistic revival, which is characterized by thick brush-strokes of bright, intense color quickly applied.

In compositions like *Manhattan Acrobat* Fetting takes this approach one step further. He often uses banal subjects rather than scenes of deliberate violence, distorting these everyday themes with freakish assemblages and fevered brushwork. The anxiety his works stir in the viewer stems not from the narrative of the paint-ing but from the way the brushstrokes dominate and dictate the composition. The vibrant color explodes powerfully from the canvas.

Since 1983 Fetting has divided his time between New York and Berlin. His move to America resulted in many paintings of cityscapes such as

Manhattan Acrobat. The violent orange-red color sets the painting aflame, but the larger-than-life acrobat performs his routine oblivious of the fire engulfing him. The alien figure is disturbingly graceful, and the elongated limbs and fingers add a frightening sensuality. The dark blue and black of the skyscraper in the background creates a dead calm in the blazing canvas. Such distortions of color and form are distinguishing features of this artist's work.

Fetting places thematic emphasis on cities and focuses primarily on the male figure set in these anxious urban scenes. The elongation of his males and their graceful movements make them appear androgynous, but this sexual ambiguity is not the artist's main concern. Fetting is interested in using dramatic contrasts in color and vigorous brushstrokes to create a disturb-ingly expressive composition. Thanks to the vivid backdrop against which they are painted, Fetting's people often look like actors on a stage. This theatrical element in his paintings relates to his work in film and video.

LHG

References
Kuspit, Donald: "Rainer Fetting: The Melancholy, Sensual Self," *Contemporanea*, July–August 1988, pp. 41–45.

———: "Rainer Fetting's New York Pictures," in *Rainer Fetting: Gemälde und Skulpturen,* Staatliche Museen zu Berlin, DDR, Nationalgalerie, [March 17–April 15], 1990; Stadtmuseum Weimar (Bertuchhaus), Kabinett am Goetheplatz, [July 14–August 23], 1990.

Rainer Fetting: Holzbilder, Marlborough Gallery, New York, June 9–July 6, 1984.

Weisler, Hermann: "Determined Liv-ing Feeling: How Rainer Fetting Incorporates Time and the Present in His Pic-tures," in *Rainer Fetting: Gemälde und Skulpturen.*

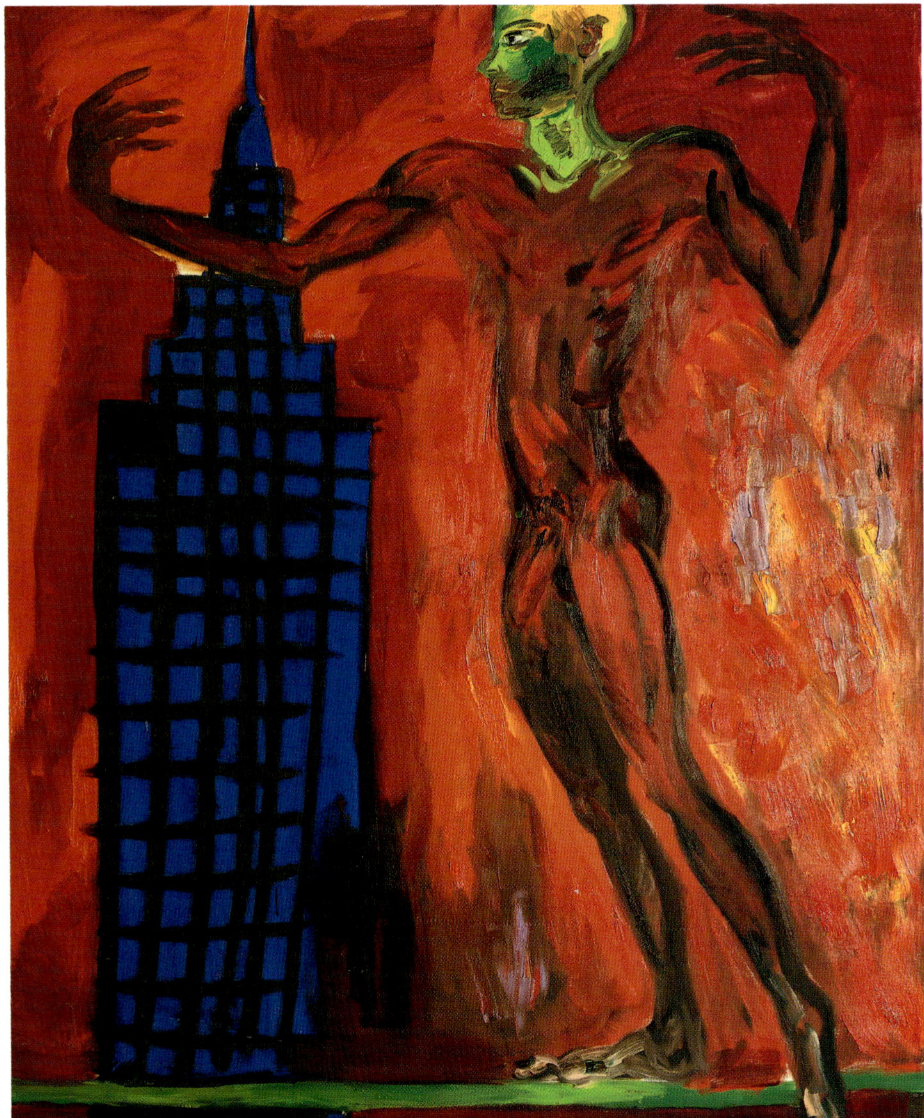

1.
Carter Ratcliff, art-
ist interview in
*Janet Fish: An
Exhibition of
Recent Paintings,*
Robert Miller Gal-
lery, New York, Feb-
ruary 5–March 2,
1985, n.p.

*Additional
References*
Cottingham, Jane:
"Janet Fish: Per-
ceptual Realist,"
American Artist,
October 1982,
pp. 44–49, 90,
and 94–95.
Gerrit, Henry:
"The Real
Thing," *Art Inter-
national,* Sum-
mer 1972,
pp. 87–91.
Lubell, Ellen:
"Janet Fish,"
Arts Magazine,
May 1979, p. 21.

Fiuggi Water, 1974
Oil on canvas, 20⅛ × 48¼
Lent by Jane and Robert Carroll

The windows of Janet Fish's childhood home were filled with bottles. Their ridges and curves glittering in the light made a lasting impression. Her paintings from the early 1970s display a wealth of objects reflecting and refracting light and color. Through closeup arrangements of bottles, glasses, honeypots, and jars, like that in *Fiuggi Water,* Fish explores a world filled with transparency.

Fish comes from a Boston family of artists; her grandfather was an impressionist painter and her mother a sculptor whom Fish credits with influence on her own work. She graduated from Smith College in 1960 and from the Yale School of Art and Architecture in 1963, where two fellow students were Chuck Close* and Rackstraw Downes* and one of her teachers was Alex Katz.* Although admiring many artists and styles ranging from Zurbarán and Hassam to de Kooning and Katz, she never considered herself "a disciple of any school or style."[1]

After working briefly as an abstract expressionist, Fish turned in the late 1960s to her own brand of realism. She consistently enlarged the scale of her subjects and maintained the expressionist fluidity in her application of pigment.

Fascinated with reflections, in the early 1970s she turned for subjects to such ordinary mass-produced glass objects as the Japanese Fiuggi containers for bottled water. Compositions like *Fiuggi Water* often create abstract designs of light and color by systematically repeating a single object larger than life to fill the canvas. The object never stands alone as an independent presence or icon but is part of an overall pattern. As each surface overlaps, catching and sharing the light, the interrelationships of forms and reflections are more important than the objects themselves.

In *Fiuggi Water* the complexity of the designs created by light passing through the facets, curves, and layers of glass is increased by the addition of water; a mirror further distorts and magnifies the illusion. The patterns ripple across the surface of the canvas like those from a pebble dropped into a still pond. No surface is dull, and even the surrounding air seems enlivened by the reflected rays of light. As the light dances through and onto each piece of glass, the energy projected defies the concept of "still life."
WGV

Janet Fish

Born 1938

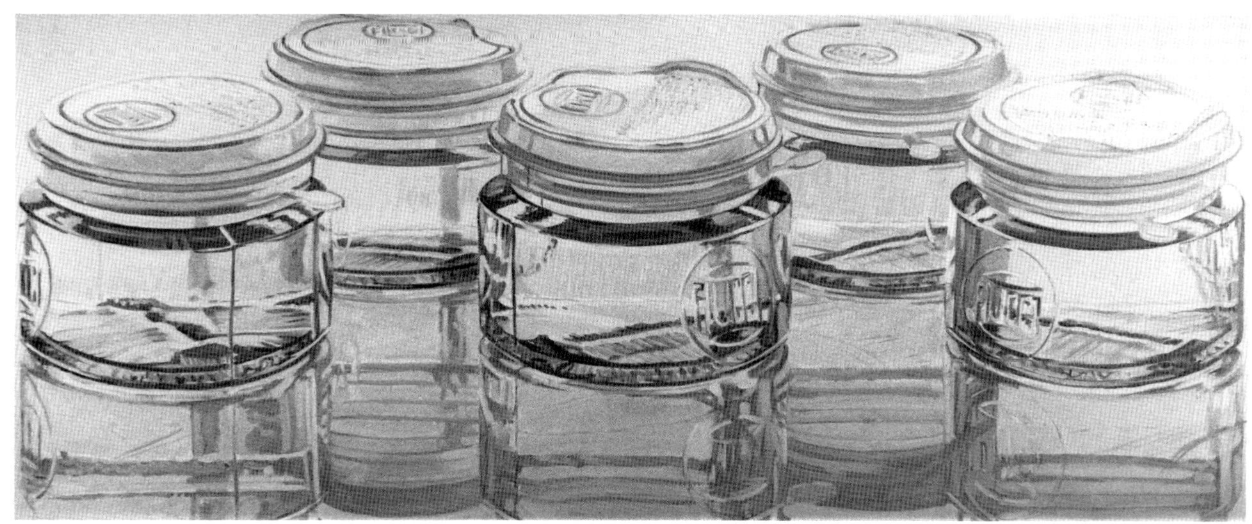

Helen Frankenthaler

Born 1928

Just Before, 1974
Acrylic on canvas, 72½ × 84
Lent by Janet W. Ketcham

At the age of ten Frankenthaler, a native of New York City, won an honorable mention in an art competition run by a Manhattan store. Her parents encouraged her to develop her painting skills, but she did not develop a passion for the arts until her senior year of high school at Dalton.

Mountain and Sea (1952), now on extended loan to the National Gallery of Art, established Helen Frankenthaler as one of the leaders among contemporary artists. Clement Greenberg, mentor to many avant-garde artists, was in her studio when she completed this work and declared her method revolutionary.[1] Because she applied thin oil washes directly onto the raw canvas, the color, acting like a stain, became inseparable from the weave of the cloth. This technique, which was immediately recognized as a significant breakthrough for artists concerned with the dichotomy between painting and drawing, influenced many other artists, including Morris Louis.*

In *Just Before* Frankenthaler repeats the method, but acrylic is the medium. In this lyrical composition the paint floods the canvas instead of staining it because the thickly applied acrylic paint is unable to penetrate so deep into the weave. Here the medium allows the artist to unite her love of painting and drawing in one work.

Frankenthaler displays large areas of deeply saturated blues and browns, intersecting the bold colors with brilliant sky blue executed with calligraphic sharpness. Her use of color is a means not only of generating the picture but also of creating a new space. The colors force the component shapes into spatial relationships.

Only when Frankenthaler is satisfied with the placement of the colors and the composition is complete does she give the work a name; it is not necessarily a specific reference to the subject of the picture at hand but is the result of an unrelated inspiration, often from nature.

Just Before was created in the 1970s when Frankenthaler began to branch out into other media, including woodcuts and sculpture. This experimentation enriched her painting style, and Frankenthaler, always open to new ideas, continues to evolve as an artist.

NJS

1.
Karen Wilkin, *Frankenthaler: Works on Paper 1949–1984,* George Braziller, Inc., and the International Exhibitions Foundation, New York, 1984, p. 31.

Additional References
Carmean, E.A., Jr.: *Helen Frankenthaler: A Paintings Retrospective,* Harry N. Abrams, Inc., New York, 1989.
Elderfield, John: *Frankenthaler,* Harry N. Abrams, Inc., New York, 1989.
Guest, Judith: "Helen Frankenthaler: The Moment and the Distance," *Arts Magazine,* April 1975, pp. 58–59.
Goodman, Cynthia: *Works of the Seventies,* Buckheim and Rowland, Inc., Ann Arbor, 1980.

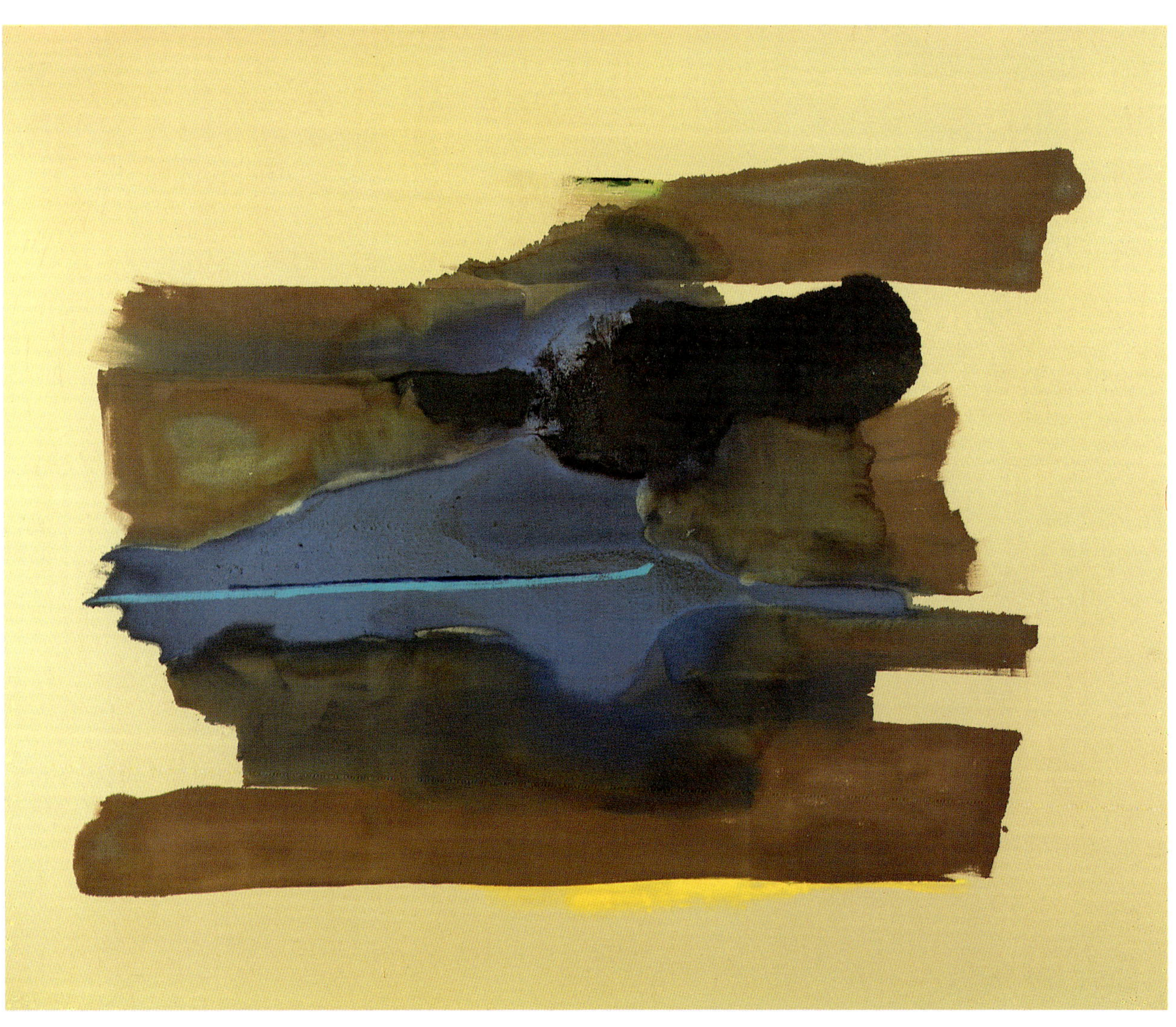

October, 1975
Oil on canvas, 52 × 44
Lent by Barbara W. and Steven Grossman

"The combination of forms and light in the land-scape produces a rush of feeling which translates into the painting," explains Jane Freilicher. "When I have stopped painting on a landscape, I go outside and I am always amazed by how much more is pouring over my head."[1]

Freilicher's rush of feeling is expressed by the painting process—free, fluid patches of gestural paint. At the same time she captures an atmospheric sense of place through her careful observation of nature. As she paints the rural landscapes around her Long Island home, major elements like houses, barns, and fields are defined through abstract gesture rather than precise contour. Essential description is included, but details are eliminated. Freilicher explains, "As soon as I do something that seems very tenuous I get bored with it . . . when I get more specific I begin to feel cloistered."[2]

A native of New York City, Freilicher became interested in art during adolescence. After studying at Brooklyn College, Columbia University, and the Hans Hofmann School of Fine Arts, Freilicher became part of New York's artistic and literary scene. In the 1950s she met Fairfield Porter,* whose landscapes have much in common with hers, especially in their combination of abstraction and realism. Freilicher also acknowledges other influences ranging from de Kooning and Pollock to Courbet and Matisse. She is particularly indebted to her teacher Hans Hofmann for his ideas on color and the dynamics of positive and negative space.

October is neither recollection nor nostalgia but pure visualization of a fall afternoon: season, time, and weather. The life of the picture comes in part from the intense autumn colors, which are faithful to nature if not exact. Instead of specific light and shadows to indicate an exact time of day, an overall light diffuses the scene, in keeping with Freilicher's belief that "light is like oxygen in a painting; without it a painting is dead, it doesn't breathe."[3]

"I'm often touched by the beauty of my subject matter and want to express it . . . flowers and landscapes are very moving; perhaps this is a kind of egoism—to want to remake it beautiful for the modern viewer."[4] As in *October,* this artist makes expression of an emotional reaction to the simple beauty of nature seem effortless.
WGV

1.
Ted Berrigan,
"Painter to the New York Poets,"
ArtNews,
November 1965,
p. 44.
2.
Ibid.
3.
Robert Doty, *Jane Freilicher Paintings,* Taplinger Publishing Co., New York, 1986, p. 52.
4.
Berrigan, p. 44.

Additional Reference
Shorr, Harriet: "Jane Freilicher," *Arts Magazine,* May 1977, p. 9.

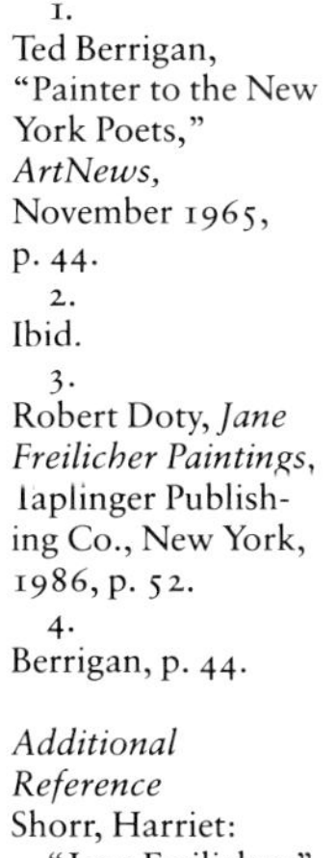

Jane Freilicher

Born 1924

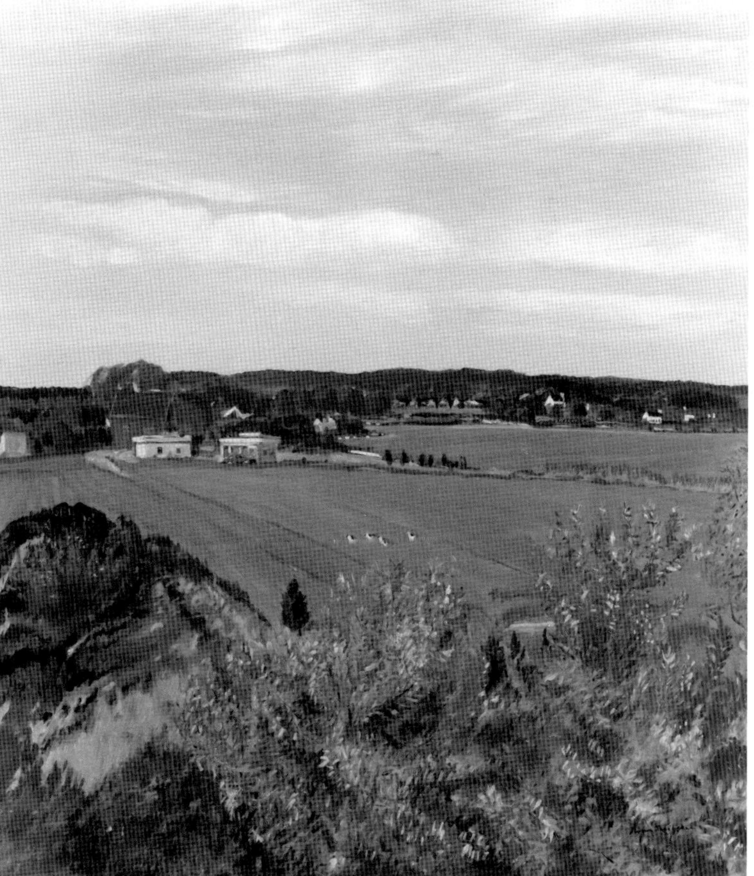

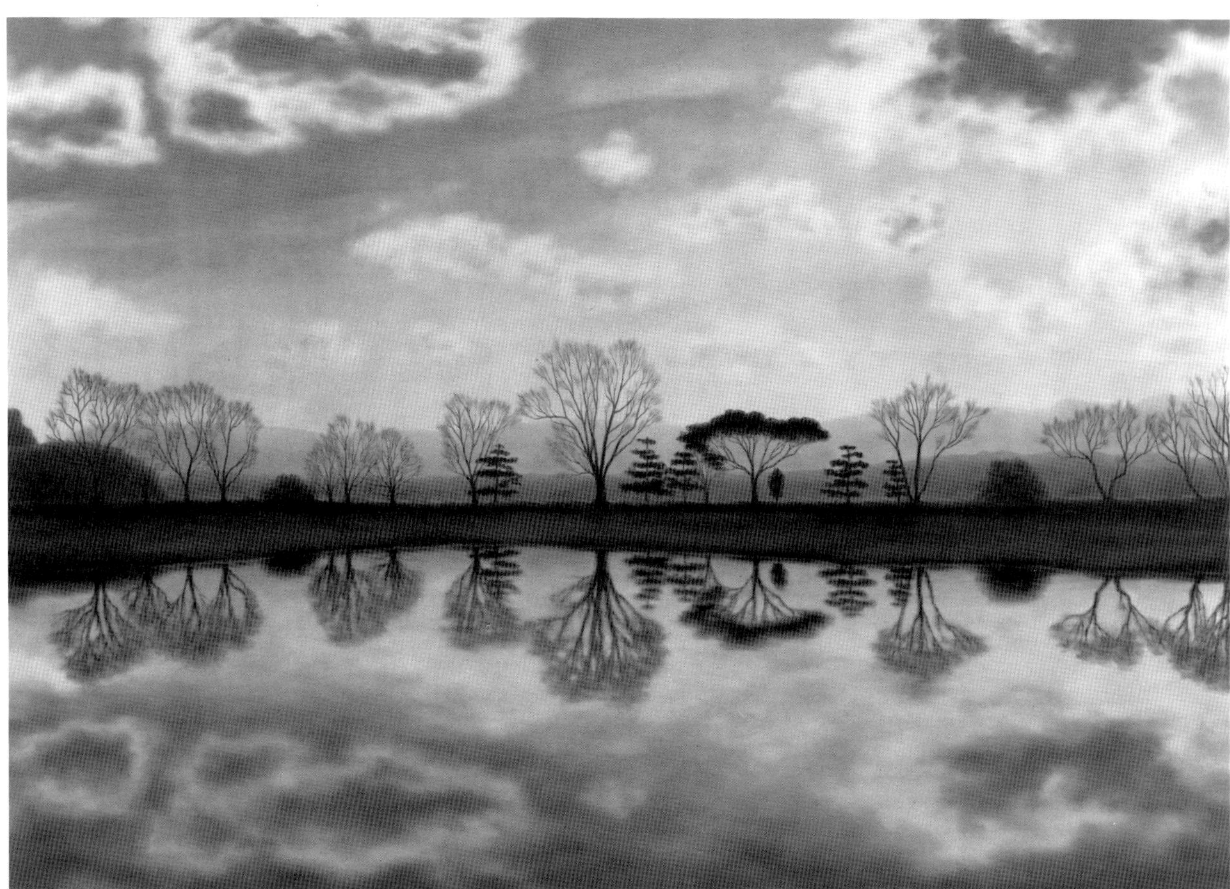

April Gornik

Born 1953

The Vernal Equinox, 1989
Oil on canvas, 77 × 106
Lent by Valerie and Charles Diker

April Gornik was born in Cleveland. She studied at the Cleveland Institute of Art and earned her Bachelor of Fine Arts degree at the Nova Scotia College of Art and Design. She started her professional life as a photographer and conceptual artist in the mid-1970s. Her attraction to landscape as a subject brought about a radical change in her work in 1977. "I had a vision in my head of something I felt I had to make. It turned out to be a landscape. It was horrifying to me—so uncool, so unhip. Landscape is the black sheep of art history."[1] Now considered a leader in the postmodern landscape movement, she has been compared with painters like Thomas Cole and Caspar David Friedrich although more than one critic has argued against such comparisons. John Loughery writes, "None of these spectacular images is part of a warmed-over or even a revised Romanticism; they are products of their time."[2]

Gornik's landscapes are creations of the imagination, pulled from memories of travels and novels, from photographs and dreams, rarely from nature. The chilling springtime landscape of *The Vernal Equinox* transcends realism. It is an unsettling portrayal of distant mountains and a peaceful lake bordered by trees. The horizon line is placed disturbingly in the exact middle of the painting. The precise exotic trees are all reflected perfectly in the dark, still waters. In its reduction of nature the painting produces a mood more austere than that evoked by even the most precise photographic landscape.

Light is ambiguous in *The Vernal Equinox.* The time of day could be dawn or dusk or some time in between. The composition is as balanced as the day in March for which it is named, when day and night are of equal length. This balance does not create a harmonious and peaceful unity, however, but a dramatic and tense schism. The architectonic symmetry establishes an ominous doubling. Combined with the fluffy clouds looming in the expansive and strangely lit sky, it projects a threatening undercurrent of potential disruption of the rarefied beauty of the scene.

The striking purity of these large-scale paintings, always devoid of human presence, is achieved through Gornik's smooth application of pigment. Her artistic hand is invisible. The flat style reinforces the illusion that there is nothing unusual about these extraordinary compositions. Yet despite its attractive colors and contemplative spaces, *The Vernal Equinox* is disquieting. Having been invited to share Gornik's private vision, the viewer is unable to interpret its symbols.

WEB

1.
Kelli Pryor, "Back to Nature," *Avenue,* February 1989, p. 136.
2.
John Loughery, "The New Romantic Landscape," *Arts Magazine,* November 1987, p. 107.

Additional References
Loughery, John: "Landscape Painting in the Eighties: April Gornik, Ellen Phelan and Joan Nelson," *Arts Magazine,* May 1988, pp. 44–48.
10 + 10: Contemporary Soviet and American Painters, Harry N. Abrams, Inc., New York, and Aurora Publishers, Leningrad, 1989.

Flight, 1964–1965
Oil on canvas, 48 × 36
Lent by Suzanne and Maurice Vanderwoude

A native of New York City who studied at the
Art Students League, Parsons School of Design,
and Cooper Union, as well as in Paris, Adolph
Gottlieb played a pivotal role in twentieth-
century American art. In 1935 he co-founded a
group of stylistically diverse independent artists,
including Mark Rothko, Arshile Gorky, and
Willem de Kooning, among others, known as
"The Ten." This first "New York School" was
dedicated to the promotion of American expressionist art.

A sojourn in Europe from 1921 to 1922
marked the beginning of Gottlieb's fascination
with European abstraction. Early in his career
this outspoken and innovative artist had rejected
popular representational artists like Reginald
Marsh and Thomas Hart Benton. Despite a
strong political conscience, Gottlieb believed
that art should not be subservient to politics but
should speak to everyone. It was his interest in
the universal expression of "emotional truth"[1]
that led him to abstraction.

Flight belongs to the Burst series, begun in
1956, which brought together several ideas
and motifs and represented the culmination of
Gottlieb's artistic development. Abstraction first
appeared in this artist's work in the 1920s. Early
paintings such as *Interior* broke with scene
painting and followed the avant-garde in its dis-
tortion of form and use of irrational space. In
the 1930s Gottlieb simultaneously developed an
interest in tribal art and the ideas of Freud and
Jung. Out of these interests came his Pictographs
of the 1940s, which present abstract symbols in
a grid format. In the Imaginary Landscapes of
the 1950s the abstract forms of the Pictographs
were separated by a single horizontal line in the
middle of the canvas.

Out of these series evolved the Bursts. Several
compositional elements from Gottlieb's earlier
work remain, but now color is his most expressive tool. As in the work of his friend Mark
Rothko, color replaces line, unifying and defining
the canvas. In *Flight,* for example, the extraordinary intensity and richness of the color has parallel expressions in Rothko's color-field works.
The color in *Flight* embodies a transcendental
spirituality, stunning in its potency yet inviting
with its deep resonance. This duality extends to
the composition. The shapes of the two central-
ized abstract forms are contrasted: the upper is
circular, luminous, and controlled; the lower
jagged and explosive. In their opposition these
large universal forms recall myths of reconcilia-
tion between the sun and the earth or between
heaven and hell. Coexisting yet separate, they
express a balance between the rational and the
irrational. Gottlieb continued to paint in the same
introspective fashion until his death in 1974.
MYZ

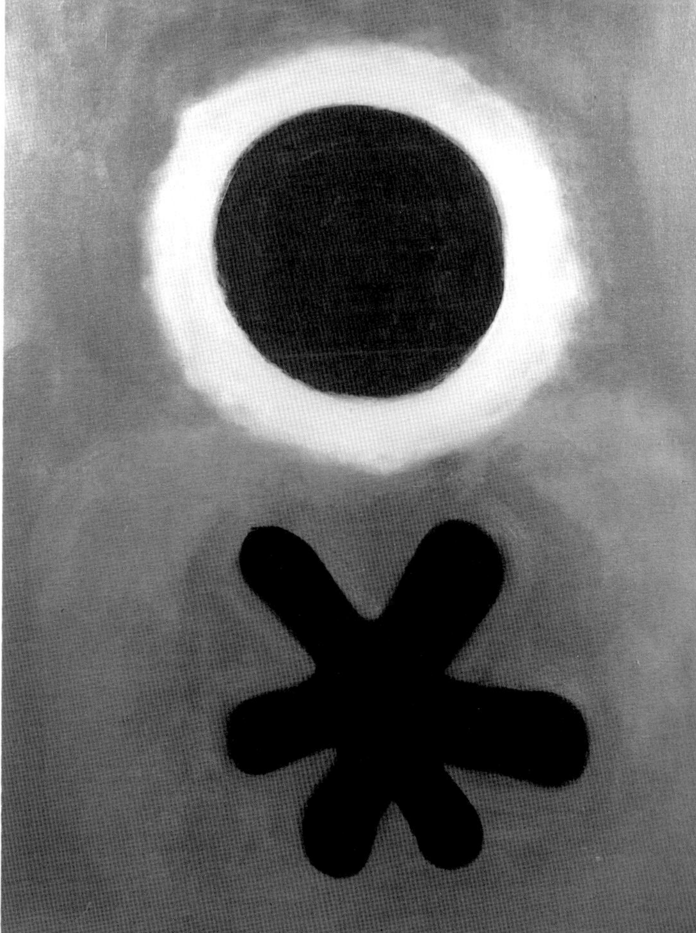

1.
Henry Flood
Robert, Jr. (ed.),
*Adolph Gottlieb:
Paintings, 1921–
1956,* Joslyn Art
Museum, Omaha,
May 12–June 24,
1979 (and later
venues), Joslyn Art
Museum, Omaha,
1980, p. 16.

*Additional
References*
Ashton, Dore:
*American Art
since 1945,*
Oxford Univer-
sity Press, New
York, 1982.
Sandler, Irving:
essay in *Adolph
Gottlieb: Paint-
ings 1945–1974,*
A. Emmerich
Gallery, New
York, 1977.

Philip Guston

1913 – 1980

Blue Sky and Green Sea, 1977
Oil on canvas, 58 × 71¾
Lent by Rena Bransten

A long artistic road had been traveled by Philip Guston before creating *Blue Sky and Green Sea,* a road with many difficulties and one not lightly taken. The son of a Russian immigrant, Guston was born in a Montreal ghetto in 1913 and moved to Los Angeles in 1919. He attended the Manual Arts High School but left before graduating and was earning his own living at seventeen. In 1935 he worked in New York on mural projects sponsored by the Works Progress Administration.

After the Second World War Guston played a leading role in the New York school of abstract expressionism. In 1960, in the middle of his "abstract" period, he said

> There is something ridiculous and miserly in the myth we inherit from abstract art: That painting is autonomous, pure and for itself, and therefore we habitually define its ingredients and define its limits. But painting is "impure." It is the adjustment of impurities which forces a painting's continuity. We are image-makers and image-ridden.[1]

Soon thereafter he began to turn out small paintings of recognizable objects—hands, shoes, books, and lamps.

There was much of the poet in Guston. He confronted abstractions of the mind and put them down on canvas. His later works, such as *Blue Sky and Green Sea*, are particularly vivid and intense, imaginative treatments of experience filled with indecipherable autobiographical allusions.

These funky images often make us laugh but also make us wonder. What are we looking at and what does it mean? An entanglement of skinny cartoon legs, bent at their knobby knees, attached to oversized shoes, some turned sideways to reveal soles like a cobbled horseshoe. Are these legs venturing out into the world from behind the slightly opened door, or are they on their way back in? There is the sense of a story unfolding, but it is only a suggestion and each of Guston's canvases seems like a single frame in a comic strip. The image is a private one, perhaps self-revealing — one used over and over again throughout the 1970s. We will have to supply the story ourselves.

Though ambiguous, the forms in *Blue Sky and Green Sea* reveal the artist's feelings. Whether the image is disturbing or amusing to the viewer, its intensity is expressed by the very active brushstrokes. The soft halftones, typical of Guston's work, along with the cadmium red, reveal a love for the sensuous quality of oil paint. Here is a work by an artist in his later years, a lifetime of thought and work behind him. Defying explanation, *Blue Sky and Green Sea* is nevertheless real, a creation of Guston's mind and heart that seems to have a life of its own.

VCK

1.
Ross Feld, *Philip Guston*, George Braziller, Inc., New York, for the San Francisco Museum of Modern Art, 1980, p. 21.

Additional References
Ashton, Dore: *Yes, but . . . : A Critical Study of Philip Guston,* The Viking Press, New York, 1976.
Mayer, Musa: *Night Studio: A Memoir of Philip Guston,* Alfred A. Knopf, New York, 1988.
Storr, Robert: *Philip Guston,* Abbeville Press, New York, 1986.

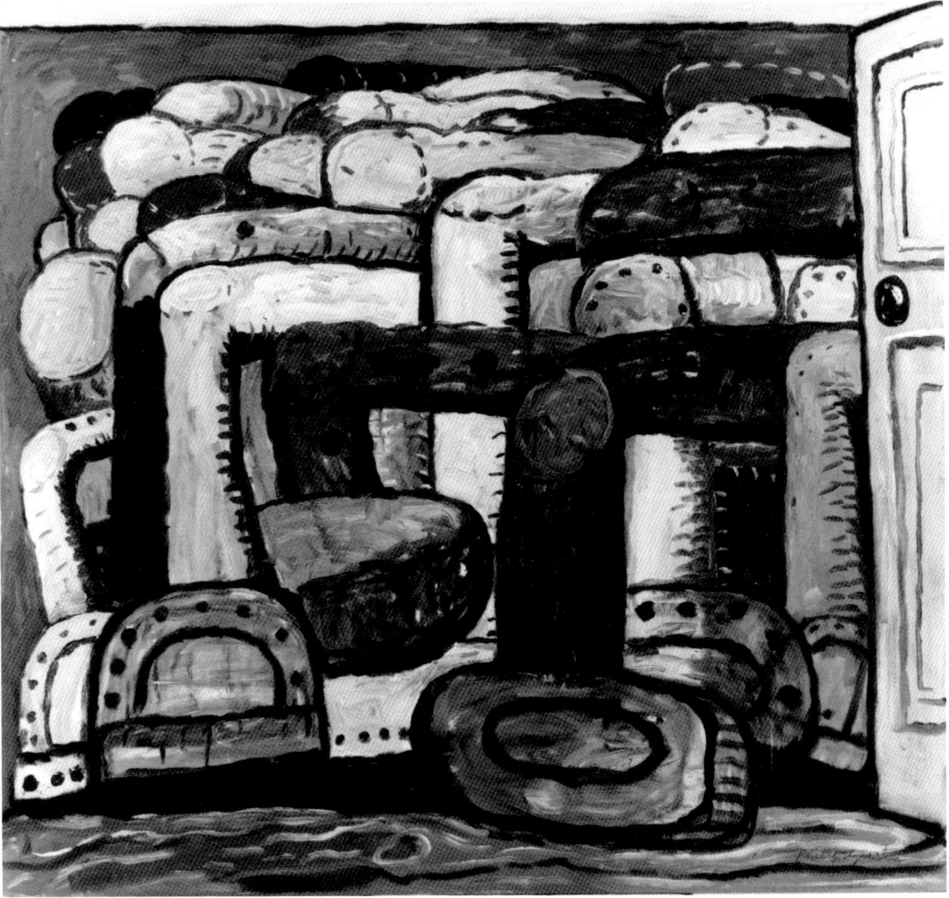

1.
For other portraits
see John McEwen,
"Introduction," in
*Howard Hodgkin:
Forty Paintings
1973–84*, George
Braziller, Inc., New
York, in association
with The White-
chapel Art Gallery,
London, 1984,
p. 10.
2.
John McEwen,
"Late Bloomer,"
Vanity Fair,
November 1984,
p. 68.

*Additional
References*
Dickhoff, Wilfried,
and Timothy
Hyman: *Howard
Hodgkin*, M.
Knoedler & Co.,
New York, 1990.
Galligan, Gregory:
"Howard
Hodgkin: Forty
Paintings," *Arts
Magazine*, March
1985,
pp. 122–125.

Mr. and Mrs. Terrance Conran, 1978–1981
Oil on wood, 39 × 49½
Lent by Loretta and Robert K. Lifton

The paintings of Howard Hodgkin are rooted in the familiar. Domestic in presentation and size, they are often domestic in subject as well. Works such as *Mr. and Mrs. Terrance Conran* conceal interior settings under a maze of patterned surfaces but also make expressive use of color to reveal the artist's emotional response to people, places, and events.

Born in London, Hodgkin received his training at the Camberwell School of Art, London, and the Bath Academy of Art, Corsham. A trustee of the National Gallery, Hodgkin was awarded the Turner Prize in 1985 for his contribution to British art. He is recognized as one of his country's most important painters and achieved international acclaim at the Venice Biennale in 1984.

Despite its apparent abstraction, *Mr. and Mrs. Terrance Conran* is in fact a kind of double portrait. Hodgkin frequently paints friends,[1] in this case a British businessman and his wife. The figures are barely discernible to the right and left of the central window-like form, a recurring motif in the artist's work that helps create a sense of space and place. With its domestic setting and strong patterning, the composition recalls the intimate interiors of Vuillard, whose work Hodgkin admires. Hodgkin paints what he feels, not what he sees, an approach demonstrated here. It is the memory of an occasion—perhaps an evening marked by bonhomie—rather than the Conrans themselves that is the subject of this warm and seductive composition.

Hodgkin works slowly, usually taking several years to complete a painting. For almost two decades he has used wood as the support for his painting. The accretion of color and patterns on top of an underlying representational image denotes, both actually and metaphorically, the impact of time on the memory of an event or feeling. And yet the final result seems spontaneous. The fauve-like colors, the sweeping brushwork, and the patterned surface contribute to the painting's vibrancy and sense of immediacy.

The presentation has a dramatic element in that the painted frame serves as a kind of proscenium for the spatial and emotional play. For years Hodgkin has employed this device to objectify both the experience depicted and the physical nature of the painting itself. The introduction of this theatrical element serves to distance both the artist and the viewer from the reconstituted emotional moment by defining our role as onlooker rather than participant. The proscenium frame also adds to the painting's presence as an object on the wall. "I have always thought of pictures as 'things,' with as much physical character as tables and chairs or cups and saucers," the artist once remarked.[2] Conceived as part of the composition, the frame or border is as integral to a work by Hodgkin as it is to a Gothic panel painting or to the Indian miniatures he collects.

EJN

Howard Hodgkin

Born 1932

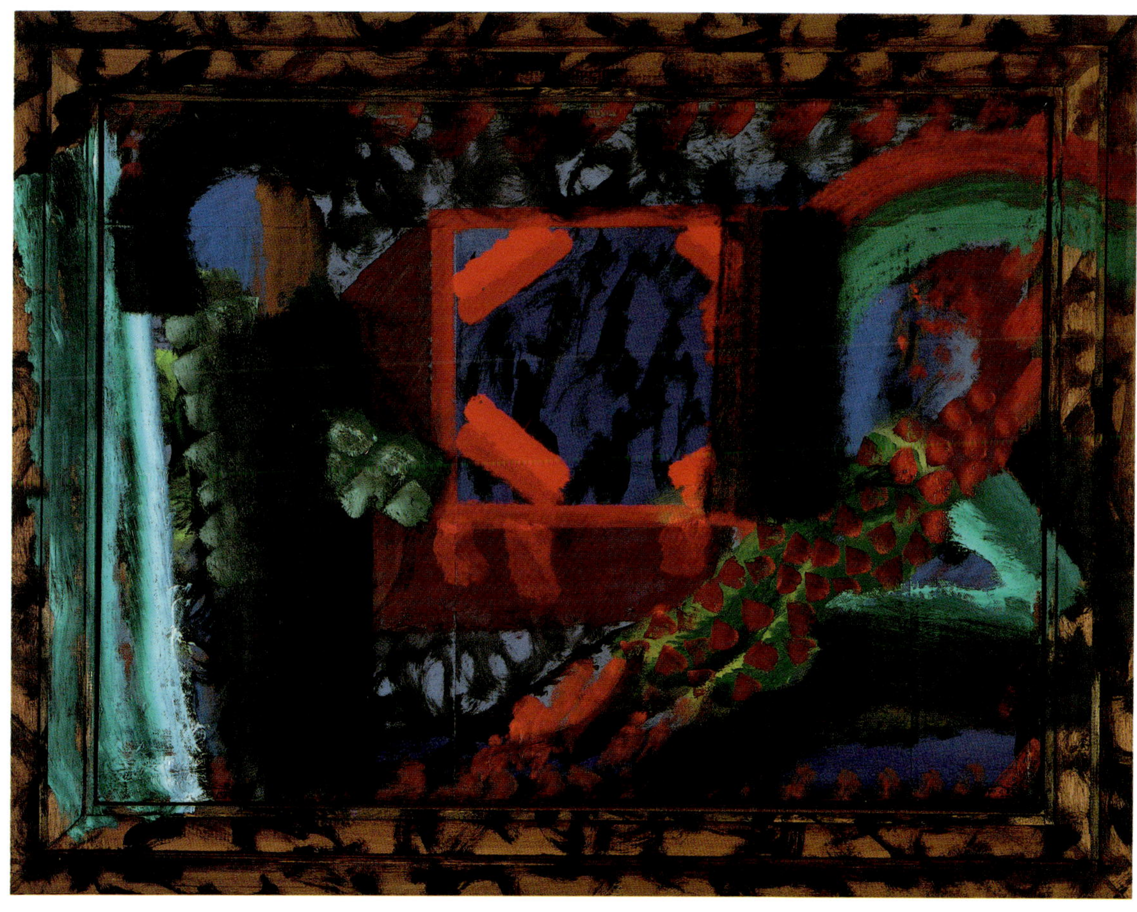

Mark Innerst

Born 1957

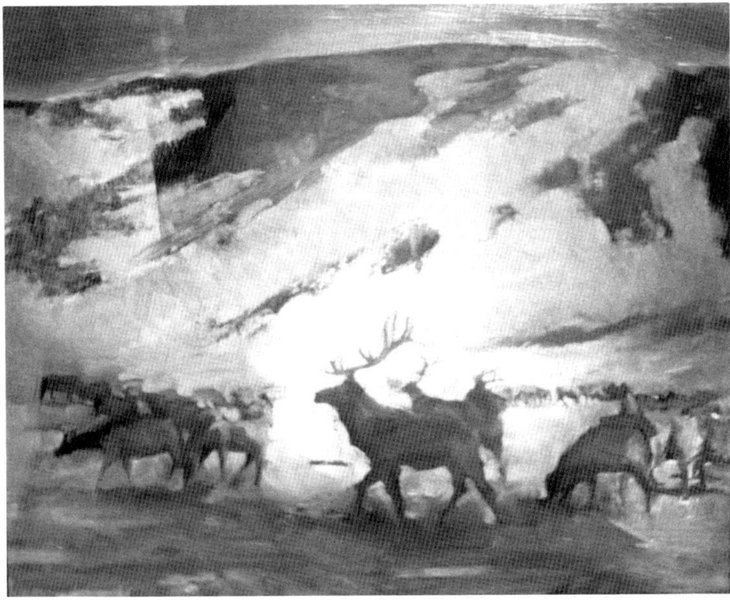

Untitled, 1983–1984
Oil and acrylic on board, 10 × 12
Lent by Jane and Robert Carroll

Mark Innerst was born in York, Pennsylvania. After graduating with a Bachelor of Fine Arts degree from Kutztown in 1980, he moved to New York, where he served briefly as Robert Longo's assistant.[1] A painter of exquisite small-scale landscapes and still lifes, Innerst belongs to a group of young artists, including Joan Nelson* and April Gornik,* who have returned to the American landscape for inspiration. Their paintings make stylistic references to nineteenth-century American landscape traditions and share such formal devices as cropped views or closed panoramas, a concern for light, intimate (or conversely expanded) scale, and elaborate framing.[2]

Innerst uses a variety of sources for his paintings. His landscapes quote the romantic realism of the Hudson River School and the radiant light and low horizons of the luminists, while the still lifes and *memento mori* paintings suggest a seventeenth-century northern European influence. More immediate and mundane borrowings are made from the movies, photographs, and the dioramas of natural history museums, but even these paintings transform their subjects into visual poems. The jewel-like quality of Innerst's work is reinforced by the "antique" frames he creates for his paintings. Often disproportionately large for the panels Innerst paints on, these frames represent encasements for precious objects. According to the artist, they are "a temptation, an affectionate rather than a cynical device."[3]

Untitled belongs to a group of works based on a diorama of elk in the American Museum of Natural History, New York.[4] The animals are shown moving across a snow field against a backdrop of mountains. In this and other paintings Innerst uses color for emotive rather than descriptive effect, building from a single-color acrylic ground or a pattern of several colors overlaid with oil glazes.[5] Panes of color—red, blue, yellow, and ochre—shine through this landscape. In some works chromatic changes are made more abruptly, as though shards of colored glass had been placed over sections of the painting, or are used to signal changes in the landscape itself. A radioactive red at the horizon may suggest apocalypse, warning of an environment at risk and the fragility of the landscape in the postindustrial world.

Despite this image's double remove from nature (the painting is based on a photograph of a staged scene), the free handling of paint and sense of open space and air persuade us of wilderness. Ironically, it can be argued that this intimately scaled painting evokes the breadth and life of the landscape more successfully than the original museum display that attempts to recreate the natural setting.

LM

1.
Barry Blinderman, "The Veil of the Soul," in *Mark Innerst: Landscape and Beyond,* University Galleries, Illinois State University, Normal, 1988, p. 12 note 5.
2.
Naomi Vine, "A Certain Slant of Light," in *A Certain Slant of Light: The Contemporary American Landscape,* The Dayton Art Institute, Dayton, Ohio, 1989, p. 22.
3.
Quoted in Blinderman, p. 8.
4.
See also, for example, cat. 6 in *Mark Innerst: Landscape and Beyond.*
5.
Lisa Dennison, "New Horizons in American Art," in *New Horizons in American Art,* Solomon R. Guggenheim Museum, New York, 1985, p. 17.

Additional Reference
Rosenblum, Robert: "Mark Innerst's Time Capsules," in *Mark Innerst Paintings and Works on Paper,* Curt Marcus Gallery, New York, 1990.

Riddle, 1986–1987
Oil on linen, 36¼ × 25¼
Lent by Loretta and Robert K. Lifton

Bill Jensen was born in Minneapolis. After graduation from the University of Minnesota in 1970, he moved to New York. Since his recovery from the illness caused by toxic materials used in his large paintings of the early 1970s, he has worked on a much smaller scale, and today his oil paintings average only 2 feet square, making him one of a few abstract painters not working on big canvases. *Riddle* is one of Jensen's larger recent paintings.

Producing fewer than ten paintings a year, the artist may spend months on a canvas and usually has several in progress at one time. When his works are shown, Jensen prefers to have them hung above the standard height (he himself is a tall man who likes his paintings to be at eye level).[1] He also likes to have them bathed with soft lighting, perhaps to enhance their magical, dreamy qualities.

Jensen's compositions combine organic and geometric shapes. Cones, ellipses, and spirals recur. The artist uses rich colors and thick textures to endow these shapes with a mystical naturalism. *Riddle,* finished in 1987, is representative of this style. The large cones in the background resemble mountains behind what appear to be creatures rising from the deep. Jensen explains, "I want my paintings to come out of the murk, the darkness, the heaviness of the earth and then shoot off."[2]

In *Riddle* color, light, and brushstroke rhythms make the sprouting forms come alive. The earthy greens and mustard yellows are typical of Jensen's palette. The three-dimensional shapes of the upper half of the composition melt into formless streams of murky color toward the bottom. Climbing upward, the yellow cocoon or germinating seedling looks as if it had been captured in the process of transformation or growth. Perhaps the title of the piece alludes to the final state of this evolving form.

CLC

1.
Eliza E. Rathbone, *Bill Jensen,* The Phillips Collection, Washington, D.C., October–November 1987, p. 8.
2.
Stephen Henry Madoff, "A New Generation of Abstract Painters," *ArtNews,* November 1983, p. 78.

Additional References
Kertess, Klaus: "Painting Metaphorically," *Artforum,* October 1981, p. 54.
Westfall, Stephen: "Into the Vortex," *Art in America,* April 1988, pp. 182–187.

Bill Jensen

Born 1945

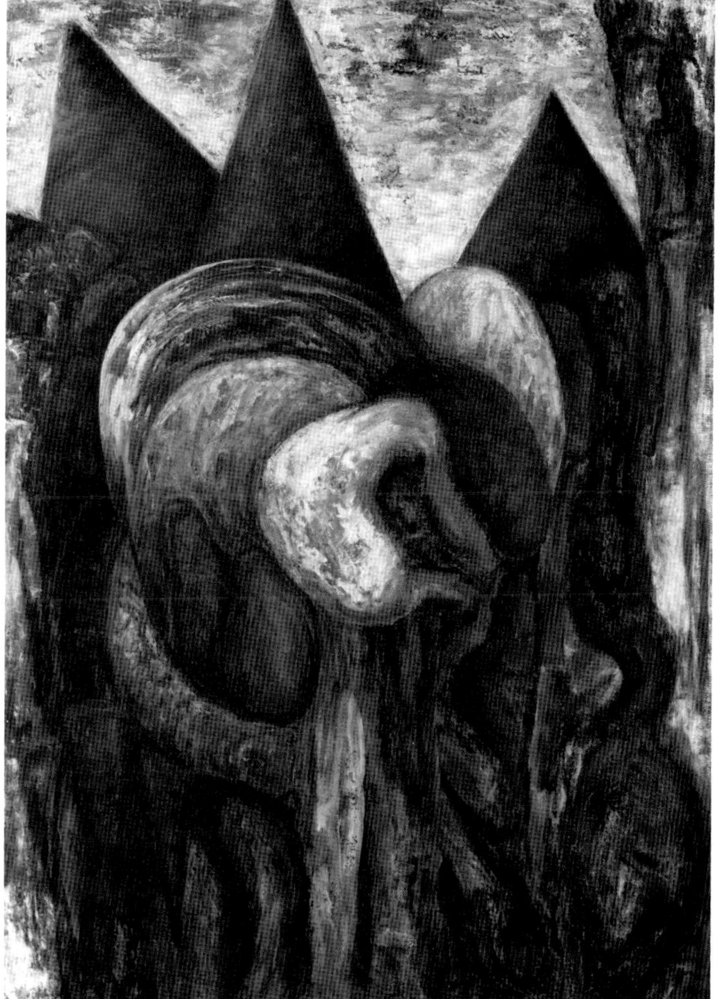

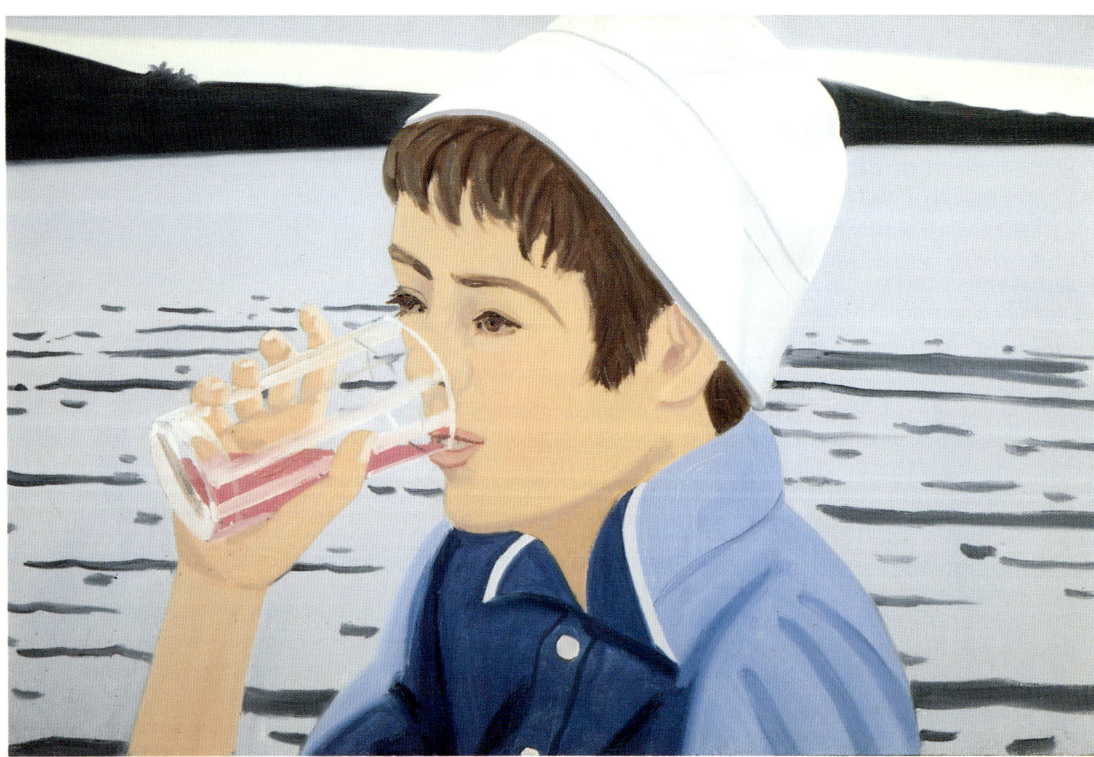

Alex Katz

Born 1927

Vincent with Glass, 1968
Oil on canvas, 30 × 44
Lent by Jane and Robert Carroll

A native of New York City, Alex Katz received his art training at Cooper Union and the Skowhegan School in Maine. In addition to painting on canvas in the mid-1950s, he experimented with collage and in 1959 began adding colored figures cut from wood and metal to his paintings. In the 1960s as Katz's work and style were evolving, his canvases got larger and he began treating light as a compositional subtext in his paintings rather than simply as a modeling device.

The preparation for one of his paintings can take longer than the painting itself. Katz frequently executes several small sketches in oil before transferring the image to a larger canvas. He always works wet on wet and rarely reworks a painting once he has put it aside.[1]

Katz paints very personal themes, easily comprehended by the viewer. His wife Ada and their son Vincent are among his favorite subjects, which also include artist friends and familiar landscapes. What makes Katz unique is his ability to take a specific everyday image, captured for a split second, and give it broad appeal.

At first glance Katz's paintings appear as straightforward as the title he gives them. *Vincent with Glass* is a classic example. Although the work depicts his son holding a glass, it is not a realistic portrayal. Katz is not interested in copying nature. The strong lines and flat colors defining forms make the images seem timeless. Devoid of modeling and shadows, *Vincent with Glass* is more a generic representation of a young boy than an illusionistic painting of a flesh-and-blood person. The artist presents us with a symbol, not a portrait. The subjects Katz paints are very personal, but he treats the images in a generalized way that makes them universal.

BH

1.
Ruth Bass, "Bland Power," *ArtNews,* April 1986, p. 111.

Additional References
Alloway, Lawrence: "The Constant Muse," *Art in America,* January 1981, pp. 110–118.
Berkson, Bill: "First Painter of Character," *Art in America,* November 1986, pp. 152–159.
Marshall, Richard: *Alex Katz,* Rizzoli International Publications, Inc., New York, 1986.

Times Square, 1965
Oil on canvas, 44 × 38
Lent by Ann and Richard Solomon

"I like to work from things that I see," Kelly said in the early 1960s. "Whether they're man-made or natural or a combination of the two.... The things I'm interested in have always been there."[1] Although the bold expanses of pristine flat color in Kelly's work make it difficult to imagine that these compositions are derived from experience, his paintings and sculptures are not inventions of the mind but intuitive distillations of visual stimuli ranging from architectural elements to shadows to the chance arrangement of cutout bits of paper.

Born in Newburgh, New York, Kelly attended Pratt Institute briefly before joining the army in 1943. It has been argued that his service with a camouflage battalion helped shape his aesthetic.[2] After the war he studied at the School of the Museum of Fine Arts, Boston, before returning to Paris in 1948. There Kelly found his artistic voice as he moved from figuration to abstraction. His compositions became starkly simple, with no sign of the artist's touch in the brushwork. Devoid of spatial illusionism, the flatly painted shapes are one with the picture plane. As objects, they project a physical presence and an artistic integrity.

When Kelly returned to New York in 1954, his minimalist works with their formalist concerns were out of step with the intensely personal action paintings of abstract expressionism. His independent spirit was soon recognized. Included in the Venice Biennale of 1966, Kelly was hailed a few years later as "one of the most enigmatic and unique forces in contemporary American art."[3]

Although *Times Square* is smaller than some of Kelly's works of the late 1960s, it displays the majestic compositional simplicity and the immaculate but anonymous surface characteris-

tic of his mature style. Typical of the period is the use of a single color set crisply against a white ground. The title is arbitrary. It could just as easily have been *Red White,* a name the artist has used for compositions with similar combinations of color.[4]

Times Square is a variation on a motif that occupied Kelly in the late 1950s—a cross placed on a white or colored ground. The central form was probably based on a sketch or collage and is therefore derived from the real world. In fact, *Times Square* is particularly close to a cutout of an envelope addressed to Kelly's friend Agnes Martin,* which inspired the sculpture *Gate* (1959) and several paintings.[5] Kelly often used the same source more than once. Here, however, the cross appears sideways as a figure-like form that pushes against the restraining edges of the canvas, virtually obliterating in the process the ground it rests on. The resulting tension between the dominant red and the underlying white transforms the static color mass into a dynamic visual force that extends beyond the confines of the picture frame.

EJN

Ellsworth Kelly

Born 1923

1.
Quoted in Diane Upright, *Ellsworth Kelly: Works on Paper,* Harry N. Abrams, Inc., New York, in association with The Fort Worth Art Museum, 1987, p. 10. See also Diane Waldman, *Ellsworth Kelly: Drawings, Collages, Prints,* New York Graphic Society, Greenwich, Conn., 1971, p. 16.
2.
E. C. Goossen, *Ellsworth Kelly,* New York Graphic Society, Greenwich, Conn., for The Museum of Modern Art, 1973, pp. 14 and 115.
3.
John Coplans, *Ellsworth Kelly,* Harry N. Abrams, Inc., New York, 1971, p. 11.
4.
For similarly titled works, see Goossen, p. 59.
5.
Upright, p. 20.

Rose, Purple, and Black, 1958
Oil on canvas, 45 × 36
Smith College Museum of Art, gift of Mrs.
Sigmund W. Kunstadter (Maxine Weil '24)

Called by Frank O'Hara the "Action Painter *par excellence,*"[1] Franz Kline is best known for the innovative black and white paintings he created from 1950 until his premature death in 1962. His early career gave little indication of the pivotal role he would play in the development of abstract expressionism. Born in Wilkes-Barre, Pennsylvania, he became interested in cartooning in high school and went on to study art in Boston and London. In 1938 he settled in New York, where he painted post-impressionist landscapes and figurative pieces.

Not until the late 1940s did Kline begin to work in an abstract style. A major breakthrough occurred at the studio of his friend Willem de Kooning in 1948 when enlargement with a Bell-Optican projector of Kline's small ink drawing of a rocking chair suggested that powerful abstract compositions could be created with strokes. Two years later, in his first one-man show, Kline's black and white paintings commanded attention.

Black and white dominated Kline's production for the next five years. Although he used color in his representational pieces of the 1940s and in his first abstractions, it was not until 1956 that color emerged as an important element in his abstract expressionist works. *Rose, Purple, and Black* therefore dates from the early stage of Kline's involvement with color. Small in scale and restrained in palette, it exhibits the pronounced structure typical of his mature style. A strong central trapezoid establishes the planarity of the composition. The black mass, bracketed by gray, white, and rose-colored passages, seems to recede into space even as its matte flatness denies visual recession. The composition suggests a mountainous landscape rent by a pass, a recurrent theme in Kline's work that may refer to the area around Wilkes-Barre and Lehighton.[2]

Kline has commented on how he "painted originally in color and finally arrived at black and white by painting the color out."[3] In *Rose, Purple, and Black* the negation of color is central to the composition's visual effect with the flat black obscuring the shiny purple underneath. Rose and gray, black and white, applied with dragging strokes, create feathery interlocking streaks of color and tone. Despite the effect of fluidity and spontaneity achieved through the energetic application of pigment, the work was not done quickly. The intricate and deliberate layering of paint undoubtedly took weeks if not months to evolve.

Not the product of artistic impulse or fleeting mood, *Rose, Purple, and Black* resonates with the emotion Kline considered critical to the success of any work of art. He admitted that his own compositions often project a sense of loneliness.[4] The depressing negativism resulting from the violent obliteration of color is nevertheless tinged with hope. The intensity of this human feeling is what touches the viewer, making the artist and his art both accessible and vulnerable.

EJN

Franz Kline

1910–1962

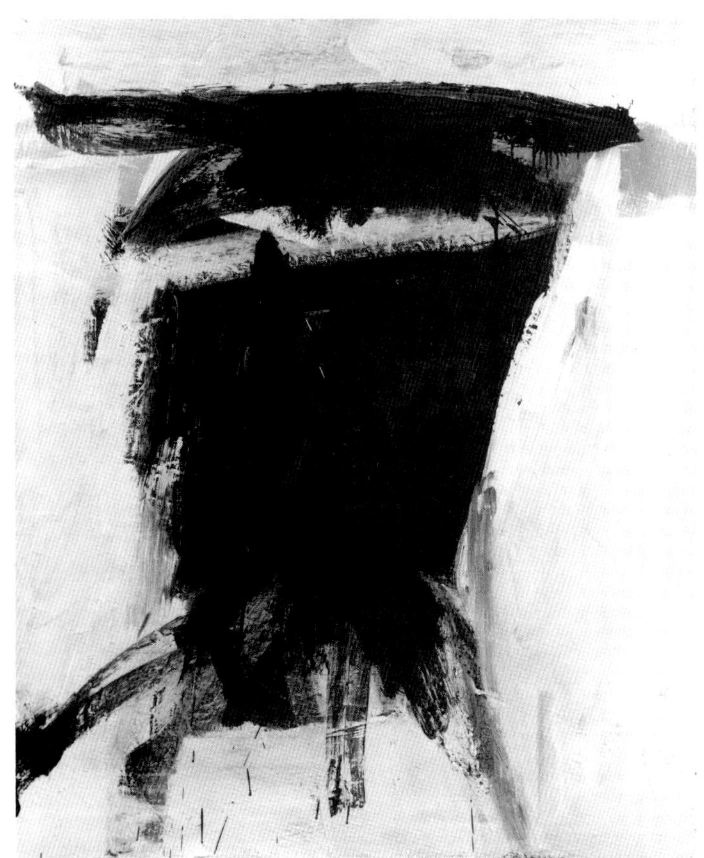

1.
Frank O'Hara, "Introduction and Interview," in *Franz Kline: A Retrospective Exhibition,* Whitechapel Gallery, London, in association with The Museum of Modern Art, New York, May–June 1964, p. 6.
2.
Harry F. Gaugh, *The Vital Gesture: Franz Kline,* Abbeville Press, New York, for The Cincinnati Art Museum, 1985, pp. 62–63.
3.
Quoted in Harry F. Gaugh, *Franz Kline: The Color Abstractions,* The Phillips Collection, Washington, D.C., February 17–April 8, 1979, p. 22.
4.
Robert Goldwater, "Introduction," in *Franz Kline 1910–1962,* Marlborough-Gerson Gallery, New York, March 1967, p. 6; also Gaugh, *The Vital Gesture,* p. 114.

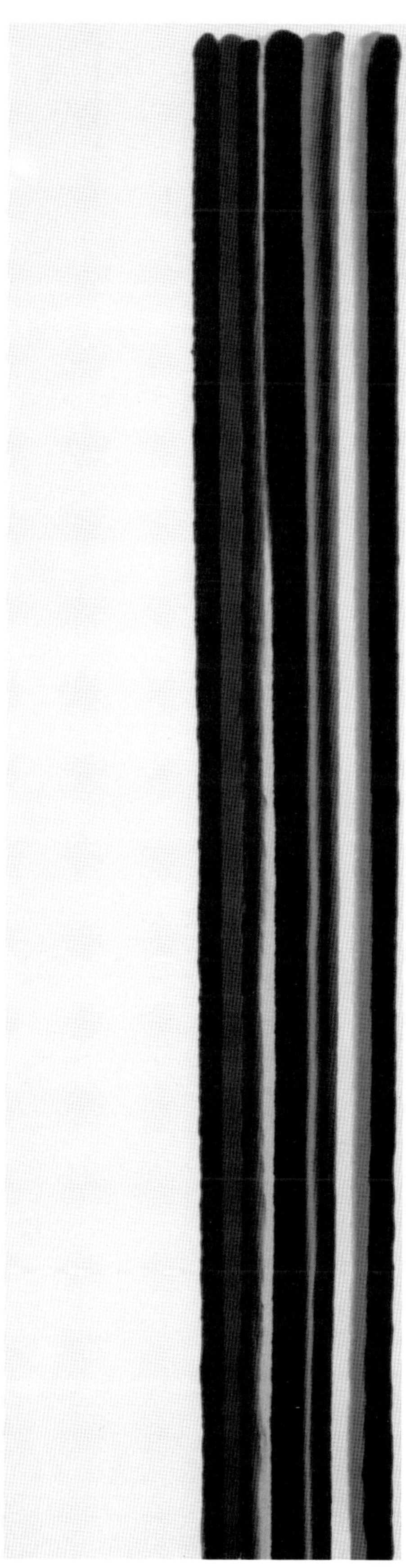

1-74, 1961–1962
Acrylic resin (Magna) on canvas, 82 × 21
Lent by Harriet Frank Rauh

Morris Louis "ranks among the supreme masters of color in modern art."[1] Louis, who emerged from provincial obscurity in the late 1950s, was born in Baltimore as Morris Louis Bernstein and spent most of his creative life in Washington, D.C. He had just begun to establish himself on the national scene when he died of lung cancer in 1962 at the age of forty-nine.

Of the 655 paintings listed in Diane Upright's catalogue raisonné, only 80 predate 1958, when Louis began to exhibit the canvases that brought him posthumous fame. Many of the works immediately preceding the Veil series of 1958–1959 were destroyed by the artist. Created with thin washes of acrylic poured onto unprimed duck canvas, the fan-like configurations of the Veils grew out of the innovative works Louis painted in 1954 after seeing *Mountains and Sea* by Helen Frankenthaler.*

The first of several important series, the Veils were followed by the Unfurled paintings, in which irregular diagonals of unmodulated color articulate the corners of a vast expanse of raw canvas. Louis began working on the Stripe paintings, of which *1-74* is an example, in 1961 and was still involved with the series when he died. The title of this composition (given after his death, like those of most of Louis's paintings) indicates that it was the seventy-fourth work to leave the estate.

Louis created about 230 paintings in the series, almost all of them vertical compositions. Generally, parallel columns of pure color are bracketed by areas of unprimed canvas at the sides and top. Fewer than a fifth have the stripes defining the left or right side, as they do in *1-74*. The orientation of these works has been the subject of debate, but Upright has shown that Louis intended the Stripes to be hung so that the portion to which the paint was first applied would be at the top.[2] The compositions vary enormously both in the placement and width of the columns and in their palettes. *1-74* achieves a visual equilibrium through the balance between the dark stripes of color on the right and the void of light on the left, a visual equilibrium that suggests a balance of the real and the spiritual, the palpable and the intangible.

The overall flowing forms of the Veil paintings are mysterious as they fuse with the cloth to produce fans of iridescent color. In the Unfurled series the monumental central void bracketed by spontaneous gestures of strong color is sublimely expansive. In contrast, the Stripes are confined and controlled, human in the rational application of color and generally in the proportions of the canvas as well. Yet there is something ritualistic about Louis's obsessive exploration of this motif which speaks for the depth of his artistic passion.

EJN

Morris Louis

1912–1962

1.
Michael Fried,
Morris Louis,
Harry N. Abrams,
Inc., New York,
c. 1979, p. 15.
2.
Diane Upright,
Morris Louis: The Complete Paintings,
Harry N. Abrams,
Inc., New York,
1985, p. 44.

Additional References
Carmean, E.A., Jr.:
"Morris Louis and the Modern Tradition," *Arts Magazine*, September 1976,
pp. 70–75;
October 1976,
pp. 112–117;
November 1976,
pp. 122–126;
and December 1976,
pp. 116–119.
Elderfield, John:
Morris Louis,
Little, Brown and Co., Boston, for The Museum of Modern Art,
1986.

Agnes Martin

Born 1912

Untitled #3, 1983
Acrylic and pencil on canvas, 72 × 72
Lent by Ann and Richard Solomon

Born in Saskatchewan, Martin came to the United States when she was twenty to attend Columbia University. After a three-year spell of teaching at the University of New Mexico, she returned to New York in 1957. Over the next decade she developed the style for which she is known. In 1967, at the height of her career, Martin abruptly left New York to return to New Mexico and stopped painting altogether, but during a seven-year hiatus produced her only series of prints, titled On a Clear Day. She now lives in an isolated adobe house built with her own hands and has the privacy she depends on for her inspiration.

Rendered in the natural light of her studio, *Untitled #3* is extraordinarily complex in its delicate handling of color and line. To appreciate the subtlety of Martin's technique one must view the work from different angles since how light falls on the surface affects the viewer's perception. At first glance one sees only a white field overlayed with faint stripes, but further investigation reveals a multiplicity of colors emerging from beneath the surface. Although Martin's range of color is limited, her handling of it is complex. White, a wide range of grays, and black dominate her palette. Martin is particularly attracted to black because she sees it as a combination of all colors. Her pigments are not flatly applied. White paintings like this one are composed of crisscross strokes of delicately tinted tones.

Although the stark simplicity and pronounced linearity of her compositions has led many critics to consider Martin a minimalist, she denies the connection. She respects the minimalist approach but believes that her method of painting is quite different. Like an abstract expressionist, which is what she considers herself, she paints broadly and freely, with a sense of spontaneity in her brushstrokes.

Martin's compositions are a result of intense contemplation of nature. They recreate the calmness of the desert or sea. She seeks to give her canvases an aura of spirituality and wants them to elicit contemplation. Martin once said in a lecture, "When I think of art I think of beauty. Beauty is the mystery of life. It is not in the eye, it is in the mind. In our minds there is an awareness of perfection."[1] It is on the possibility of perfection that she encourages viewers to reflect through the purity of her canvases.

NJS

1.
Pace Gallery Archives.

Additional References
Ashton, Dore: *Agnes Martin Paintings and Drawings 1957– 1975*, Westerham Press, London, 1977.
Grimes, Nancy: "Agnes Martin: Pace," *ArtNews*, January 1987, p. 140.
Hillerman, Anne: "A Visit with Agnes Martin," *The New Mexican*, July 26, 1974.
Stevens, Mark: "Thin Gray Line," *Vanity Fair*, March 1989, pp. 50–54.

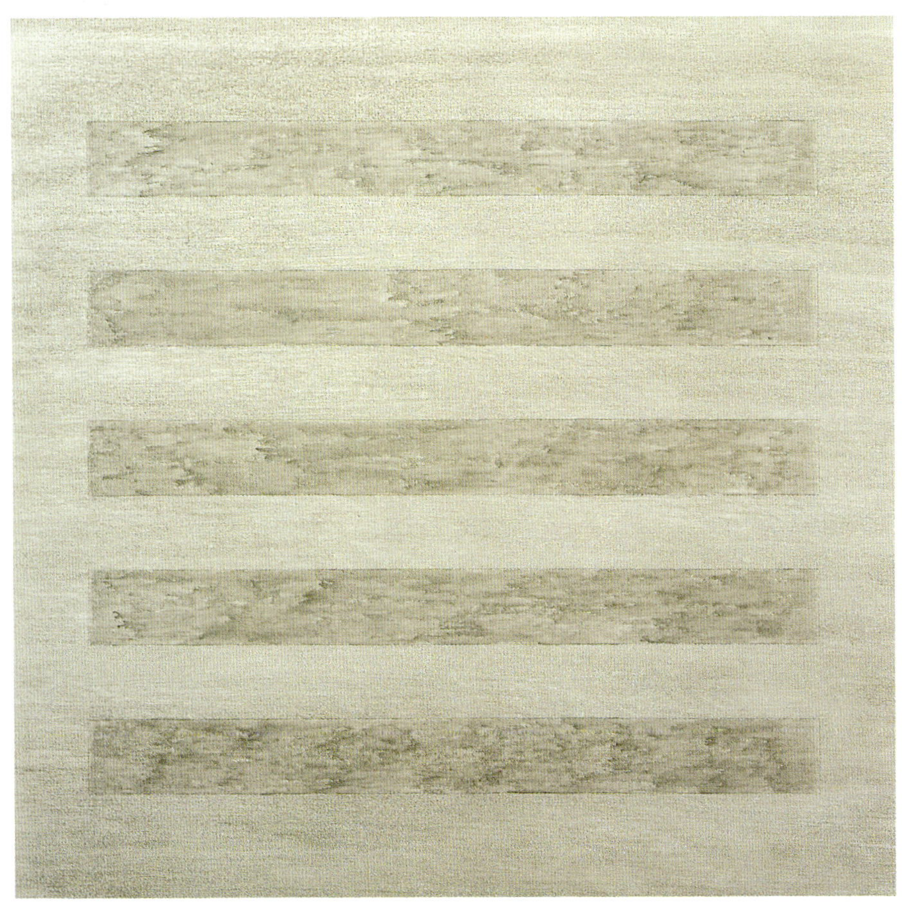

Spring Street, 1987
Acrylic on canvas, 78 × 64
Private collection, Arizona

George McNeil was born in New York in 1908
and studied at the Pratt Institute. He was one of
the founders of the American Abstract Artists in
1936. A contemporary of Franz Kline,* Jackson
Pollock, and Willem de Kooning, McNeil received
little attention until recently renewed interest in
neo-expressionism brought him recognition.

Although McNeil's style has remained constant over the years, his works of the late 1950s
and 1960s are more suggestive of landscapes than
recent paintings like *Spring Street* which center
around the human figure. The expressive primitivism of some of his images here and elsewhere
is reminiscent of the work of Jean Dubuffet.*

Spring Street has the same hallucinatory quality as *Demonic Disco* (1984), *Dionysus Disco*
(1982), and *Professor Unrath* (1981). His art is
a response to the urban excitement and vitality
of New York City. The vibrant colors and jarring
juxtapositions of *Spring Street,* an actual street
in SoHo, capture the cacophony of Manhattan's
contemporary art district.

McNeil's vigorous brushwork—broad, free,
and bold—energizes dynamic compositions in
which child-like figures of varying size coexist
in an irrational space. Cars are placed upside
down at the top of the composition while Diony-
sian characters of the night occupy the center
and corners. The confusion of this frenzied scene
is conveyed by McNeil's rich and vibrant palette
and its explosive use of reds, oranges, purples,
and other intense colors. Anxiety and absurdity
exist simultaneously in metamorphosed figures
with distorted forms and facial expressions. This
chaotic and multicolored street scene, with its
jumble of crudely drawn people and signs, contains many of the visual elements characteristic
of McNeil's art from the last decade.

GL

References
Cameron, Dan:
   "Content in Con-
   text: The Retro-
   spective of Leon
   Golub and
   George McNeil,"
   Arts Magazine,
   March 1985,
   pp. 115–117.
Henry, Gerrit:
   "George
   McNeil," *Arts
   Magazine,*
   December 1984,
   p. 19.
*George McNeil:
   Abstractscapes
   and Figures,*
   University Art
   Gallery, Univer-
   sity Center at
   Binghamton,
   State University
   of New York,
   February 20–
   March 31, 1985.
George McNeil,
   *Expressionism
   1954–1984,*
   Artists' Choice
   Museum, New
   York, Septem-
   ber 22–
   November 10,
   1984.

George McNeil

Born 1908

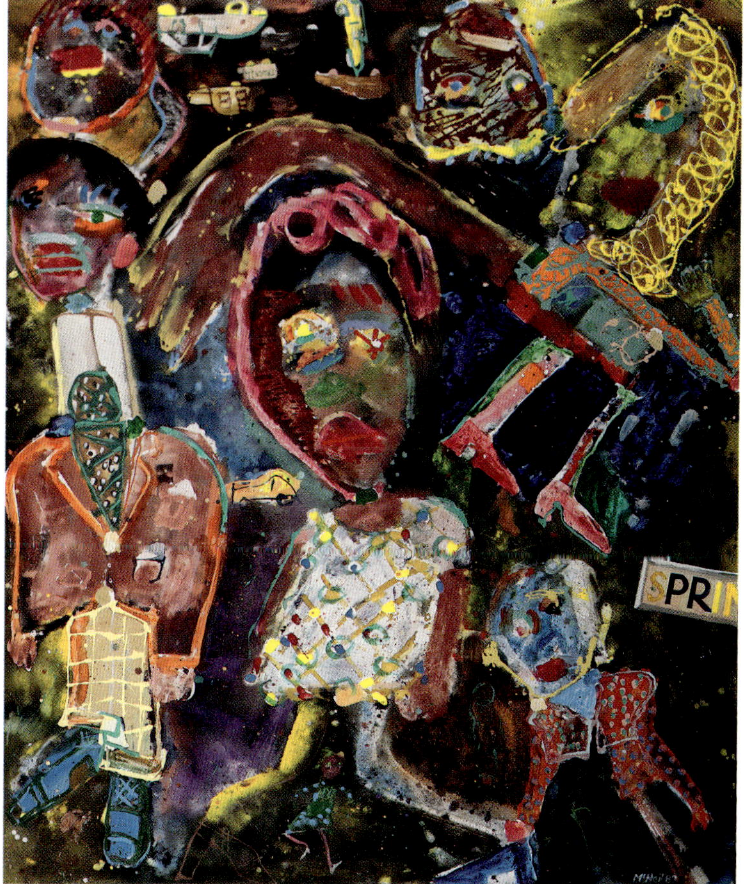

Joan Mitchell

Born 1926

Untitled, 1960
Oil on canvas, 50 × 38
Smith College Museum of Art, purchased with funds given by Mrs. John W. O'Boyle (Nancy Millar '52)

Joan Mitchell spent part of her undergraduate years at Smith before earning her Bachelor of Fine Arts degree from the School of the Art Institute of Chicago in 1947. *Untitled* was painted a year after she went to Paris, a move that separated her from the New York of Pollock, Kline,* Rothko, and de Kooning with which she had been associated since the early 1950s. Writing about the positive influences exerted on Mitchell's painting after leaving New York, John Ashberry said, "The exalting and deadening effects of an abundance of cash and action are alike absent from her work. It looks strong and relaxed, classical and refreshing at the same time."[1]

Mitchell dislikes being called a second-generation abstract expressionist. Broadly speaking, she is a landscape painter. *Untitled,* for instance, captures the essence of a landscape—brown earth, green trees, yellow and pink flowers, blue sky—with quick energetic brushstrokes, gestures as fresh and rejuvenating as a spring day. It is as though we were looking at a bouquet of wildflowers or a muddy garden path from a distance through a distorted rain-splattered lens.

Color, balance, solidity, and energy are all here; lacking only is the representation of recognizable forms.

Mitchell paints indoors in a studio and claims she hates nature.[2] "I paint from remembered landscapes that I carry with me—and remembered feelings of them, which of course become transformed. I could certainly never mirror nature. I would like more to paint what it leaves me with."[3]

She is left with canvases that are alive with tangles of calligraphic strokes, thickly applied high-intensity colors, thinly painted pastel threads, and expressive drips. The effect is spontaneous and seemingly instinctive but not chaotic since the harmony and lyricism of her compositions can result only from paint applied with a reason. A recent interview adds, "What keeps all this ferocious and obviously painstaking decision-making together is the breath of canvas emanating from behind the paint."[4]

Mitchell's formats have expanded to include multiple canvases, and her compositions now contain broader patches of paint. Considered as a whole, however, her paintings have changed little over her long career. She continues to affirm that paintings are occurrences and that their primary subject is the act of painting itself.
WEB

1.
John Ashberry, "An Expressionist in Paris," *ArtNews,* April 1965, p. 63.
2.
Edward Bryant, *Forty Artists under Forty,* Whitney Museum of American Art, New York, 1962, p. 56.
3.
Ibid., p. 29.
4.
Peggy Cyphers, "NY in Review," *Arts Magazine,* January 1990, p. 96.

Additional Readings
Bernstock, Judith: *Joan Mitchell,* Hudson Hills Press, New York, 1988.
Westfall, Stephen: "Then & Now: Six of the New York School Look Back," *Art in America,* June 1985, pp. 112–121.

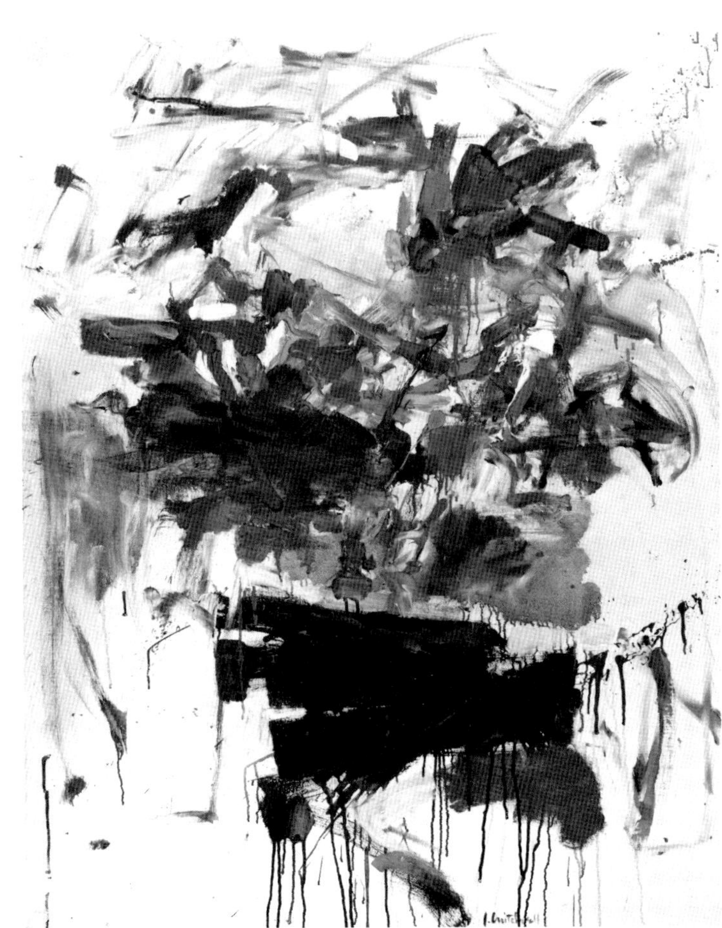

Black and White No. 3, 1966
Acrylic on canvas, 66 × 50
Lent by Rena Bransten

A native of Aberdeen, Washington, Motherwell graduated from Stanford University, studied philosophy at Harvard University Graduate School, and then worked under Meyer Schapiro at Columbia. He has taught at Black Mountain, Hunter, and Columbia.

Because Motherwell is considered a spokesman for abstract expressionism, his ideas provide insight into his art. As he himself has noted, however, his paintings speak louder than his words.

> Barnett Newman for years has said that when he reads my writings, he learns what I have been reading, but when he wants to know what I am really concerned with at a given moment, he looks at my pictures. He's right.[1]

Black and White No. 3 is but one example of the power of Motherwell's visual statements. The painting was done in 1966, the year of his major retrospective at the Museum of Modern Art. It was a time of transition for the artist, whose creative process often moves in stages—the tragic Elegy to the Spanish Republic series and the broad color fields of the Open series being best known.[2]

A bold black "x" slashes across the white canvas of *Black and White No. 3* while expressive orange-red strokes form a recognizable "4." A horizontal yellow line dissects the weighty lower portion of the painting. Motherwell has explained that in his limited palette, black and white are the protagonists and ochre always represents the earth.[3] The iconic "4" is grounded by the line of earth on which it stands. Behind the figure rises a silhouetted shape, the lines of which organize the white area. The dynamic play between the negative and positive spaces created by the black and white "protagonists" is equaled by a playfulness in the application of paint—the red color drips; the black is roughly applied. The brightness and intensity of the colors combined with the large scale of the "4" give a child-like air to the work.

Black and White No. 3 is most closely related to a series of works Motherwell began in Italy during the summer of 1960, but it employs a vocabulary of color and form that has been consistent throughout his career. The use of black and white, for example, and the calligraphic quality of the brushwork are ubiquitous elements. Repeated shapes and thematic similarities in his paintings hint at potentially symbolic meanings in the abstracted forms. Take the use of "4," for example. Motherwell claims that the image "has baffled curious iconographers" since it first appeared early in his career.[4] *The Figure 4 on an Elegy,* a 1960 work on paper and one of Motherwell's "supreme favorites,"[5] is similar to *Black and White No. 3*, but the latter reads as a freer and more independent interpretation of the motif, one in which the shapes of the slashing black strokes and the number seem more balanced. Whatever symbolic meaning "4" may have, its visual purpose is to electrify and activate the composition with its hot color and familiar shape.

WEB

1.
Frank O'Hara, *Robert Motherwell,* Stedelijk Museum, Amsterdam, 1966, n.p.
2.
Robert Hughes, "Robert Motherwell," in *Nothing if Not Critical,* Alfred A. Knopf, New York, 1990, p. 292.
3.
Stephanie Terenzio, *Robert Motherwell & Black,* The William Benton Museum of Art, Storrs, Conn., 1980, p. 8.
4.
H.H. Arnason, *Robert Motherwell,* Harry N. Abrams, Inc., New York, 1982, p. 142.
5.
Ibid.

Additional References
Arnason, H.H.: "Robert Motherwell: 1966–1976," *Art International,* October–November 1976, pp. 9–25 and 55–56.
Ashton, Dore, and Jack Flam: *Robert Motherwell,* Abbeville Press, New York, 1983.
O'Hara, Frank: *Robert Motherwell,* The Museum of Modern Art, New York, 1965.

Robert Motherwell

Born 1915

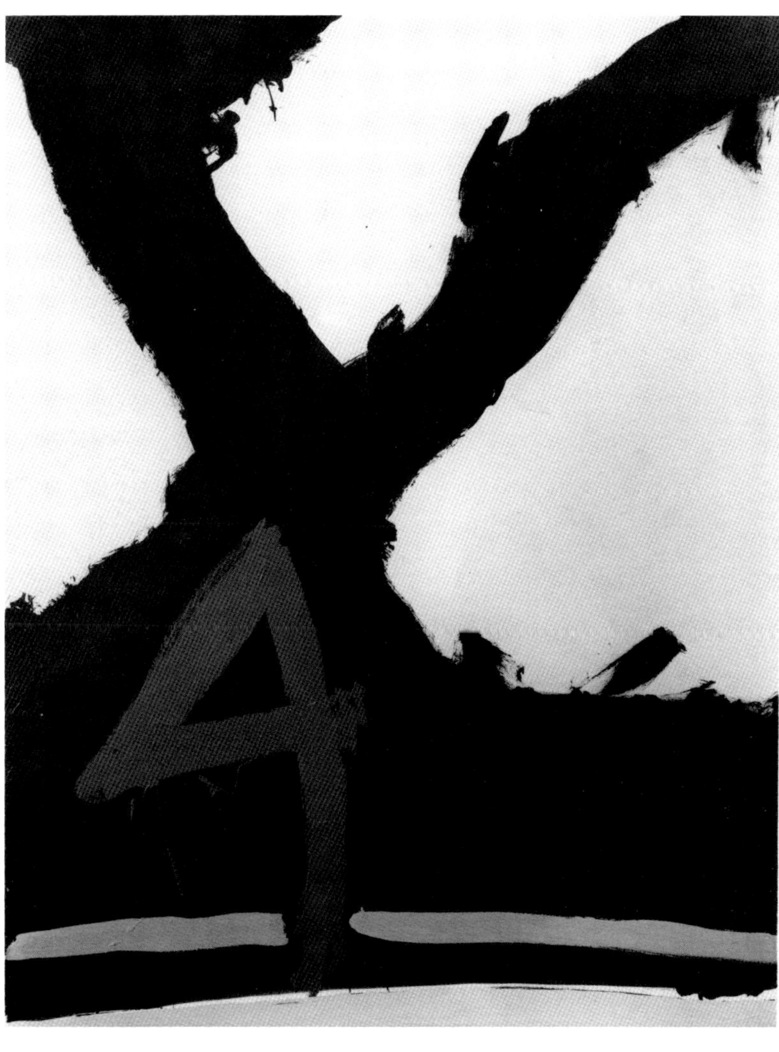

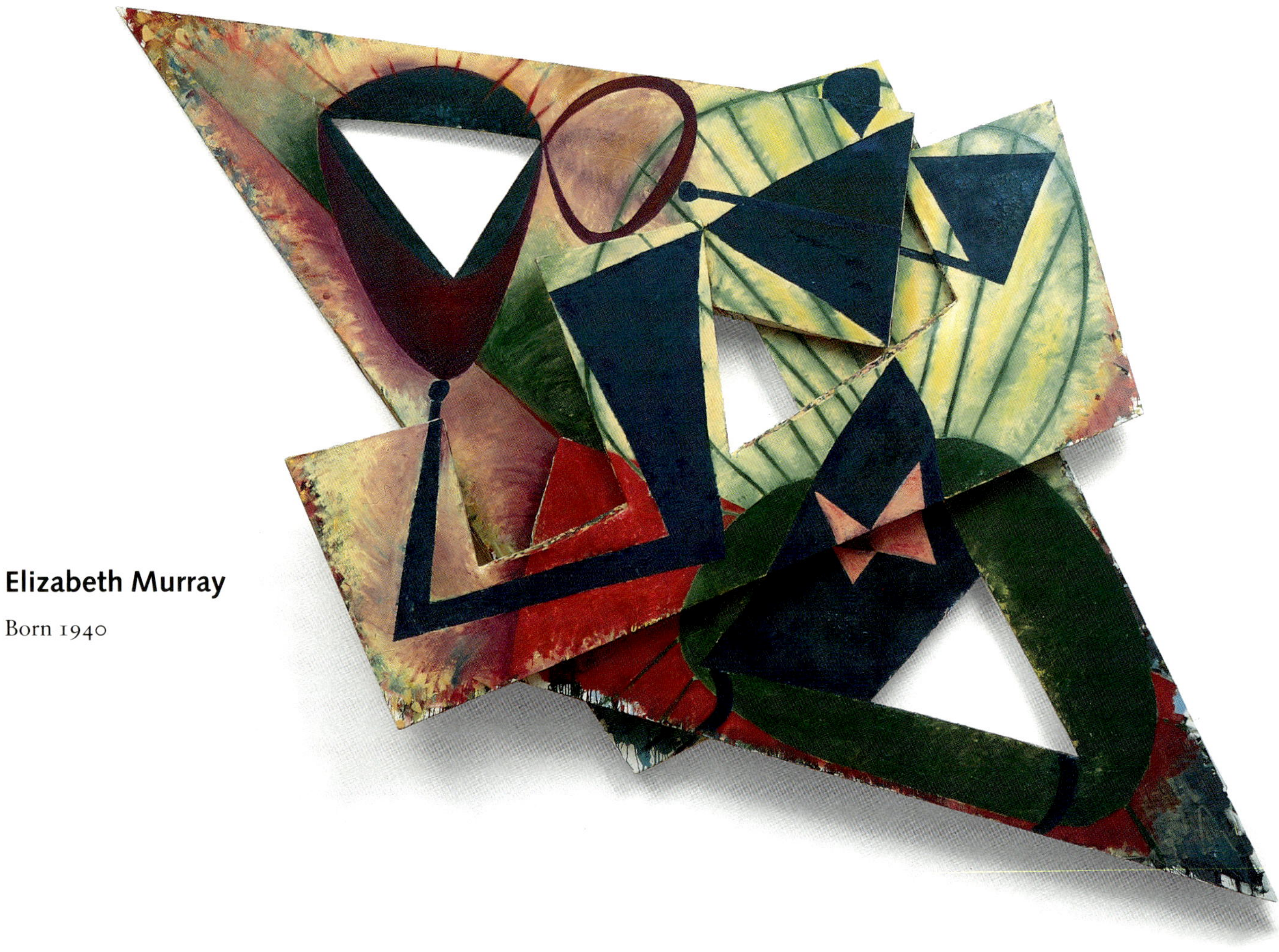

Elizabeth Murray

Born 1940

Her Story, 1984
Oil on canvas (in three parts), 105 × 132
Lent by Loretta and Robert K. Lifton

With its bold color and constructed surfaces, Elizabeth Murray's art shares certain affinities with neo-expressionism and modernism. Artistically influenced by both movements, Murray is a dedicated formalist interested in articulating the basic elements of a work—paint, surface, and support.[1]

Murray was born in Chicago. She received a Bachelor of Fine Arts degree from the School of the Art Institute in 1962 and a Master of Fine Arts from Mills College in 1965; two years later she moved to New York.

Her Story consists of three powerful interlocked polygonal canvases. Although the inventiveness of the surfaces and the combination of geometric and biomorphic forms make the imagery difficult to discern, the artist says that *Her Story* is really a portrait of her mother, who enjoyed reading to her children. The woman sits on a green chair and lifts a large cup in one hand. A book made up of superimposed pink triangles rests on her lap. The triangular shapes, which recur in the dress, the head, and the hands,[2] also form three gigantic letters A-A-E emerging from the exuberant and brilliantly colored canvases as an emotionally charged cry.[3]

Other works by Murray show the same emotional intensity. The bulbous forms of *Can You Hear Me?* (1984) and *Sentimental Education* (1982) projecting out into real space reflect an interest in cartooning and an admiration for the sculpture of Claes Oldenburg.*[4] These are not images designed to amuse, however; the jagged lines and invasive shapes of the overlapping canvases convey tension and anxiety. *Her Story* makes it clear that despite its abstraction, Elizabeth Murray's art is rooted in the experiences of her own life.

GL

1.
Roberta Smith, "Motion Pictures," in Sue Graze and Kathy Halbreich, *Elizabeth Murray: Paintings and Drawings,* Harry N. Abrams, Inc., New York, in association with The Dallas Museum of Art, 1987, p. 9.
2.
Graze and Halbreich, pp. 74 and 130.
3.
Smith, p. 23.
4.
Robert Storr, "Shape Shifter," *Art in America,* April 1989, p. 217.

Additional References
Early Works by Five Contemporary Artists . . . , New Museum, New York, November 11–December 30, 1977.
Simon, Joan: "Mixing Metaphors: Elizabeth Murray," *Art in America,* April 1984, pp. 141–145.
Varnedoe, Kirk, and Adam Gopnick: *High and Low: Modern and Popular Culture,* The Museum of Modern Art, New York, October 1990–January 1991.

1.
Wanda M. Corn,
*The Color of
Mood: American
Tonalism 1880–
1910,* California
Palace of the Legion
of Honor, San Fran-
cisco, January 22–
April 2, 1972, p. 1.
2.
Michael Boodro,
"Joan Nelson,
Second Nature,"
ArtNews, Sep-
tember 1990,
p. 145.
3.
Lisa Dennison,
*New Horizons in
American Art,*
Solomon R.
Guggenheim
Museum, New
York, 1985, p. 88.
4.
Boodro, p. 146.
5.
Donald Kuspit,
Joan Nelson,
Robert Miller Gal-
lery, New York,
March 6–31, 1990,
and Michael Kohn
Gallery, Santa
Monica, March
10–April 7, 1990,
n.p.

*Additional
References*
Haus, Mary Ellen:
  "The Unnatural
  Landscape,"
  ArtNews, Janu-
  ary 1988, pp.
  129–132.
Loughery, John:
  "Landscape
  Painting in the
  Eighties: April
  Gornik, Ellen
  Phelan and Joan
  Nelson," *Arts
  Magazine,* May
  1988,
  pp. 44–48.

Untitled No. 128, 1987
Oil and wax on wood, 14 × 16
Lent by Rima Ayas and Ronald W. Moore

In her short career Joan Nelson has produced an extraordinary group of landscapes. Untitled, intimate in scale, luminous, and layered with emotion, they represent an artist unique in her vision. They contain art-historical references to so many places and times that perhaps even she would be surprised at the names invoked by her critics: Courbet, Turner, Raphael, Zurbarán, Ruisdael, Claude Lorrain, her contemporary Mark Innerst,* and many others. One might even suggest that in their quiet and subtle beauty Nelson's landscapes are related to paintings by the American tonalists of the late nineteenth and early twentieth centuries, who "were not inter-ested in the grandiose drama of nature, but were attracted to its most suggestive moments."[1] The group included Thomas Wilmer Dewing, Childe Hassam, and Dwight William Tryon, an artist associated long and closely with Smith College.

Nelson was born in California, but her family moved to St. Louis when she was eleven. She began to study art in junior college and received the Bachelor of Fine Arts degree from Washing-ton University in 1981. In college her exposure to contemporary art movements was largely through the art press. After college she moved to New York to study at the Brooklyn Museum Art School, where she was awarded the Max Beckmann Memorial Scholarship. In a recent interview she said of her time at Brooklyn, "Mostly what I learned from the program was that I couldn't do anything anyone else was doing. You could paint anything. What mattered was the attitude."[2] Her first group exhibition was held in 1982 at the Nature Morte Gallery in New York, and her first one-woman show at the P.P.O.W. Gallery in New York in 1987. Since then there have been many group and solo exhi-bitions of her work. She presently lives and works in Brooklyn.

Nelson's paintings of the mid-1980s were larger than her present work and consisted of architectural structures in desolate landscapes devoid of any human presence. She has called these places "insipid monuments to neglect."[3] Many were done in egg tempera and plaster on Masonite or board. *Untitled No. 128* is typical of the paintings of the later 1980s—smaller in scale and carried out in wax, tempera, and plaster on wood, often with scoring of the surfaces. Landscape and skyscape or trees silhouetted against the sky, frequently from unusual per-spectives, these paintings are meant to "elicit a response more complicated and emotional than that prompted by merely a framed view, a win-dow onto a scene that might or might not exist."[4] The levels of meaning relate to the absence of man, his destruction of the environment, and his failed attempt to regain his place in the natural order. Joan Nelson's recent works are "a form of mourning for a vanishing nature—a nature that is vanishing from our emotional lives as well as literally."[5]

MG

Joan Nelson

Born 1958

David Park

1911–1960

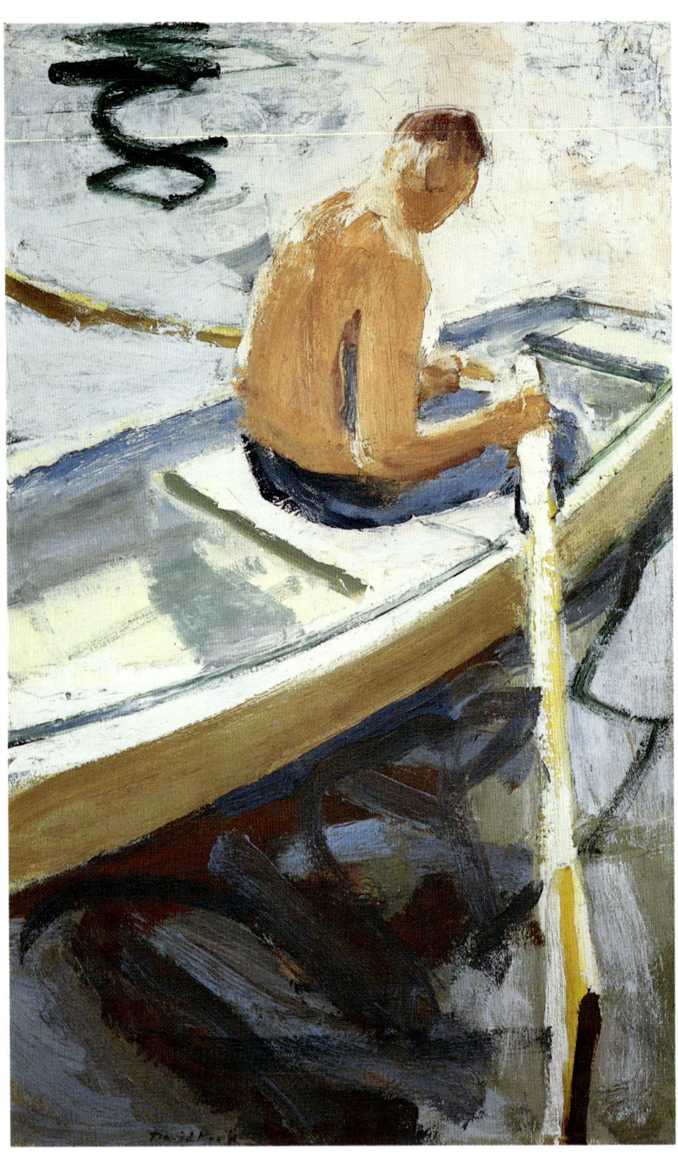

Rowboat, 1954–1955
Oil on canvas, 48 × 29½
Lent by Jane and Robert Carroll

At a time when many painters were experimenting with abstract expressionism David Park was rejecting nonobjective art. Park grew up in the Back Bay section of Boston and first visited the West Coast on a visit to his aunt in 1928. He attended the Otis Art Institute briefly but moved to Berkeley, where he studied at the University of California. In 1944 Park began teaching at the California School of Fine Arts in San Francisco, which was to become the breeding ground for his figurative style.

Early in his career Park was influenced by the work of such realists as Courbet and Eakins, especially in his aim to depict common people engaged in leisurely or everyday activities. Another influence was Diego Rivera. After a brief flirtation with abstraction, in 1949 Park developed his characteristic style, which, however, retained many traces of his nonobjective painting, particularly the use of heavy impasto and textured surfaces.

Park's figures and objects are not naturalistic. Instead of making his subjects conform to preconceived or imitative forms, he allows his works to generate their own shapes spontaneously. Color also becomes an active structural element in the creation of space and expression of attitudes. The artist once remarked about his shift from abstraction to figuration

> I saw that if I would accept subjects I could paint with more absorption, with a certain enthusiasm for the subject which would allow some of the aesthetic qualities, such as color and composition, to evolve more naturally. With subjects, the difference is that I feel a natural development of the painting rather than a formal, self-conscious one.[1]

In *Rowboat,* a product of Park's early figurative style, heavy, thick paint is applied in long, wide brushstrokes that dominate the work. The elimination of a horizon line releases the figure into an undefined and boundless space. This painting displays Park's fondness for boats, a remembrance perhaps of childhood summers spent in New Hampshire.[2] Both the rowboat motif and the title recur throughout his oeuvre. Park continued to paint figurative subjects until his untimely death in 1960.

LHG

1.
Richard Armstrong, *David Park,* University of California Press, Berkeley, Calif., in conjunction with the Whitney Museum of American Art, 1988, p. 42.
2.
Ibid., p. 40.

Additional References
Jones, Caroline A.: *Bay Area Figurative Art,* University of California Press for the San Francisco Museum of Modern Art, San Francisco, 1990.
Mills, Paul: *The New Figurative Art of David Park,* Capra Press, Santa Barbara, 1988.
Park, David: *The David Park Scroll/David Park,* Bedford Arts Publishing, San Francisco, 1989.

1.
John Ashbery, in
John Bernard Myers
et al., *Fairfield Porter
(1907–1975):
Realist Painter in an
Age of Abstraction,*
Little, Brown and
Co., Boston, 1982,
p. 49.
2.
Ibid., p. 57.
3.
Ibid.

*Additional
References*
Benedict, Michael:
  "Fairfield Porter:
  Minimum of
  Melodrama,
  ArtNews, March
  1964, pp. 36–38.
Downes,
  Rackstraw:
  "Porter: The
  Painter as Critic,"
  Art Journal, Sum-
  mer 1978,
  pp. 306–312.
Finkelstein, Louis:
  "The Naturalness
  of Fairfield
  Porter," *Arts
  Magazine,* May
  1976,
  pp. 102–105.

View, 1971
Oil on canvas, 38 × 56
Private collection, Arizona

Fairfield Porter's landscapes evoke a familiar place—inviting, peaceful, and bathed in an atmosphere of ease. With brushstrokes freely applied, the artist captures a momentary glimpse of a serenely beautiful scene.

Born in Winnetka, Illinois, Porter studied art history at Harvard and established himself as an art critic and writer. Mainly self-taught, he began painting in the 1950s during a period dominated by abstract expressionism. An admirer of de Kooning, whom he met in the late 1930s, Porter was greatly influenced by the physicality of his work, particularly de Kooning's visible brush-strokes and self-expression through the active application of paint.[1]

Fluid patches of rich paint reduce elements of the landscape, like the water, meadow, and island in *View,* to flat planes of color. Such details as trees and flowers are expressed by bright dashes of paint. As in many of Porter's works, the scene as a whole does not feel arranged; it is simply organized by the horizontals and verticals in the window frame. Porter is not immersed in detail; he simplifies and abstracts the form.

Porter's compositions are rooted in personal experience and sentiment. He painted scenes around his home in Southampton, New York, and a family-owned island in Maine, perhaps the location of *View.* Although his oeuvre includes still lifes, interiors, and portraits as well as land-scapes, his approach has been consistent, always showing his delight in studying the changing seasons, color, and light in nature around him. "Why did one think of doing anything else when it was so natural to do this?" Porter wondered after viewing an exhibition of paintings by Vuil-lard and Bonnard in 1938.[2] Like these French artists, whose attention to color and light he shares and whose works inspired his love of visual reality combined with an expressive medium, Porter captures the intimate scenes of life, often seen through windows and doors.

Porter's art is not conceptual: it is about the delicate subject of beauty, not about ideas. His paintings capture the beauty of a familiar scene often overlooked precisely because of its famil-iarity. When Porter said, "I painted a picture recently. A great big painting. And it's because I looked out the window and saw it as if for the first time, in a new way. I saw it as something integral,"[3] he could have been talking about *View,* with its calm, undisputed beauty.
WGV

Fairfield Porter

1907–1975

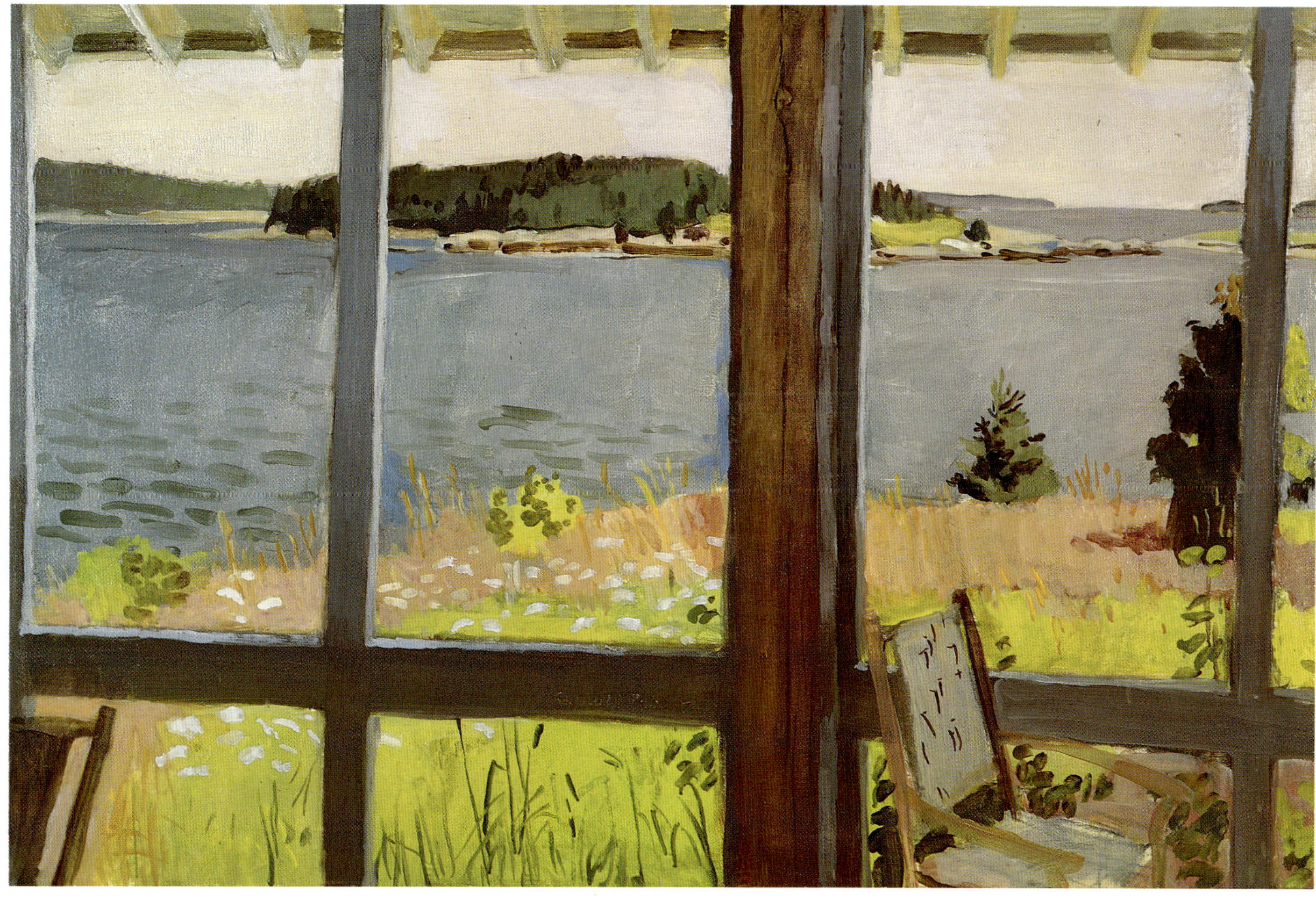

Architonguture, 1983
Oil and spray paint on canvas, 53 × 41
Lent by Barbara Jakobson

Saturday morning cartoons watched inches away from the television screen, Disney World, Hanna-Barbera, plastic dinosaurs, trash and graffiti—what do these things have in common? They are all used by Kenny Scharf and he is having fun while creating art.

Scharf lived in Los Angeles, where he was born, until he went to the School of Visual Arts in New York. In the four years before he graduated in 1980 Scharf became interested in graffiti, creating his own on empty billboards and building facades. He painted images of cartoon characters, like Judy Jetson, surrounded by weird, colorful, animated little shapes. Scharf also "customizes" ordinary objects like clock radios and toasters with paint and the addition of elements such as small plastic trinkets. He has recently begun to decorate the frames of his paintings.

In the early 1980s Scharf became involved with performance art. His installation pieces consisted of black light shining on found objects covered with phosphorescent paint. He also continued to incorporate graffiti art he admired in his compositions, spray-painting both frames and canvas. At times he would add plastic toy dinosaurs and babies to his paintings.

In *Architonguture* his original cartoon characters float in an imaginary space. The title, also of his creation, describes a composition of architectural shapes combined with crazy-looking creatures with long tongues. The texture of Scharf's paintings is smooth, not a brushstroke visible. While the artist acknowledges a debt to surrealism,[1] there are no profound ideas behind the work. The images in Scharf's art, while a product of his imagination, clearly reflect the influence of West Coast popular culture, television, and fantasy.

BH

Kenny Scharf

Born 1958

1.
Stephen Westfall, "Surrealist Modes among Contemporary New York Painters," *Art Journal,* Winter 1985, pp. 315–316.

Additional References
Haring, Keith: "Kenny Scharf," *Flash Art,* January 1985, pp. 14–17.
Marzorati, Gerald: "Kenny Scharf's Fun-House Big Bang," *ArtNews,* September 1985, pp. 72–81.
O'Brien, Glen: "Review," *Artforum,* March 1985, p. 92.

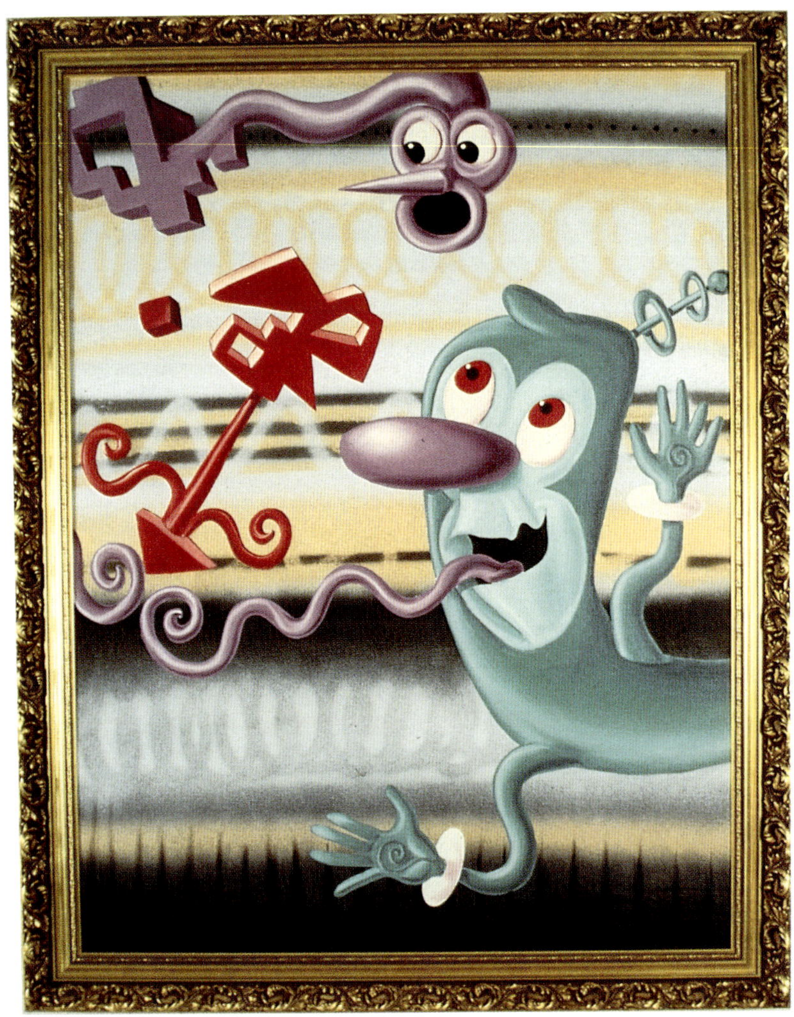

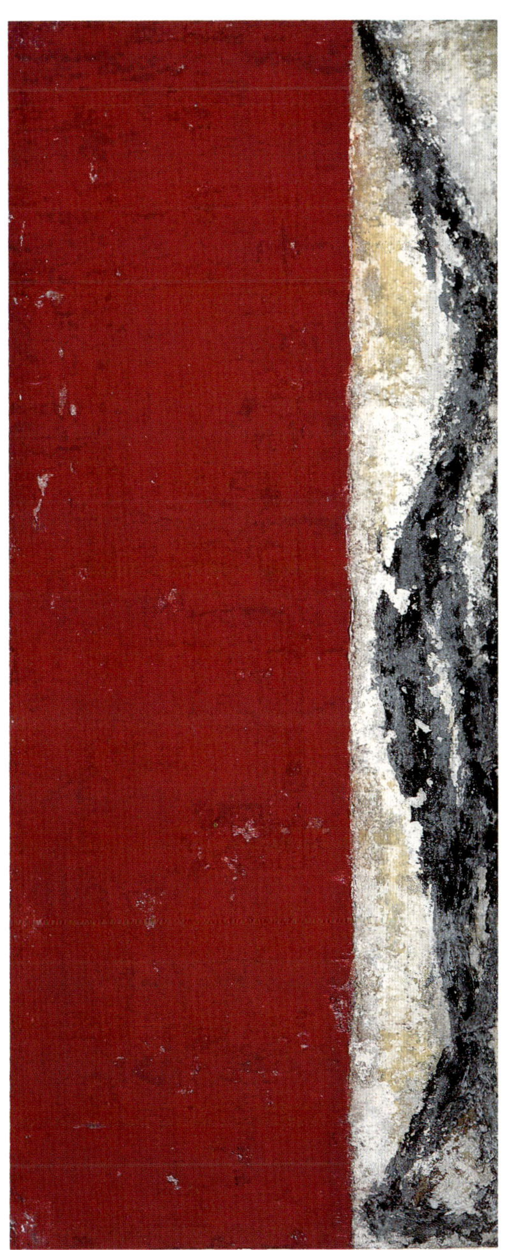

Red Flower, 1987
Acrylic on canvas, 39 × 16
Private collection, Arizona

José Maria Sicilia emerged in the 1980s as one of the leading young painters of Spain. Born in Madrid in 1954, he studied at the San Fernando Institute of Fine Arts from 1975 to 1979. Sicilia moved to Paris the following year and has lived there ever since.

Before Sicilia began the series of works to which *Red Flower* belongs, he experimented with a range of subjects. Favorites included still lifes of tools and kitchen utensils and urban scenes of Madrid and Paris. The cityscapes in particular translated a strong emotional response into visual terms.

Red Flower, one of the artist's most recent paintings, belongs to the Flower series, begun in 1984. The work reveals to some extent how the original conception of the series has changed and how the earlier compositions and the new variations differ. In the Tulip series of 1985 the flower was expressed by vigorously painted overlapping geometric forms floating on a light field. In more recent pictures the abstracted flower is often depicted as a rectangle of color, as it is in *Red Flower.* The stem is suggested by a dark undulating line, its soft edges adding to the visual fragility in this element of the composition. *Yellow Flower, White Line Flower,* and *Black Flower,* although executed in the same year as *Red Flower,* are even farther removed from representation. Fundamentally abstract paintings, they emphasize formal aspects of the composition such as the texture created by a thick application of pigment. They seem to have moved a long way from the initial inspiration.

In Sicilia's work blacks, whites, earth tones, and dramatic reds dominate the pictorial space. The pigment appears dry, suggestive of the dusty earth which gives birth to life. The variety in arrangement, texture, and hue provides unexpected combinations. *Red Flower,* a fusion of broad textured areas and simple colors, is a vibrant composition that captures the viewer's attention.

Light is the fulcrum of Sicilia's art. He plays with its ambiguities without revealing its source. The canvases with the darkest colors also seem to glow with an intense inner light, creating a powerful tension with these contrasting tonalities. Although works such as *Red Flower* may have been inspired by the artist's response to color in nature, subject matter is not Sicilia's main concern. Issues of structure, space, and form are among the recurrent visual problems he has been analyzing since the outset of his career.

GL

José Maria Sicilia

Born 1954

References
Calvo Serraller, Francisco: *José Maria Sicilia: Peintures de 1987,* Palacio de Velazquez, Madrid, April–May 1987 (and later venues).
Gambrell, Jamey: *José Maria Sicilia: Recent Paintings,* Blum/ Helman, New York, December 2, 1987–January 2, 1988.
Grout, Catherine: "José Maria Sicilia," *Flash Art,* April 19, 1980, pp. 56–58.
Peppiat, Michael: "José Maria Sicilia: Escaping the Tyranny of Style," *Art International,* Spring 1989, pp. 71–77.

My Temple/My Totems, 1983
Mixed media on canvas, 60 × 120
Private collection, Arizona

Born in Highland Park, New Jersey, Snyder
studied at Syracuse University under Robert
Morris.* She first became known for her Stroke
paintings. On large canvases Snyder analyzed
and dissected lines of paint from various per-
spectives and angles. Like notes of music on the
staff, Snyder's strokes were painted over an
underlying grid drawn on the canvas with pencil
that remained visible in areas not covered with
pigment.

After the Stroke paintings her work changed
significantly. The range of materials and media
expanded, as did her imagery, which frequently
made powerful feminist statements. Snyder
turned within herself to find inspiration. Looking back at this transition, she explains, "I had
nowhere to go but into my own past again,
into my own iconography."[1] *My Temple/My
Totems* is representative of these autobiographical compositions.

The painting contains two images used
repeatedly in Snyder's works: a house and a
skull-like head with vacant eyes and gaping
mouth. The large head, based on an African
mask, dominates the center of the composition
and is contained within the schematic outline
of the house. The house may well represent institutions which restrict or repress human expression, suggested here by the screaming head.
Snyder's child-like style heightens the message
of helplessness and frustration while the immense
size of the painting reflects the importance to the
artist of fighting against repression.

Organic elements—mementos perhaps of the
artist's life—appear in each corner. Although
unidentifiable, these forms, through their mystery and placement, add to the voodoo quality
and psychological intensity of the work. Snyder's
choice of colors and paint application further
raises the pitch. The vibrant pigments, applied
quickly with broad strokes, seem to drip and
run. The artist has built up the surface by layering the paint and by attaching other materials
to the canvas. This process of accumulation
seems to be a collage of memories with pieces
from the artist's life. The freedom of execution
underscores the bold insistence of the magical
but frightening image.
CLC

Joan Snyder

Born 1940

1.
Hayden Herrera,
*Joan Snyder: Seven
Years of Work,*
Neuberger Museum,
State University of
New York at
Purchase, Janu-
ary 17–March 4,
1978, p. 20

*Additional
References*
Henry, Gerrit:
"Joan Snyder:
True Grit," *Art
in America,* Feb-
ruary 1986, pp.
96–101.
Herrera, Hayden:
"Joan Snyder at
Carl Solway,"
Art in America,
May–June 1976,
pp. 103–104.
Walls, Michael:
Joan Snyder, San
Francisco Art
Institute, San
Francisco,
November 3–
December 14,
1979.

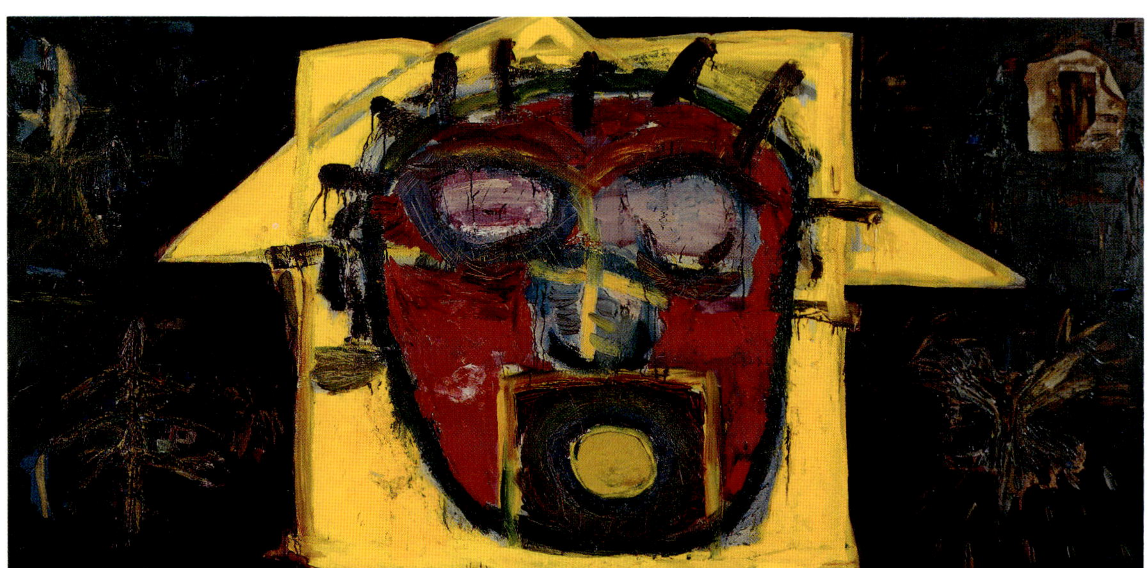

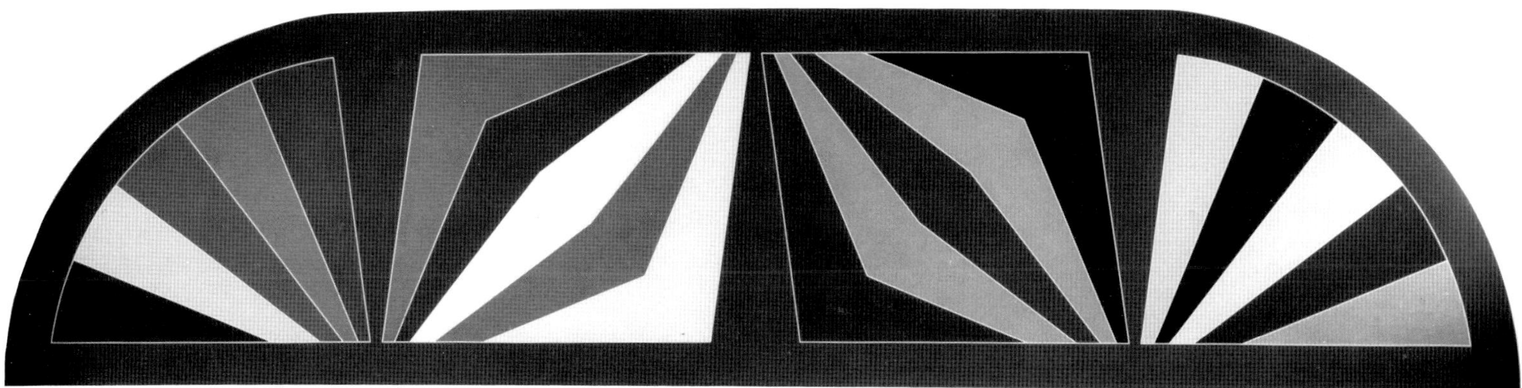

1.
William Rubin,
Frank Stella,
The Museum of
Modern Art, New
York, 1970,
pp. 127–149.
2.
Ibid., p. 135.
3.
William Rubin,
*Frank Stella (1970–
1987),*
The Museum of
Modern Art, New
York, 1988, passim.

*Additional
References*
Leider, Philip: *Stella
since 1970,* The
Fort Worth Art
Museum, Fort
Worth, 1978.
Rosenblum, Robert:
Frank Stella, Pen-
guin Books,
Harmondsworth,
Middlesex, 1971.
Rubin, Lawrence:
*Frank Stella:
Paintings 1958
to 1965—A Cata-
logue Raisonné,*
Stewart, Tabori
& Chang, New
York, 1986.

Damascus Gate (Variation III), 1969
Polymer and fluorescent polymer paint on
canvas, 120 × 480
Smith College Museum of Art, gift of the artist

Frank Stella's Black series of 1958–1960 marked
the beginning of a major career that has spanned
three decades. These elegantly spare works, composed of monochromatic bands separated by
thin stripes of bare canvas, signal a stylistic
break with the painterly, gestural canvases of the
abstract expressionists that had influenced Stella
during his years as a student at Princeton from
1954 to 1958. The series of works Stella produced in the 1960s redefined painting in terms
of the relation of the painted surface to the boundaries of the canvas. In his Aluminum pictures
of 1960 the traditional rectangular support is
notched or cut away to reflect the abstract pattern
of painted bands. The first of Stella's "shaped
canvases," they introduced the more radical
structural breaks that would follow as paintings
assumed the shape of crosses (Copper series,
1960–61), polygons (Purple series, 1963), or
flying wedges (Notched V series, 1964–1965).

Stella's developing interest in the affective use
of color in the mid-1960s culminated in the
decorative chromatic bursts of the Protractor
series of 1967–1971, to which *Damascus Gate
(Variation III)* belongs. Named for cities in Asia
Minor with circular plans, they are the first of
Stella's paintings to adopt a curvilinear format
and architectural scale. In this series the paintings are based on the unit of the semicircle and
divided into three design groups: "interlaces,"
in which bands of color interweave, "rainbows,"
based on concentric color arcs, and "fans,"
distinguished by wedge shapes that radiate from
the base of the protractor.[1]

Damascus Gate (Variation III) is a fan painting. As the title suggests, its arching structure
recalls a monumental gateway or entry. The
internal geometry of the painting is determined
by two contiguous protractors overlapped by a

third, inverted, with its base at the top of the
canvas; the color wedges of the protractors fan
out and meet, forming the distinctive shapes
contained in the two central fields of the painting.
As in the first Black series pictures, the white
unprimed canvas demarcates the painted areas.
It was Stella's working practice to use manufac-
turer's colors, but for the Protractor paintings
the artist sometimes mixed his own pigments,
combining acrylic and fluorescent media[2] to
achieve the volatile and almost vertiginous color
relationships that characterize a work like
Damascus Gate. Although the composition is
abstract and nonillusionistic, a two-dimensional
surface reinforced by the flat application of
paint, it not only dominates the wall but com-
mands space well into the room by the dizzying
force of its colors.

The early 1970s marked a new beginning or a
second career for Stella, when his paintings began
to build away from the wall, first as shallow
reliefs in the Polish Village series (1971–1973).
The Exotic Bird series (1976–1980), colorful
mixed-media reliefs incorporating curves and
painterly marks, announced an evolution toward
the more baroque configurations of Stella's metal
relief paintings of the late 1970s and 1980s.[3]
LM

Frank Stella

Born 1936

Donald Sultan

Born 1951

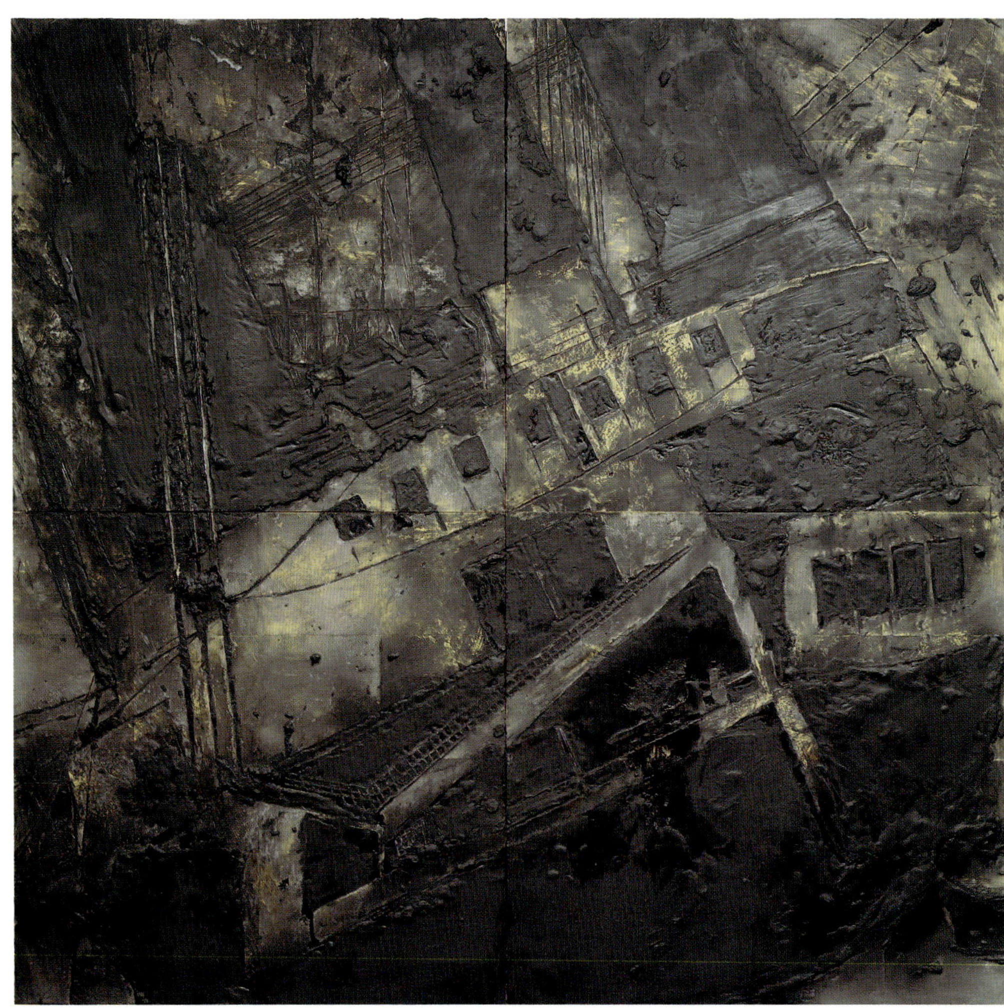

Ferry, 1987
Latex on tile on Masonite, 96 × 96
Private collection, Arizona

Donald Sultan was exposed to art at an early age through his father, an amateur painter and passionate admirer of the work of Jackson Pollock. Born in Asheville, North Carolina, Sultan attended the University of North Carolina at Chapel Hill. He first wanted to be an actor but once he realized that actors do not have complete control over their artistic expression, he decided to study art history and painting instead.

After receiving a Bachelor of Fine Arts degree in 1973, Sultan undertook graduate study at the School of the Art Institute of Chicago. There he created paintings using a variety of materials as well as splatter paintings influenced by Pollock. These efforts led to his Debris works, consisting of objects glued onto a solid support such as

wood, which in turn led to his present method.

For subject matter Sultan relies on newspapers for inspiration and visual material. He is particularly attracted to such catastrophic events as fires and explosions. *Ferry,* for example, is based on a newspaper photograph showing a ship at sea which nearly capsized in a storm. Sultan says that the intricate method by which he uses a photograph as a point of departure for his own creativity prevents him from merely illustrating an event.[1] He sets Masonite tiles in a grid-like shape, draws the image of the illustration selected directly on the tile with black crayon, and then removes unnecessary lines by scraping them off with a razor blade. He calls this a "cartoon" in conscious reference to the method of the old masters.[2] After applying paint the artist adds tar to the picture to make the "doomsday" subject matter abstract and to create a chiaroscuro effect. The contrast of darks and lights brings out the underlying form of the painting.

Although Sultan begins his paintings with a representational image, his work is essentially abstract. He believes that abstraction must begin with the form of the image, and his method underscores his commitment to that process.
NJS

1.
Interview by NJS with the artist, October 26, 1990.
2.
Barbara Rose, *An Interview with Donald Sultan,* Elizabeth Avedon, New York, 1988, p. 85.

Additional Reference
Henry, Gerrit: "Dark Poetry," *ArtNews,* April 1987, pp. 104–111.

1.
Ronald Penrose,
Tàpies, Rizzoli
International Publi-
cations, Inc., New
York, 1978, p. 120.

*Additional
References*
Gimferrer, Pere:
*Tàpies and the
Catalan Spirit*,
Rizzoli Interna-
tional Publica-
tions, Inc., New
York, 1975.
Lascaut, Gilbert:
"Thinking with
Tàpies," *Cimaise*,
April–May 1988,
pp. 5–16.
Lebovici, Elisabeth:
"Antonio
Tàpies," *Beaux
Arts Magazine*,
November 1985,
pp. 38–42.

Grey Brown Lid, 1966
Mixed media on canvas, 33¾ × 57½
Lent by Elizabeth and Maurice Pinto

One of the most prominent living Spanish artists, Antoni Tàpies has been a key figure in shaping the direction of contemporary art in his country. Such stylistic innovations as the use of unorthodox materials and repetitive symbolic elements have engaged the general public and elicited widespread admiration. Tàpies has also influenced many young artists, including José Maria Sicilia.*

A native of Barcelona, Tàpies devoted himself wholly to painting after giving up the study of law at the University of Barcelona. His art is a complex combination of geometric forms in which primitivism and abstraction merge. His use of unconventional materials like earth and sand and the symbolic nature of his images are distinguishing characteristics of his mature style.

Grey Brown Lid presents a duality of conflicting concepts that reappear in *Closed Doors* (1971), *Double Oval in Blue* (1959), and other works. Tàpies has always been fascinated by the symmetry and confusion created by mirror images, with their power to reflect and distort reality. The composition of *Grey Brown Lid* and to some extent the title offer insights into the dualities that occupy Tàpies's art. While some writers refer to the image as a bed, others have called it a lid.[1] The stony quality and earth tones argue against its being a bed; still, the placement of the two symmetrical pillow-like objects suggest a place of rest. This particular "bed," however, can also be read visually as the lid or slab of a tomb. Turned around, the shapes of *Grey Brown Lid* also recall a pair of doors, perhaps hiding some terrifying secret or leading into the unknown. Whatever the significance of these impenetrable forms, they project a sense of mystery and foreboding. Like much of Tàpies's work, this composition offers the viewer admittance to an unknown world where enigmatic questions are raised if not necessarily answered.
GL

Antoni Tàpies

Born 1923

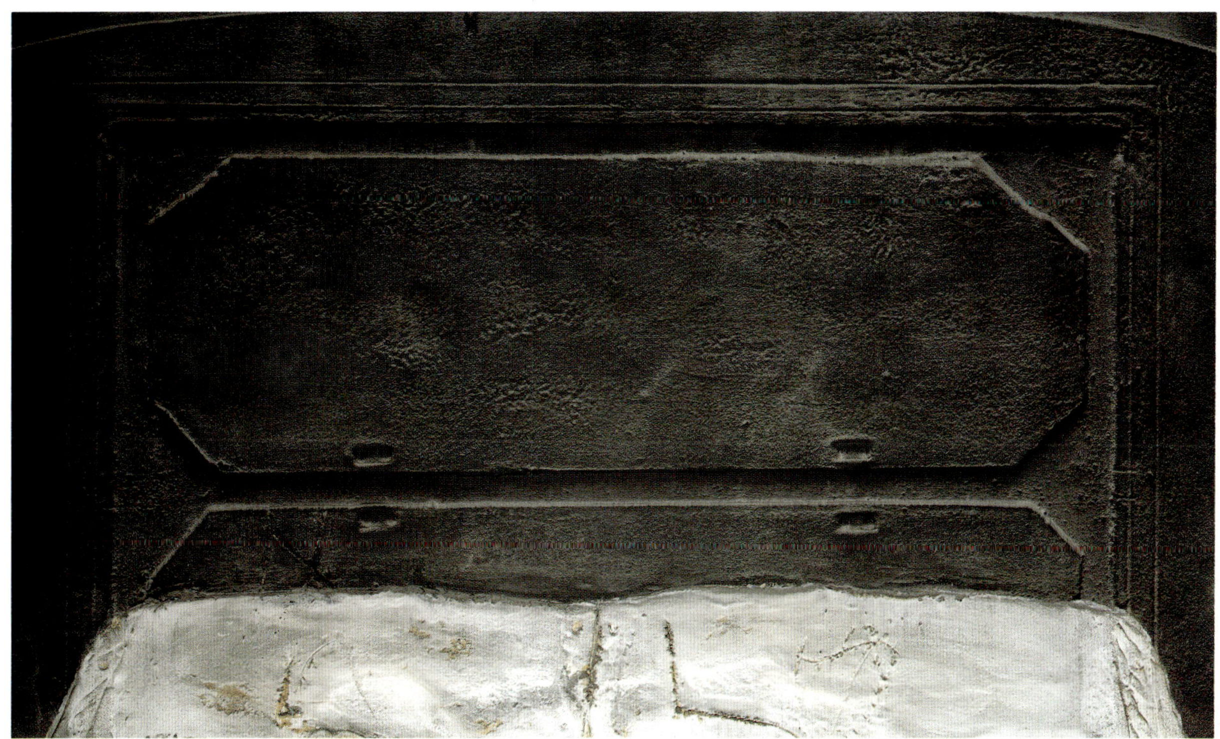

Wayne Thiebaud

Born 1920

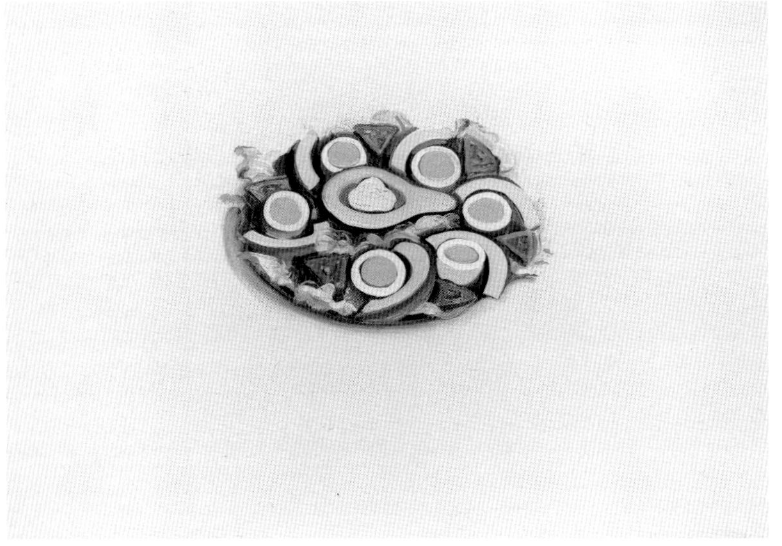

1.
Bill Berkson,
"Thiebaud's Van-
ities," *Art in
America*, December
1985, p. 115.

*Additional
References*
Cooper, Gene:
"Thiebaud,
Theatre, and
Extremism," in
Wayne Thiebaud,
Phoenix Art
Museum, 1976.
Hoving, Thomas:
"Time for
Thiebaud:
America's Best
Overlooked
Painter," *Con-
noisseur*, Sep-
tember 1985,
pp. 76–79.
Moorman, Mar-
garet: "Review,"
ArtNews, Sum-
mer 1986,
pp. 142–143.

Avocado Salad, 1962
Oil on canvas, 20 × 28
Lent by Mr. and Mrs. Morton Sosland

A window full of shoes, a pile of ties, a display of food on a table, a portrait of a woman in a bathing suit eating an ice-cream cone, cityscapes of San Francisco—all these are among the subjects of Wayne Thiebaud's paintings.

Born in California and educated at Long Beach City College and California State College, Sacramento, Thiebaud did not start painting until he was thirty. Earlier he had done animation for Walt Disney, cartoons for Rexall Drugs, and illustrations for movie posters. His background in commercial art is apparent in his paintings. Although Thiebaud is often mistaken for a pop artist because of his themes, the subjects are of less interest to him than formal concerns of color, composition, and brushwork.[1]

Avocado Salad is a typical Thiebaud work of the early 1960s. The paint is very thick, creating a rich texture and making the brushstrokes and hand of the artist apparent. A platter brimming with avocados, hard-boiled eggs, tomato wedges, and lettuce rests on a solid light-blue background, an unusual color for this artist, who generally uses white. Only part of the platter shows, and because it casts no shadow on the background, it seems to be floating in undefined space.

What makes Thiebaud unique is his style of painting. Very sensitive to color harmonies and contrasts, he paints thickly and heavily. Although he uses the true colors of the object he is painting, the result is not at all realistic and verges on the disturbing. Whether they are cupcakes, hot dogs, or avocado salad, his dishes are anything but appetizing.

Although there are no shadows in *Avocado Salad*, Thiebaud is often concerned with them in other paintings, where they may even become a sort of subtext, a form almost separate from the subject. Even if the light on an object is painted realistically, Thiebaud may introduce shadows that negate that lighting. Both his use of shadow and the isolation of the subject on a blank background give his work a surreal quality.
BH

Form and Sepik Mask, 1984
Oil on linen, 84 × 66
Private collection, Arizona

John Walker was born in Birmingham, England, and educated at the Birmingham School of Arts and the Académie de la Grande Chaumière in Paris. A graphic artist as well as a painter, Walker has traveled widely and taught at many institutions, principally in England, the United States, and Australia. He has been a visiting professor at the Cooper Union and the Yale School of Art and Architecture and currently lives in New York.

Beginning as an abstract painter, Walker now seeks to unite the abstract with the representational. Just as he reconciles the two painting styles on one canvas, *Form and Sepik Mask* may be viewed as an attempt to reconcile the art of two different cultures, a dominant theme in his work of this period. Yet, as Memory Holloway eloquently summarizes, Walker's works invite multiple readings.

> They can be seen as pure abstraction, as objects in space, as referents to the art of the past, and more recently to the tribal art of Australia and Oceania. If there is one characteristic which these images share it is their ambiguity. They take up residence with the literal figure of Goya's Duchess of Alba and with New Guinea masks from the Sepik. Yet the artist consistently transforms the recognizable into its traces, into images which only distantly recall the initial impetus which gave them life. That is one aspect of Walker's work. The other, equally important, is the constant working and reworking of a theme, as though to perfect it, to relocate the same shape against more luxuriant grounds, to clothe the shape with more opulence and to reinvest it with new meaning.[1]

Ambiguous, even mysterious, *Form and Sepik Mask* deals with issues that Holloway raises while posing other questions as well. The Alba form has been a consistent motif in Walker's paintings since the late 1970s and dominates the smaller Sepik mask. The two elements are abstracted, transformed into "traces," and thus enhanced by not being precisely recognizable. The juxtaposition of these forms, which seem to face each other, raises questions for the viewer. With which form should the viewer identify? The answer— or answers—remain unclear. In western art the Alba form and its historical overtones may be better known to the viewer, but the anthropomorphic Sepik mask is also immediately familiar.

Formally the painting is also ambiguous, particularly in its spatial configuration. It is possible to read either a foreground, middle ground, and background or a flattening out of space in which the figures appear on a ledge or stage-like ground in front of a flat backdrop. Or both these possibilities may coexist. What is not ambiguous is the force the painting exerts upon the viewer. The surface is strongly tactile and the colors warm. Yet it is not entirely confrontational, requiring contemplation.

AT

1.
Memory Holloway, *John Walker: Prints & Drawings 1977– 84,* The Tate Gallery, London, 1985, p. 4.

Additional References
Ashton, Dore: *John Walker: Paintings from the Alba and Oceania Series 1979–84,* Hayward Gallery, London, 1985.
Flam, Jack: *John Walker,* The Phillips Collection, Washington, D.C., 1982.

John Walker

Born 1939

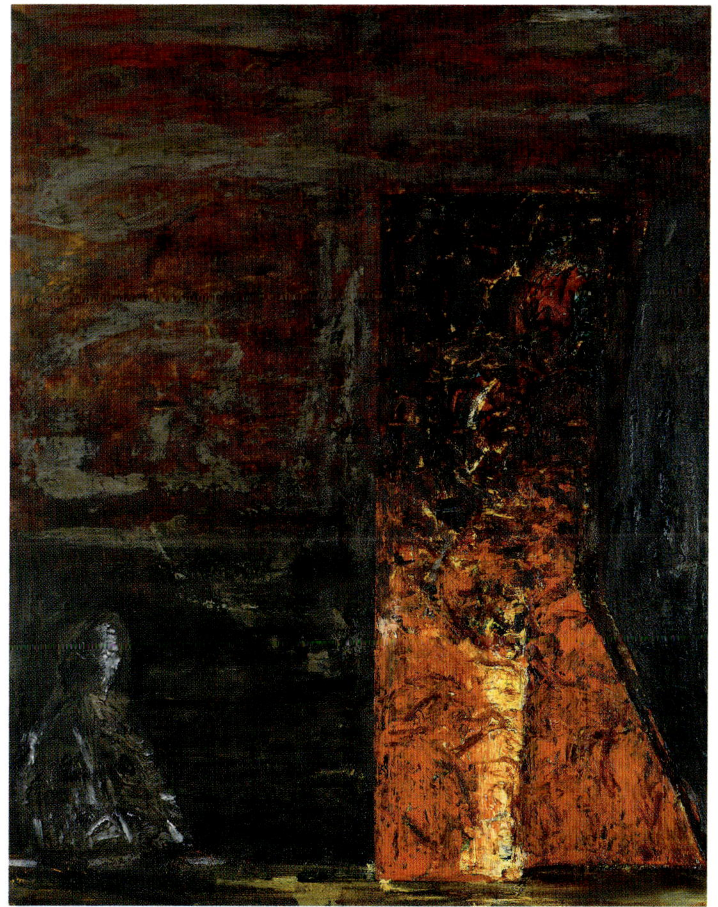

Andy Warhol

1928–1987

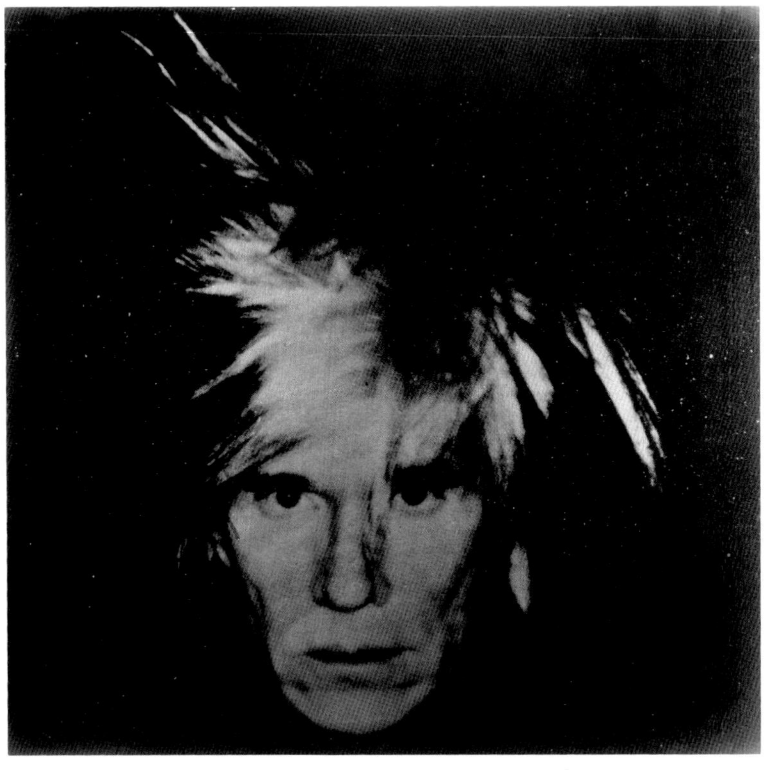

Self-Portrait, 1986
Silk-screen ink on synthetic polymer paint on canvas, 40 × 40
Lent by Mr. and Mrs. Marshall Cogan

One of the most enigmatic and best-publicized personalities of this century, Andy Warhol is closely identified with the avant-garde of the 1960s. Born Andrew Warhola in Pittsburgh of Czechoslovakian immigrants, he studied pictorial design at the Carnegie Institute of Technology, graduating in 1949. He worked in New York as an illustrator for *Glamour Magazine* in 1949 and 1950 and was successful as a commercial artist through most of the 1950s. In the early 1960s he began a series of paintings and drawings based on comic strips and advertisements. Along with Roy Lichtenstein, Tom Wesselmann, Claes Oldenburg,* and Robert Indiana, Warhol emerged as a leading exponent of pop art, which was often characterized as an attempt to break with the dominant abstract expressionist style. Pop artists returned to the object as subject, deriving images from popular culture.

Warhol achieved fame in the 1960s with his paintings of Campbell's Soup cans and Green Stamps, endlessly repeated, the sculptures of Brillo Pad boxes, and the paintings based on photographs of such celebrities as Elvis Presley, Marilyn Monroe, and Elizabeth Taylor. Warhol surrounded himself in his studio, "The Factory," with members of the fringe culture associated with that decade. When a deranged "star" of one of his underground movies tried to kill Warhol in 1968, it took him months to recover physically; he probably never did recover emotionally.

In the 1970s and 1980s Warhol's energy was concentrated on portraits and on *Interview,* the magazine he founded in 1969. He was best known in the 1980s for his commissioned silk-screen portraits based on photographs and for his role in the New York social scene. He died in 1987 of complications following gallbladder surgery. A major retrospective of his work was held in 1989.[1]

Death, an important theme in Warhol's art,[2] first appeared in 1962 in *129 Die (Plane Crash)* (Museum Ludwig, Cologne) and was treated in the Disaster paintings of the 1960s, the Electric Chair series, and the paintings of Jackie Kennedy based on photographs taken immediately after the assassination of the President. The theme recurs in the skull paintings of the mid-1970s and in the last self-portraits.

In this black *Self-Portrait* Warhol's head, visualized almost as a skull, is eerily isolated from the rest of the body. Wearing one of his signature silver wigs, the artist stares directly at the viewer with a disturbing sadness and an almost palpable awareness of mortality. The self-portraits made in the year before Warhol's death "are not the paintings of some reticent, evasive young innocent but of ravaged maturity."[3]

MG

1.
Kynaston McShine (ed.), *Andy Warhol: A Retrospective,* The Museum of Modern Art, New York, February 6–May 2, 1989.
2.
See especially Trevor Fairbrother, "Skulls," in Gary Garrels (ed.), *The Work of Andy Warhol,* Bay Press, Seattle, 1989, pp. 93–114.
3.
McShine, p. 21.

Additional References
Bockris, Victor: *The Life and Death of Andy Warhol,* Bantam Books, New York, 1989.
Ratcliff, Carter: *Andy Warhol,* Abbeville Press, New York, 1983.

1.
Edwin Denby, interview, in *Neil Welliver: Paintings 1966–1980*, Currier Gallery of Art, Manchester, N.H., 1981, p. 23.

Additional References
Downes, Rackstraw: "Welliver's Travels," *ArtNews*, November 1967, pp. 34–36, and 75–76.
Medoff, Eve: "Neil Welliver: Painting—Inclusive and Intense," *American Artist*, April 1979, pp. 48–53.
Goodyear, Frank H., Jr.: *Contemporary American Realism since 1960*, New York Graphic Society, Boston, 1981.

Winter Stream, 1976
Oil on canvas, 96 × 96
Smith College Museum of Art, gift of Mrs. Leonard S. Mudge in memory of Polly Mudge Welliver '60

Whether Neil Welliver's subject is a stream, field, or forest, his landscapes express the beauty and power of a world untouched, unpolluted, and unconstrained by man. The fluid brushstrokes, expressive color, and large scale create an image as airy and open as the outdoors. Through intricate patterns of twigs and branches and the play of light on water and snow, Welliver celebrates the complexities of nature. True wilderness and natural beauty leap from the canvas.

Welliver, who was born in Millville, Pennsylvania, studied at the Philadelphia Museum School and the Yale School of Art and Architecture. As a child he had fallen in love with nature as he explored the woods around his rural home. This fascination returned in the 1960s when he began to paint bucolic scenes, children, and bathers. Gradually, however, the artist moved on to pure landscapes charged with energy. Panoramic views like *Clouds over Grieg's Bog* (1970) avoid a closeup view of nature while

other works, like *Winter Stream,* in which the water almost rushes out of the canvas, submerge us in it.

Throughout the late 1960s and 1970s Welliver emphasized abstract expressionist methods, particularly the gestural application of paint, to create uniquely vigorous images of the natural world. Even today he avoids copying nature's hues. "To imitate nature you'd need a tube of air," says Welliver.[1] Instead he chooses colors that remind him of the true natural tone but are more intense and startling, like the bright blue in the chunks of ice in *Winter Stream.* For Welliver, winter emphasizes the luminosity and intensity of color. In this work the artist plays with the effects of light reflected off the snow and the details enhanced by the sun's cold glare.

Welliver lives on a farm in Maine where he raises his own food, generates his own power with windmills, and forbids lumbering, hunting, and snowmobiling on his property. As he strives to protect nature in its pure, unspoiled state through his mode of life, he also preserves it on canvas.
WGV

Neil Welliver

Born 1929

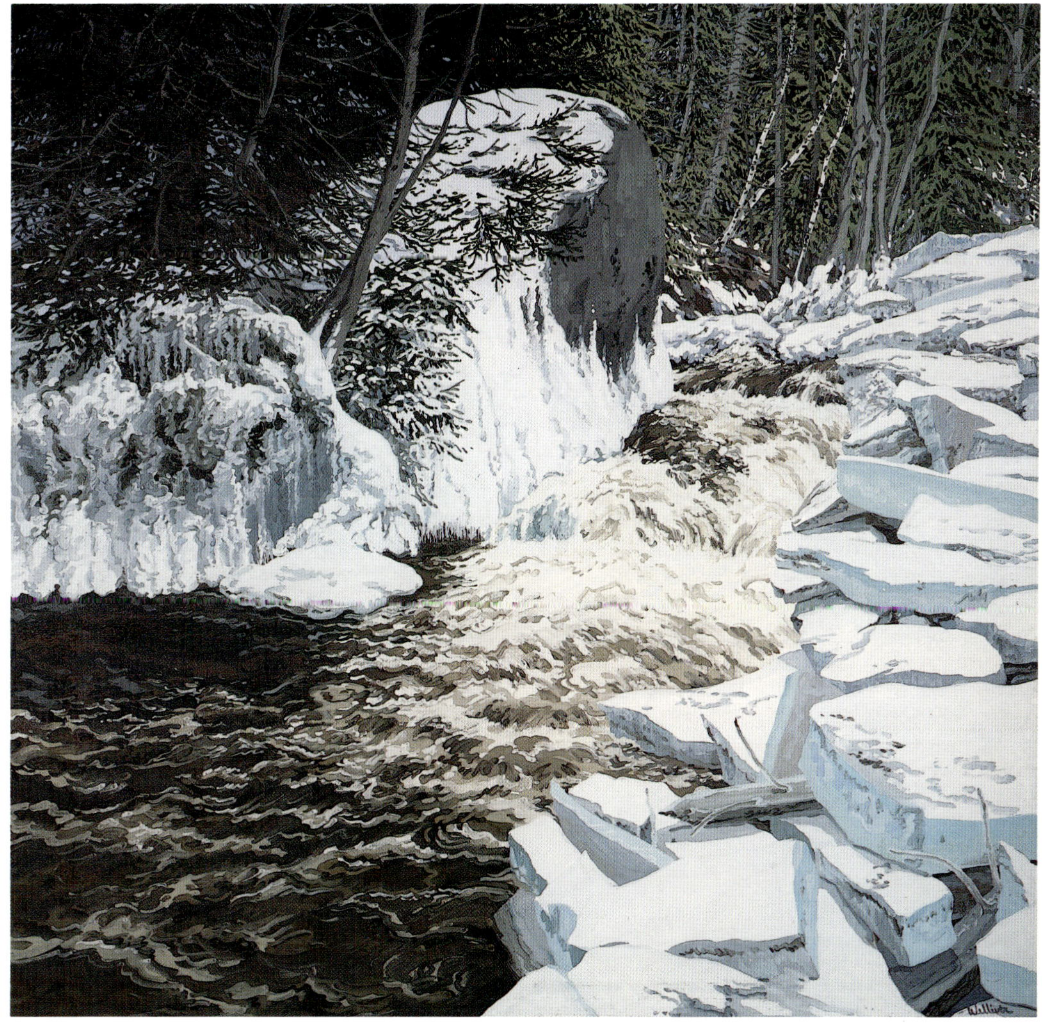

Han Xin

Born 1955

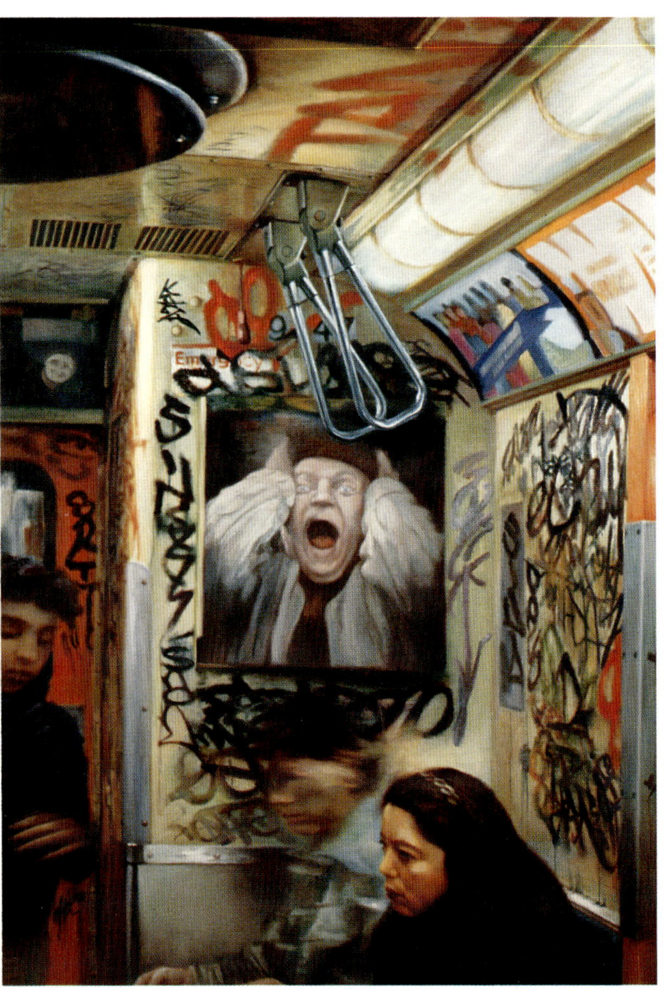

That Unbeatable Feeling, 1987
Oil on canvas, 68 × 47⅜
Xin Ji 心 迹 [Heart Traces] Collection

In the early 1970s Han Xin was the youngest
member of a group of Shanghai artists labeled
"black painters" by government leaders who
objected to their bourgeois styles and subjects at
a time when propagandistic socialist realism was
the only official mode of expression and access
to international art severely limited. Basically
self-taught, Han Xin was finally allowed to
attend Beijing Central Academy of Fine Arts. In
1982 he left China to study at Oakland College
of Arts and Crafts, from which he received the
degree of Master of Fine Arts.

Han Xin's paintings have evolved from small-
scale realistic works into large confrontational
canvases like *That Unbeatable Feeling.* "Gone
is the prettiness of his work in China; he has
heightened the direction of his original vision."[1]
His series on the subculture of the New York
subway faithfully renders the conflicts inherent
in an alarming but mundane scene of everyday
life.

That Unbeatable Feeling is painted as though
from a photograph. The blurring of the seated
man suggests that he moved too fast for the camera to freeze his image precisely, and the cropped
figure of the young boy on the left seems candid
in its arbitrariness. Although the flat brushstrokes
add to the realistic portrayal of space, the artist
is clearly interested in presenting more than a
photographic view of life in New York. The
scene—recognizable to anyone who has traveled
on the subway—is at the same time a terrifying
nightmare.

The hallucinatory image reflected in the shiny
metal panel in the center of the composition
looks like a modern reincarnation of the being
in Edvard Munch's *The Scream.* Unnoticed by
his fellow passengers, the disturbing figure floats
in a spaceless vacuum somewhere inside the
subway car underneath a graffiti-covered
"Emergency" sign.

The uneasy, "unbeatable" feeling arises from
the enigmatic presence that skews the rest of
an otherwise commonplace scene. The bright,
jarring colors and the line of white lights impart
a sense of motion and speed as the train hurtles
through cavernous underground space. The agi-
tated calligraphic lines of graffiti enliven the surface of this painting, creating a claustrophobic
effect within the space of the composition. Their
gestural forms, some of which resemble Chinese
characters, hint at a pictographic language whose
meaning is unknown.

WEB

1.
Joan Lebold Cohen,
*Artists from
China—New
Expressions,* Sarah
Lawrence College
Art Gallery,
Bronxville, N.Y.,
September 29–
November 22,
1987, n.p.

*Additional
References*
Cohen, Joan
  Lebold: *Painting
  the Chinese
  Dream: Chinese
  Art Thirty Years
  after the Revolu-
  tion,* Smith
  College Museum
  of Art,
  Northampton,
  Mass., May 19–
  September 12,
  1982.
———: *The New
  Generation of
  Chinese Art,*
  Smith College
  Museum of Art,
  Northampton,
  Mass., January
  12–February 21,
  1990.

Sculpture

Copper-Zinc Plain, 1969
Copper and zinc plates, eighteen of each
$\frac{3}{8} \times 72 \times 72$
Private collection, courtesy of Sperone
Westwater

The minimalist Carl Andre was raised in
Quincy, Massachusetts, and is a graduate of
Phillips Andover Academy. Characteristics of his
work are flatness, modular compositions that
are arranged rather than joined, and the use of
ordinary interchangeable forms and materials.
Influenced by the reductive geometry of Frank
Stella,* whom he met in 1958, Andre relies on
personal exploration and experience; for example, his work as a brakeman on the Pennsylvania
Railroad from 1960 to 1964. Although "he had
already begun to work with preexisting, stan-
dardized materials, four years of coupling and
uncoupling freight cars confirmed him in his use
of regimented, interchangeable units."[1]

In considering *Copper-Zinc Plain* the following statements by the artist are valuable:

> The Course of Development
>   Sculpture as form
>   Sculpture as structure
>   Sculpture as place[2]

> My work is atheistic, materialistic, and commu-
> nistic. It's atheistic because it's without transcendent
> form, without spiritual or intellectual quality.
> Materialistic because it's made out of its own mate-
> rials without pretension to other materials. And
> communistic because the form is equally accessible
> to all men.[3]

> I believe in using the materials of society in the form
> the society does not use them.[4]

The transition from sculpture as form to structure as place means leaving aside the traditional
notions of sculpture, moving from vertical
anthropomorphic structure to flat horizontal
arrangements of modular pieces. *Copper-Zinc
Plain* makes this transition at the lowest level
available—laid out, $\frac{3}{8}$ inch high, upon the floor.
Communistic also in its cellular modularity, the
work is materialistic in bespeaking its own substance and remaining, as it is titled, copper, zinc,
plain.

The sculpture emanates from *37 Pieces of
Work*, a larger construction created for Andre's
1970 solo exhibition at the Solomon R.
Guggenheim Museum. That piece consisted of
thirty-six "plains," each made up of thirty-six
12-inch squares $\frac{3}{8}$ inch thick. The six plains

each of single metals (aluminum, copper, steel,
lead, magnesium, and zinc) and thirty plains containing alternating combinations of the metals
in pairs made up in their totality the thirty-
seventh plain. Mathematically the sculpture's
dimensions were unitary and multiplicative. The
foot-square metal plates were arranged in plains
equaling 6 square feet; the thirty-six plains
together equaled 36 square feet. As a result of
their unitary and interchangeable natures, the
individual metals and plains do not rely on each
other for completion unless juxtaposed. Thus
each plain is a separate entity, as *Copper-Zinc
Plain* illustrates.

Following his dictum "sculpture as place,"
Andre emphasizes the geographic nature of these
sculptures by labeling them "plains" rather than
"planes." The plains are meant to be walked on,
like an expanse of flat geography. The changes
in the surface of the metal plates caused by this
viewer interaction enrich the sculpture with tem-
poral change. Andre believes that the viewer can
distinguish the different properties of the metals
by walking over them. Indeed, viewer interaction
is essential. "Andre's works come into existence
only when necessary. When not on exhibition,
the pieces are dismantled and cease to exist
except as ideas."[5]

AT

Carl Andre

Born 1935

1.
David Bourdon,
"The Razed Sites
of Carl Andre," in
Gregory Battcock
(ed.), *Minimal Art:
A Critical Anthol-
ogy*, E.P. Dutton
& Co., New York,
1968, p. 104.
2.
Ibid., p. 103.
3.
Ibid., p, 107.
4.
David Bourdon,
*Carl Andre
Sculpture 1959–
1977*, Jaap Rietman,
Inc., New York,
1978, p. 14.
5.
"The Razed
Sites...," p. 107.

*Additional
Reference*
Tuchman, Phyllis:
"An Interview
with Carl Andre,"
Artforum, June
1970, pp. 55–61.

Arman

Born 1928

The Seven Muses, 1964
Watch wheels in polyester resin
33½ × 25¾ × 1½
Lent by Rosa and Aaron H. Esman, M.D.

Born Armand Fernandez in Nice, Arman studied
at the École Nationale des Arts Décoratifs in
Nice and the École du Louvre in Paris. He is now
an American citizen and divides his time between
this country and France. In his first exhibition in
1956 he signed his work with his given name.
When the "d" was accidentally dropped from a
catalogue two years later, he became "Arman."
By this time he was creating *cachets,* inked
impressions of rubber stamps on paper. These
led to the *allures d'objet,* marks made by items
being dipped in ink or color and then pressed,
rolled, or splattered onto a surface. In 1959 he
first arranged actual objects in works called
accumulations. He also began making *colères* by
burning or smashing such things as violins and
typewriters.

At first, Arman made *accumulations* with
trash or old objects, but when he visited the

United States in 1961, he turned to industrial
materials that were often small and shiny. At
about the same time he also started suspending
objects in polyester resin.[1] *The Seven Muses* is
thus one of his earliest compositions making use
of these materials and this method.

In addition to watch wheels, Arman has used
a variety of items—gas masks, cameras, paint
tubes, pencils, teapots, forks, nails, toy guns,
ball bearings, and even garbage. Arranged in
piles, stuffed in boxes, embedded in polyester, or
set in concrete, these *accumulations* become
expressions of our time.

> I didn't discover the principle of *accumulation,* it
> discovered me. It has always been obvious that soci-
> ety feeds its sense of security with a pack-rat instinct
> demonstrated in its window displays, its assembly
> lines, its garbage piles. As a witness of my society,
> I have always been very much involved in the
> pseudobiological cycle of production, consumption,
> and destruction. And for a long time, I have been
> anguished by the fact that one of its most conspic-
> uous material results is the flooding of our world
> with junk and rejected odd objects.[2]

Thanks to the materials he uses, Arman's
work is frequently linked to the "ready-mades"
of Marcel Duchamp.[3] While acknowledging the
influence of Dada and surrealism, Arman uses
man-made objects to make art; he does not ele-
vate the single manufactured item to the level of
art. The proliferation of forms prevents this. In
The Seven Muses the watch wheels retain their
physical identity but take on new meaning
through the play of light on their shiny surfaces.

Arman's titles frequently provide commen-
taries on his pieces (it is not explained why he
refers to only seven of the nine muses). "The
titles I give show to what degree I can be sensitive to the humorous, aggressive, or poetic con-
tents of a certain number of objects."[4] The title
of *The Seven Muses* is poetic but tinged with
irony as Arman associates the goddesses of
learning and art with small mass-produced
mechanisms.

EJN

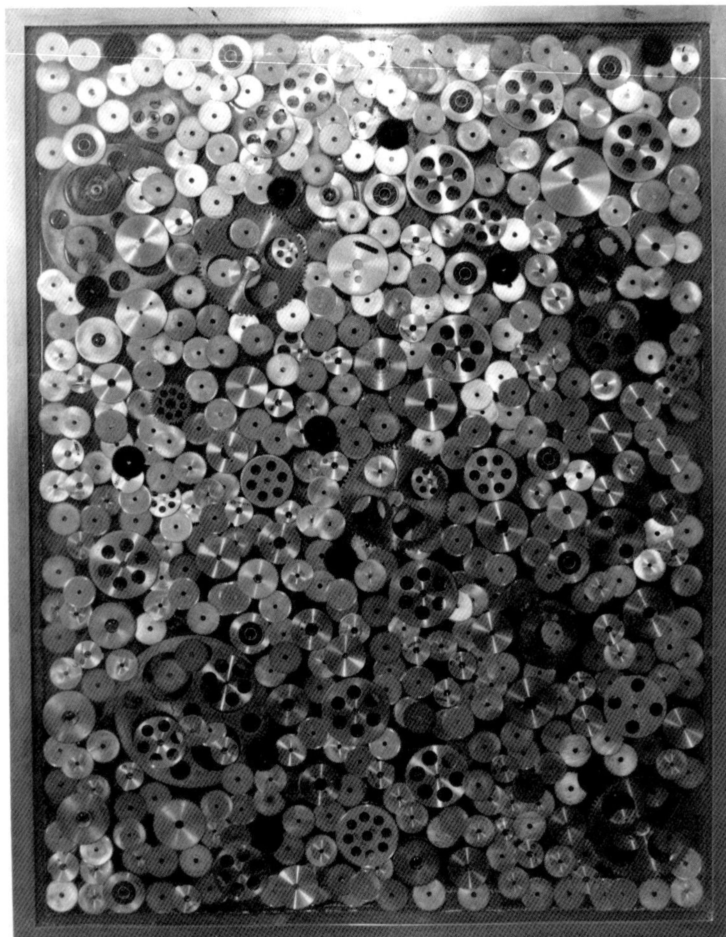

1.
G.R. Swenson,
"Arman and Esthetic
Change," *Quadrum,*
1964, p. 87.
2.
Quoted in Henry
Martin, *Arman,*
Harry N. Abrams,
Inc., New York,
c. 1973, p. 56.
3.
Jan van der Marck,
"Logician of Form/
Magician of Ges-
ture," in *Arman
Selected Works:
1958–1974,* La
Jolla Museum of
Contemporary Art,
La Jolla, Calif., Sep-
tember 15–
October 29, 1974
(and later venues),
p. [1].
4.
Alain Jouffroy,
"Arman," *L'Oeil,*
June 1965, p. 48.

*Additional
References*
Jones, Peter:
"Arman and the
Magic Power of
Objects," *Art
International,*
March 25,
1963, pp. 40–43.
Putnam, Jacques:
"Les Moments
d'Arman,"
L'Oeil, Feb-
ruary–March
1972, pp. 20–29.

Anonymous Woman #16, 1987
Mixed media (photograph, drawing, resin, lead,
red resin, mirror, glass, hubcap, and wood)
29½ × 25¼ × 21½
Lent by Rosa and Aaron H. Esman, M.D.

Bill Barrette was born in Providence and
attended the School of Visual Arts in New York
from 1968 to 1971. Besides being an artist he
works as a restorer and photographer in the
Egyptian Department of the Metropolitan
Museum of Art. He recently published a study
of the sculpture of Eva Hesse,* for whom he
served as studio assistant.

Anonymous Woman #16 was among the first
works the artist made using enlargements of
nineteenth-century daguerreotypes of nameless
sitters. In this case the hubcap obscures the
woman's body and part of her face, emphasizing
her anonymity. Before this series Barrette's constructions frequently alluded to Egyptian art,
either in form or content. The present piece
builds on some of the ideas he explored in his
earlier work, particularly the use of objects
suggesting cultural accumulation and the passage
of time.

Elaborately framed, the distressed photographic enlargement in *Anonymous Woman
#16* projects out from the wall on a box-like
form. The open structure invites the viewer to
peer around the sides. A recurring feature of
these assemblages is the lens, centered here in
the middle of the hubcap, encouraging the viewer
to look through the photograph to what lies
beyond. As with other pieces in the series, our
inward gaze is directed at a small image at the
back of the construction, in this case the photograph of a man.

Barrette's assemblages have been compared
with those of Joseph Cornell and Marcel
Duchamp.[1] Sharing in their iconography an
enigmatic quality with the art of Cornell, they
also recall Duchamp's *Étant Donnée* by turning
the viewer peeping through the lens into a kind of
voyeur. The mystery in Barrette's work, however,
comes primarily from the juxtaposition of incon-
gruous objects in elegant but simple structures.

Works such as *Anonymous Woman #16* have
been likened to a camera and to the eye.[2] In fact,
the hubcap with its radiating elements actually
looks like an eyeball, the lens occupying the
place of a pupil in the iris.[3] A further optical
parallel exists between the interior photograph
of the man and the image thrown on the retina.
The viewer's eye therefore mirrors the construction of the box. These formal elements argue
that *Anonymous Woman #16* and related pieces
are essays on the way we see. But Barrette's
assemblages deal as much with conditioned perception as with physical sight. Not only do the
layered images serve as visual metaphors for
layers of awareness, but the mixture of old and
new suggests that time and experience affect our
understanding of what we see.

EJN

1.
Ken Johnson, "Bill
Barrette," *Art in
America*, December
1988, p. 152; John
Yau, "Bill Barrette,"
Artforum, October
1990, p. 167. See
also Terry R. Myers,
"Bill Barrette's
Anonymity," in *Bill
Barrette*, fiction/
nonfiction, New
York, March 7–
April 1, 1989, n.p.
2.
Elizabeth Hayt-
Atkins, "Bill
Barrette,"
ArtNews, Septem-
ber 1988, p. 163;
also Myers, n.p.,
and Yau, p. 167.
3.
Hayt-Atkins,
p. 163.

Bill Barrette

Born 1947

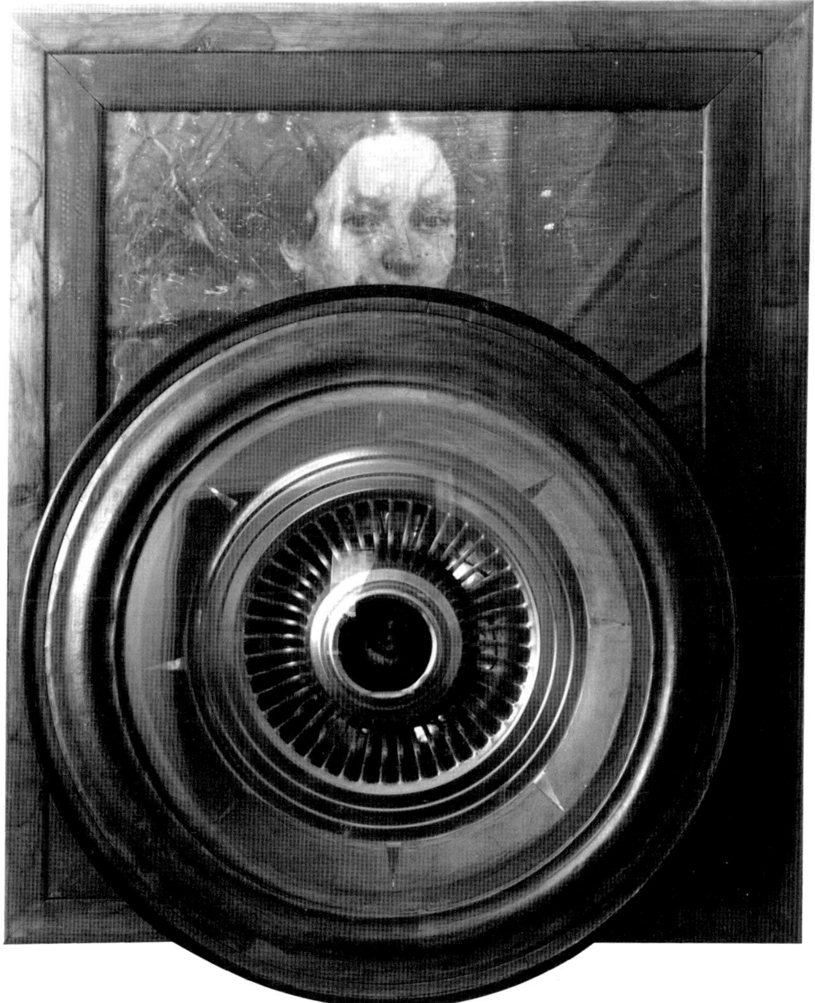

Untitled [Construction: Wall Relief], 1960
Welded steel, canvas, parchment, and copper
wire, 31½ × 31¾ × 13½
Lent by Suzanne and Maurice Vanderwoude

Lee Bontecou was born in Providence and grew
up in Nova Scotia. She attended the Art Students
League in Manhattan and the Skowhegan School
in Maine. A Fulbright grant enabled her to
spend 1957–1958 in Rome, where she constructed cement and bronze birds and animals
by attaching sections to an armature. The canvas
reliefs were first shown at the Leo Castelli Gallery in 1959. *Untitled* belongs to the initial phase
of the artist's exploration of form and materials.
She continued to make related pieces throughout the 1960s.

Bontecou's wall reliefs are neither sculptures
nor paintings but something in between, break-
ing down barriers and challenging assumptions
about the nature of art.

> I'm afraid I am rather vague about expressing
> philosophies of art and especially about my own
> work. I can only say that I do not know if what I am
> doing is art nor do I have any real concern. I just
> want to do what I believe and what I want to do,
> and what I must do to get what I want—something
> that is natural and something that exists in us all.[1]

> My concern is to build things that express our
> relationship to this country—to other countries—to
> this world—to other worlds—in terms of myself.
> To glimpse some of the fear, hope, ugliness, beauty
> and mystery that exists in us all and which hangs
> over all the young people today. The individual is
> welcome to see and feel in them what he wishes in
> terms of himself.[2]

Like most of the wall reliefs in this series,
Untitled has a central black hole formed by pieces
of wire radiating from this void or encircling it.
The wire framework rises from a square metal
frame, and the radial and concentric lines generally meet at right angles. Stretched between the
wires are pieces of canvas that differ slightly in
texture and color; twisted bits of thin wire attach
the cloth to the wire framework. The sections of
cloth generally slope away from the hole, creating
a cone or mound shape. These planes suggest
mountain terraces or a patchwork quilt. The
whole construction looks like something that
has been pulled, stretched, and finally turned
inside out.

The artist intends the object to confront the
viewer at eye level. It is a powerful image, something mysterious and primordial that seems to
exist apart from everything else. It is so totally
assertive that the form is only about itself.

A single, unified image, *Untitled* is nevertheless a complex one, formally and emotionally.
The angles, the edges, the slopes, and the shapes
of the canvas pieces all vary. The subtleties and
complexities within the basic structure add to its
potency as a work of art but also trigger powerful
emotions in the viewer, who is invited to enter
and internalize this web-like piece. What do we
feel as we view the aggressiveness of the barbed
wire, the void of the black hole? Do certain
associations with life, death, sex come to mind?
At the outset the mysterious unknown of this
wall relief projects a feeling of wariness, which
may extend to fear.

VCK

Lee Bontecou

Born 1931

1.
Dorothy Miller
(ed.), *Americans:
1963*, The Museum
of Modern Art,
New York, 1963,
p. 12.
2.
Ibid.

*Additional
References*
Johnson, Ellen H.
(ed.): *American
Artists on Art
from 1940 to
1980*, Harper &
Row, New York,
1982.
Judd, Donald: "Lee
Bontecou," *Arts
Magazine*, April
1965, pp. 16–21.
Myers, Terry R.:
"From the Junk
Aesthetic to the
Junk Mentality,"
Arts Magazine,
February 1990,
pp. 60–64.

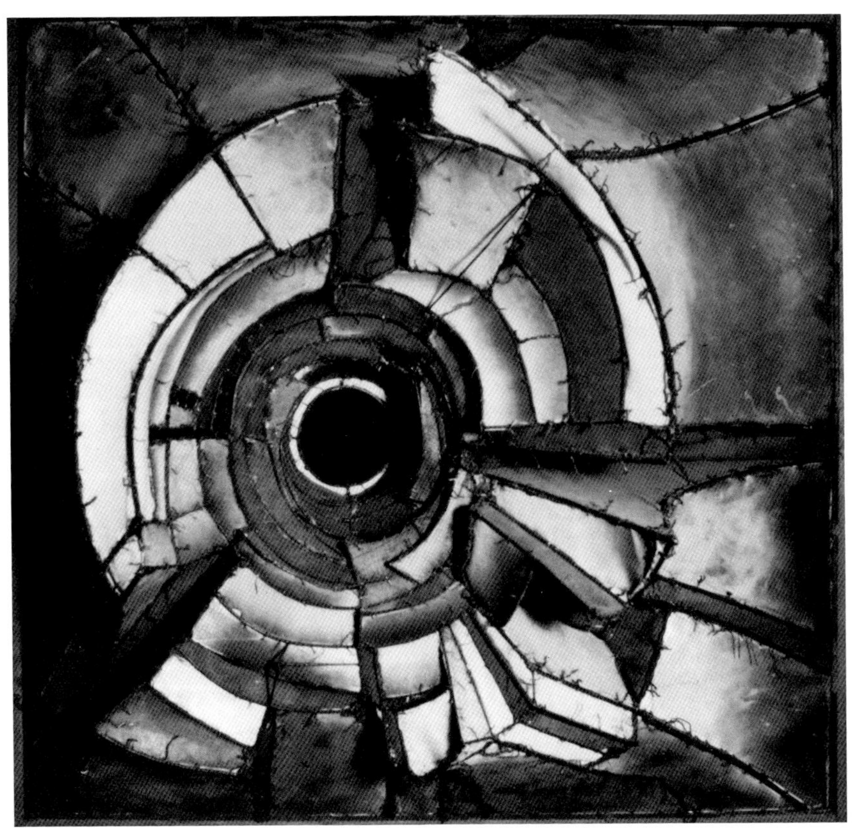

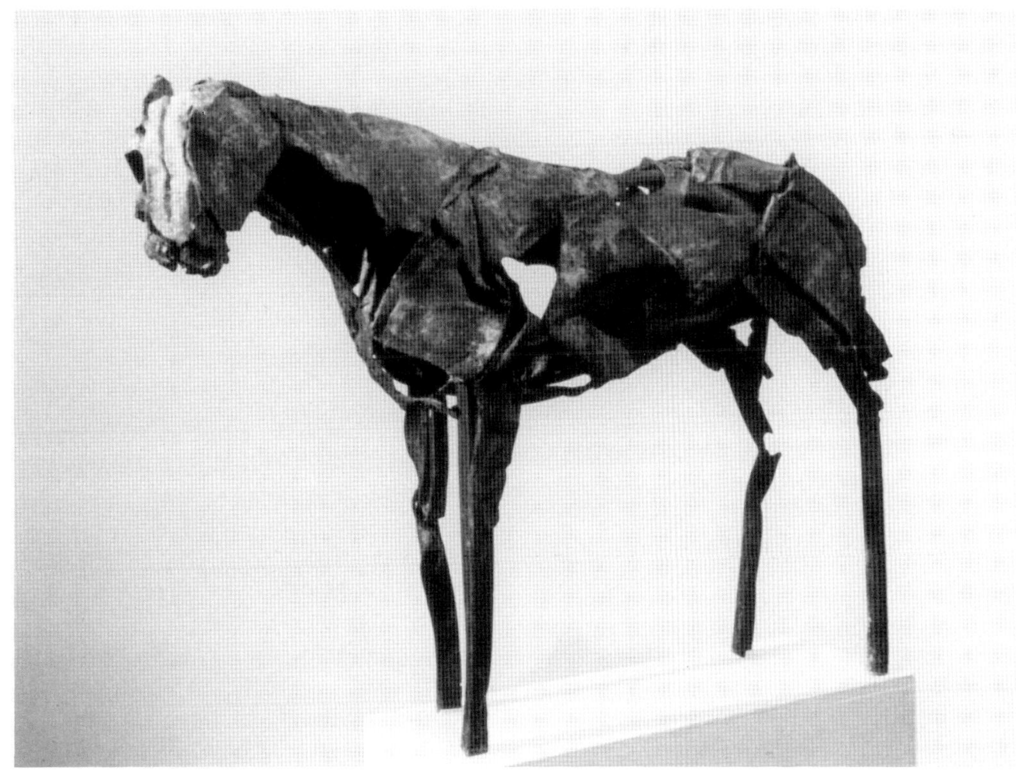

Deborah Butterfield

Born 1949

Untitled No. 1 [Derby Horse], 1985
Cast bronze, 32 × 45 × 8½
Third of an edition of five
Lent by Judith Plesser Targan

Deborah Butterfield was born in San Diego and, like many young girls who grew up in the West, went through a phase of being obsessed with horses. Her obsession continued into adulthood, however, and she now sculpts horses in a wide range of materials.

Butterfield studied ceramics at the University of California, Davis, graduating in 1972. She also attended the Skowhegan School in Maine and received her Master of Fine Arts in sculpture from Davis the following year. In 1973 Butterfield started creating horse sculptures which she describes as a sort of self-portrait meant also to depict the way horses look. These first works were solid constructions of chicken wire and plaster that emphasized the external features of a horse. Many were life-sized portrayals in different lifelike postures.

In 1977 Butterfield and her husband, the artist John Buck, moved to a farm in Montana, where she could watch her horses daily and use them as actual models.[1] As she began exploring such unorthodox materials of construction as sticks and mud, her sculpture became more abstract.

Now that Butterfield works in metal, her representation of horses has changed again, and the sculptures resemble drawings in three dimensions. Where earlier she focused on the entire horse, now she is concerned with the skeleton schematically: the backbone, leg bones, neck, and head may be indicated simply by a metal beam or pipe. She also uses found metal objects like oil drums in her sculptures.

Butterfield's metal sculptures are suggestive of life and death.[2] They are meant to capture a momentary action of a horse forever in a sculpture. *Untitled No. 1* is part of Butterfield's Derby Horse series. Although the standing horse appears to be constructed of scrap metal, it is actually cast bronze. The legs are simple beams or poles, bent at the joints as real bones would be; the neck is slightly twisted, suggesting life and movement; and the skeletal and muscular structure are evoked by the choice of material.

BH

1.
Avis Berman, "A Decade of Progress, but Could a Female Chardin Make a Living?" *ArtNews,* October 1980, p. 75.
2.
Marcia Tucker, "Equestrian Mysteries," *Art in America,* June 1989, p. 156.

Additional Reference
Martin, Richard: "A Horse Perceived by Sighted Persons: New Sculptures by Deborah Butterfield," *Arts Magazine,* January 1987, pp. 73–75.

Anthony Caro

Born 1924

Water Street Side Show, 1980
Brass and bronze, cast and welded
$12\frac{1}{2} \times 33 \times 18$
Lent by Judith Plesser Targan

By the early 1960s Anthony Caro had emerged as one of the most influential English sculptors of the twentieth century. Born near London, he prepared for a career in engineering at Christ's College, Cambridge, but then he studied drawing and sculpture under Charles Wheeler at the Royal Academy from 1947 to 1952. For three years he worked part time as an assistant in the studio of Henry Moore.* Caro began exhibiting in 1955 and had his first one-man show in Milan in 1956. In 1959 he paid his first visit to North America.

The year 1959 was crucial in another sense, for it was then, after his exposure to the work of David Smith and other American sculptors in metal, that Caro abandoned figurative sculpture in favor of total abstraction. His work of the 1950s was still largely concerned with the human form, expressionistic in style, and usually modeled in clay. Unlike Moore, who never completely rejected the human figure, Caro began in the early 1960s to seek out the expressive possibilities of purely abstract forms and to work directly with steel, brass, and bronze—cast, assembled, bolted, and welded. At the same time he rejected the convention that sculpture must rest on a pedestal. The products of his mature style are made to sit on the floor, a table, or the ground. *Water Street Side Show* is one of many small table sculptures from the 1970s and 1980s. The title, like that of many of Caro's works, is for identification only and refers to no specific object, event, or place. Like Moore's abstract reclining figures of the 1960s and 1970s, the work is a construction in which the spaces are as important as the solids.

> The experience of viewing a Caro is not holistic; his constructions can be comprehended only through prolonged viewing, through the study of individual parts and the gradual synthesis of those elements. Only by dissecting and reassembling the image are we able to grasp it as a unified whole.[1]

Despite his return to the human form in the early 1980s,[2] Caro's enduring and continuing contribution to contemporary art is as an abstractionist. In a 1984 interview he summarized his thinking about sculpture:

> Sculpture is enriched by no longer being restricted to the figurative. It doesn't have to resemble anything, to represent anyone or anything; and I believe we have only just started along the road to discovery.[3]

MG

1.
Diane Waldman, *Anthony Caro,* Abbeville Press, New York, 1982, p. 131.
2.
An exhibition of Caro's recent figurative sculptures and drawings, "From the Figure," was held at the Acquavella Gallery in New York, April 26–May 24, 1986.
3.
Phyllis Tuchman, "An Interview with Anthony Caro," *Art in America,* October 1984, p. 149.

Additional References
Fenton, Terry: *Anthony Caro,* Rizzoli International Publications, Inc., New York, 1986.
Rubin, William: *Anthony Caro,* The Museum of Modern Art, New York, 1975.

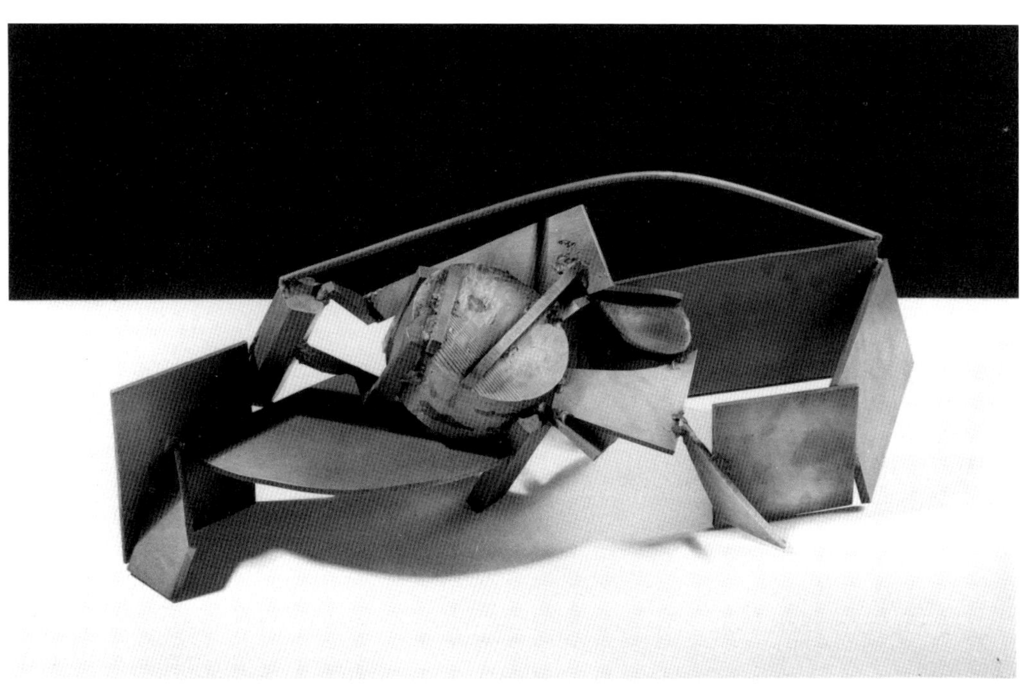

Night Head, 1971
Stoneware and oxide, 28 × 19 × 19
Lent by Suzanne and Maurice Vanderwoude

Mary Frank was born in London and studied
at the Hans Hofmann School in New York.
Although she works in a variety of media, she
established her reputation with ceramic sculpture. *Night Head* is one of a series of split heads,
an innovative form she chanced upon in the late
1960s and continued to make well into the 1980s.
About the initial work she commented

> I was not happy with this head, she looked both
> old and young. I tried to destroy it by cutting it in
> half with a wire. And then by being willing to give
> the piece up as lost, I found something.[1]

Accidental discoveries play a large role in
Frank's creative process. She works quickly, a
practice she may have picked up during her
marriage to photographer Robert Frank, and
she works best in an atmosphere where the unexpected is encouraged. This element of chance is
evidenced by the cracks that occur during firing,
which become as much a part of a completed
sculpture as the original concept. Frank's conscious gesture, the torn edges and fingerprints
left in the fired clay, convey the physicality of her
creative process.

There is a mythic quality to Frank's figures
(mostly female) that suggests something lost, as
if the pieces were actually ancient Greek or
Egyptian sculptures long buried underground.
In *Night Head* the graceful and eerily serene face
looks like the only remnant of a figure that has
decomposed and returned to the earth. This
mask-like face, staring past us into an unknown
world, appears to be in the midst of a mystical
transformation. Like all Frank's ceramic sculpture, *Night Head* is constructed from clay slabs,
which both support the modeled face and form
part of the piece, becoming in turn cascades of
hair, a mountain range, or the flat plane of a canvas on which the artist has painted a figure. The
heaviness of the medium and the unfinished surface of the sculpture give this work tactile immediacy, but for all its weight and durability, the
form appears to be a fragile, precarious balance.

Frank's sculptures reflect a sensitivity to the
human body and an awareness of its expressive
capabilities. In part this may be due to her training under Martha Graham. The result is figures
that are poised and graceful, as if caught in the
midst of flowing motion. Frank's forms maintain
a centered whole and even in repose are intensely
powerful. Like an accomplished modern dancer,
Night Head is open to the viewer: we can look
into its very structure and see the clay supports
which serve as its muscle and bone.

WEB

Mary Frank

Born 1933

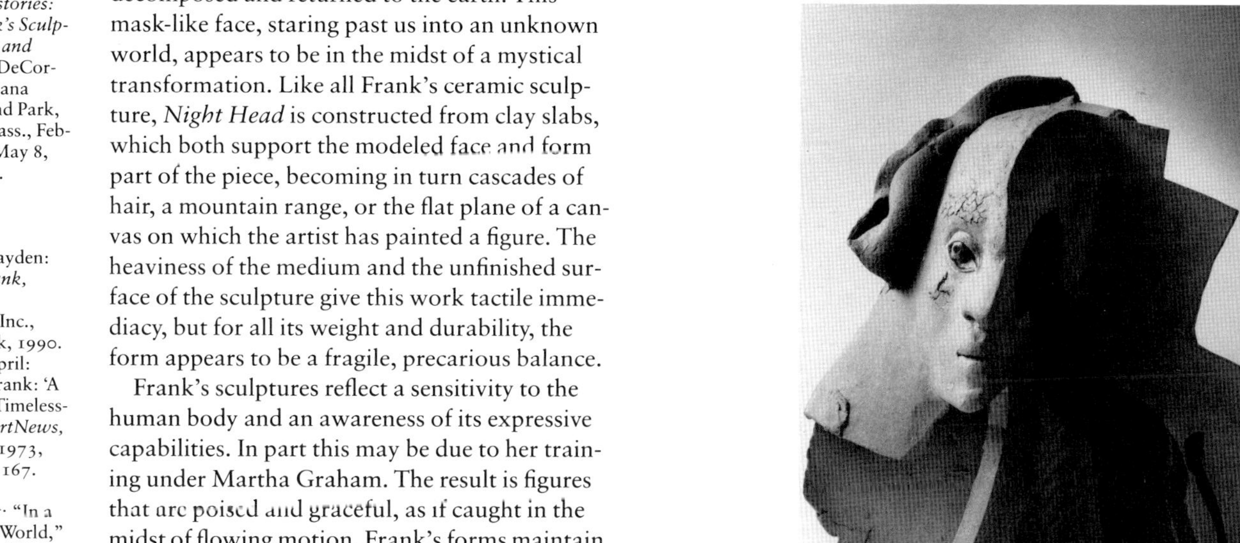

1.
Hayden Herrera and
Stella Kramrisch,
*Natural Histories:
Mary Frank's Sculp-
ture, Prints and
Drawings,* DeCor-
dova and Dana
Museum and Park,
Lincoln, Mass., Feb-
ruary 27–May 8,
1988, p. 14.

*Additional
References*
Herrera, Hayden:
   Mary Frank,
   Harry N.
   Abrams, Inc.,
   New York, 1990.
Kingsley, April:
   "Mary Frank: 'A
   Sense of Timeless-
   ness,'" *ArtNews,*
   Summer 1973,
   pp. 165–167.
Moorman,
   Margaret: "In a
   Timeless World,"
   ArtNews, May
   1987, pp. 90–
   98.
Sawin, Marticia:
   "The Sculpture
   of Mary Frank,"
   Arts Magazine,
   March 1977,
   pp. 130–132.

Viola Frey

Born 1933

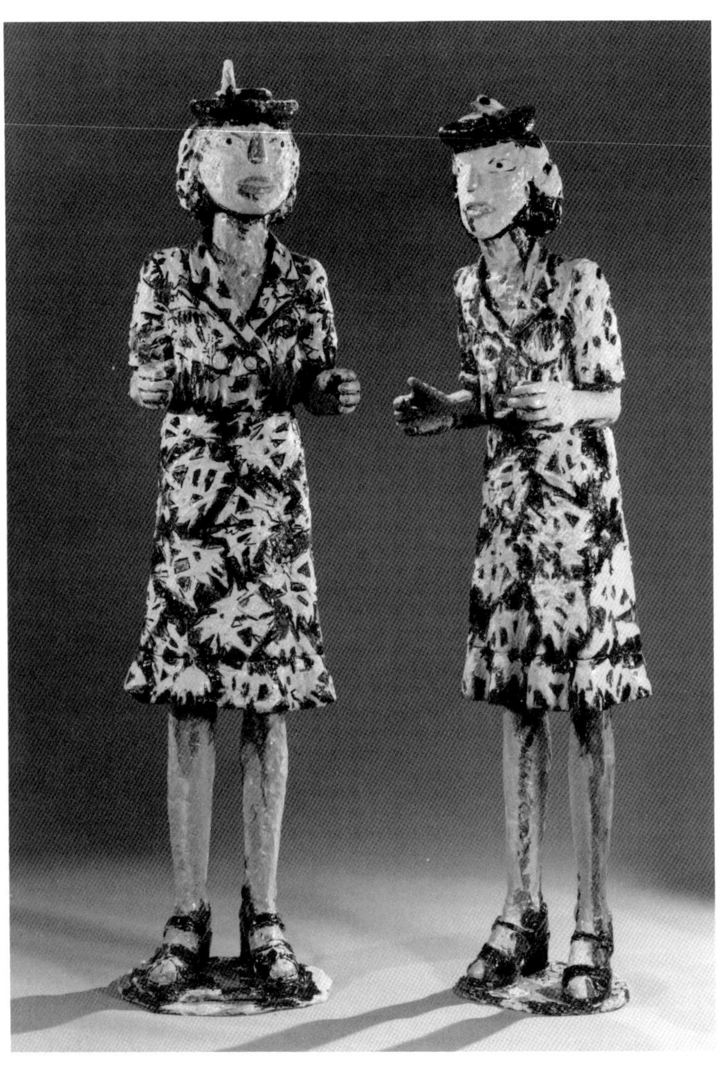

Double Grandmothers in Black and White Dresses, 1982
Glazed ceramic, 86 × 20 × 20
Lent by Rena Bransten

Monumental figure sculpture has been an integral part of western art since antiquity. In resurrecting this ancient tradition Viola Frey shatters the boundaries between past and present, painting and sculpture, and art and craft. Frey's figures may be larger than life, but unlike idealized antique statues or the confident forms of the Renaissance they appear emotionally weak and vulnerable. This paradox of heroic scale and human frailty is central to Frey's work.

These massive and vibrantly painted ceramic *Grandmothers* seem timeless and archetypal despite their ordinary middle-class twentieth-century dresses and hats. They also represent Frey's interest in the elderly, whom she sees as a group attempting to salvage a sense of dignity in the face of an uncaring society. Although the awkward and frail stance conveys some sense of the hardships of the aged, the monumental size of the figures dignifies them. Despite their conventional dress, they do not project the sweet sentiments and comforting feelings usually associated with grandmothers. In fact, they appear intimidating, even challenging.

Frey is well known for her innovative use of polychromatic ceramic, in which she incorporates all the resources of drawing and paint. A Californian who studied at the California College of Arts and Crafts and took her Master of Fine Arts degree at Tulane, she has become an important member of the sculptural movement that began on the West Coast in the 1950s with Peter Voulkos, Kenneth Price, and Robert Arenson, a development arising in part out of West Coast dissatisfaction with the narrow East Coast definition of fine art. Encouraged by the less formal Californian way of life, these artists sought to explore the unique qualities of clay, previously associated with craft. They exploited its special appeal: its metaphorical association between nature and man and its plastic qualities.

Grandmothers reveals a keen sensitivity on the part of Frey, both to the medium and to basic human emotion, captured in the subtle postures and gestures of the figures. They are stagnant, devoid of life; yet from their facial expressions we sense their fervent desire to break free.

Such figures engage the viewer in perplexity: should we laugh at these grandmothers, empathize with them, or be disturbed by them? Clear, however, is the human quality of these silent witnesses to the ironic realities that define our time.
MYZ

References
Kimmelman, Michael: "Viola Frey," *The New York Times,* May 26, 1989.
The Los Angeles Times, May 6, 1988, part VI, pp. 20–21.
Miedzinski, Charles: "Images of Paradox," *ArtWeek,* September 21, 1985.
Ceramic Sculpture, The Whitney Museum of American Art, New York, 1981.
Viola Frey, The Whitney Museum of American Art, July 25–September 30, 1984.

Four Figures on a Pedestal, 1950
Bronze, 29¼ × 16⅛ × 6
Fifth of an edition of six
Lent by Mr. and Mrs. Irving W. Rabb

The elongated, wasted bodies of Giacometti's
Four Figures on a Pedestal are the hallmark of
his post-1945 sculpture. Although this artist had
achieved considerable recognition for his surrealist sculptures before the Second World War,
the works he created between 1946 and 1952
established him as one of the leading sculptors
of the century.

Giacometti's family, from a small town in
Switzerland, included a post-impressionist
painter (his father, Giovanni Giacometti) and a
fauvist painter (his godfather, Cuno Amiet).
A brother Diego was Alberto's studio assistant
for over forty years. When Giacometti began
painting in the early 1920s, his style was neo-
impressionist, but soon his work took on a primi-
tive quality.

By the 1930s the painter was simultaneously
trying his hand at sculpture. With this creative
versatility came a dramatic shift in style and
a complete rejection of realistic representation.
The 1930 joint exhibition in Paris with Joan
Miró resulted in an invitation from Salvador
Dali for Giacometti to join the surrealists. During
his active association, which lasted about four
years, Giacometti created *Woman with Her
Throat Cut* and *The Palace at 4 A.M.* By 1935 the
artist's dissatisfaction with surrealism led him
to return to a more representational style.

The time of the Second World War, spent
mostly in Switzerland with family and friends,
was a period of artistic stagnation. The burst of
creative energy that followed when the artist
returned to Paris gave birth to the elongated
figural sculptures with jaggedly modeled surfaces
for which he is best known. Although *Four
Figures on a Pedestal,* an excellent example of
this phase, was a work of the imagination, it
refers to four prostitutes from a neighboring
brothel in Paris. It has been said that this particular work reveals Giacometti's "ambivalence
toward women, whom he tended to both despise
and adore."[1] The artist himself has remarked

> I have often thought of the four figures on the base
> somehow as the devils that came out of the box and
> of women that I saw sometimes in reality, attractive
> and repulsive at the same time.[2]

Giacometti depicts his female subjects in
straight, upright immobile postures, whereas his
male figures are shown striding. The bulky rectangular base of this work serves as both balance
and anchor, rooting the figures in their immobil-
ity. Giacometti intended works like *Four Figures
on a Pedestal* to be viewed from a distance.
Recognizable from afar, the forms become
increasingly abstract as the viewer approaches
them.

LHG

1.
Valerie J. Fletcher,
*Alberto
Giacometti: 1901–
1966,* for the
Hirshhorn Museum
and Sculpture
Garden by the
Smithsonian Institu-
tion Press,
Washington, D.C.,
1988, p. 153.
2.
Ibid.

*Additional
References*
Hohl, Reinhold:
*Alberto
Giacometti,*
Harry N.
Abrams, Inc.,
New York, 1971.
Lord, James:
*Giacometti: A
Biography,*
Farrar, Straus,
and Giroux, New
York, 1985.
Selz, Peter, and
Alberto
Giacometti:
*Alberto
Giacometti,* The
Museum of
Modern Art,
New York, 1965.

Alberto Giacometti

1901–1966

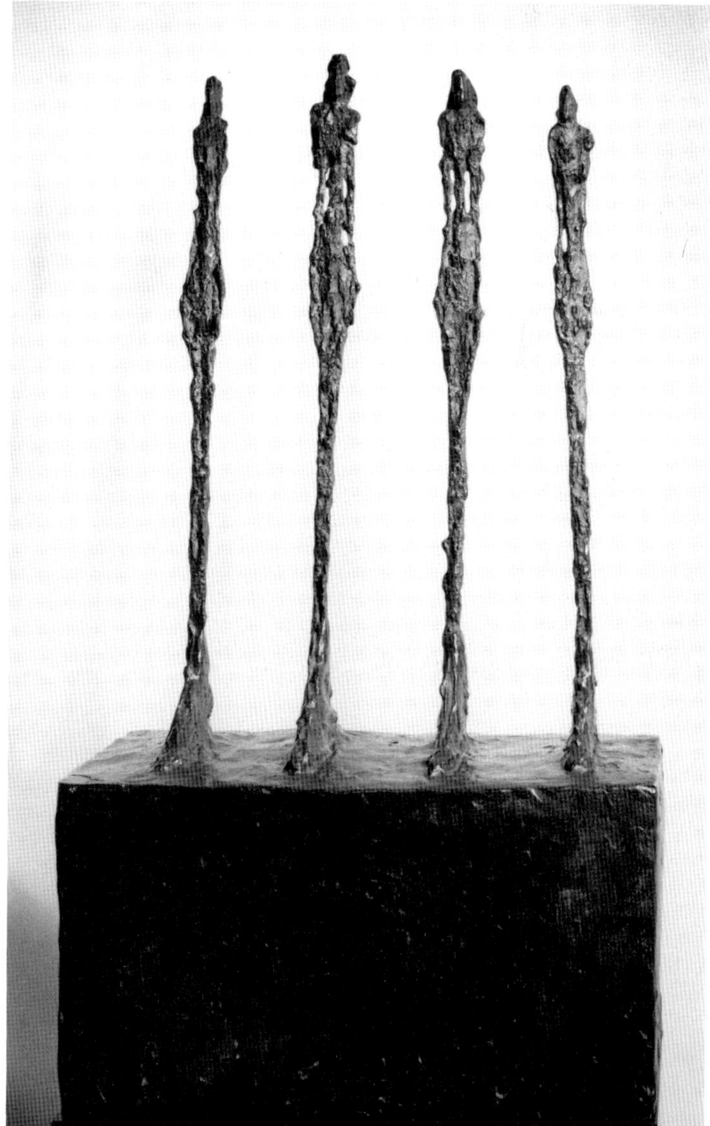

R.O., 1968
Leather over wood with metal, 16 × 6¾ × 8¼
Lent by Suzanne and Maurice Vanderwoude

Nancy Grossman is best known for her meticulously crafted heads bound in leather and studded with metal. These sculptures suggest the self-perpetuating nature of violence: they are "metaphors for the violence men do simultaneously to themselves and others."[1] As Grossman says, these images "are not *being* tied up. They are tied up."[2]

Grossman was born in New York City and grew up on a farm in Oneonta, New York. She returned to the city to study at Pratt Institute, where she received her Bachelor of Fine Arts degree in 1962. She began as a painter in 1963, painting what she called "internal landscapes" and female figures in an abstract expressionist vein. In that same year she produced a series of lithographs dealing with tensions between men and women. Looking back, she states, "I was always involved with the lack of communication on every level."[3] After 1965 Grossman's work became increasingly three-dimensional and aggressive. She made collages overloaded with leather, metal, and cloth. She calls some of these works, which are full of sexual and visceral imagery, "women landscapes."

To buy herself uninterrupted time for her art Grossman worked intensively for a year as an illustrator, but when she came back to her work in late 1967 she felt alienated from it. She began making drawings of closed up heads which eventually took three-dimensional form. *R.O.* (the letters are a man's initials) is an early example of these victim-victimizer sculptures: mute and blind, he passively resigns himself to his imprisonment. A skintight black leather hood conceals even his ears and chin. His face, which at first appears uncovered, is masked with rust leather. Only his nose is bare but it is harnessed by a complex pattern of straps and buckles, which crisscross his head and hitch under his chin. Even his neck is belted. His brows are heavy and brooding; his mouth just the suggestion of a crack beneath the rust-colored leather.

Grossman's later heads begin to struggle in fury and desperation. They develop resentful eyes and horrible grimaces; horns begin to sprout from their crowns; their noses are replaced by guns. Bodiless, they are denied sex as a weapon, which contributes to their pent-up violence. In some of her rarer full-figure sculptures and drawings Grossman clearly portrays the perversion of sexuality which links it to frustration and violence. In a 1973 drawing, *Portrait of A.E.,* she presents a naked man in profile: the gun protruding from his face mirrors his erect penis.

Grossman continually affirms that her work is highly personal—"just where I am myself is where my work is."[4] However, her work is also greatly misunderstood. It is *not* an autobiography of perversion or a documentation of the sadomasochistic subculture.[5] As John Canaday suggests, Grossman expresses horror and cruelty "in terms of physical suffering inflicted by the devices she invents."[6] This horror and cruelty is not limited to the fringes of society by any means. Her leather and metal accoutrements are a means of expressing the violence, both internalized and externalized, which erodes the humaneness of all society.

Nor is her work an anti-male statement by a bitter woman. This is most evident in her 1971 sculpture of a tormented man, noble and tragic in his struggles. With his chest thrown out and arms clasped about his head, the massive figure has been likened to Michelangelo's *Dying Slave.* Grossman's

exquisite portrayal of the male body, as well as her empathetic treatment of the male as both victim and victimizer can be interpreted as an outcry transcending sexual bounds against all forms of human degradation.[7]

ss

Nancy Grossman

Born 1940

1.
Cindy Nemser, "Nancy Grossman," *Art Talk: Conversations with 12 Women Artists,* Charles Scribner & Son, New York, 1975, p. 343.
2.
Ibid.
3.
Ibid. p. 336.
4.
Ibid.
5.
Stephen Westfall, "Nancy Grossman," *Arts Magazine,* February 1981, p. 28.
6.
John Canaday, "The Least Cruel Artist Alive," *The New York Times,* November 28, 1971, p. D2.
7.
Nemser, pp. 327–328.

Additional Reference
Alvin, Martin: *Recent Figure Sculpture,* Fogg Art Museum, Cambridge, Mass., 1972.

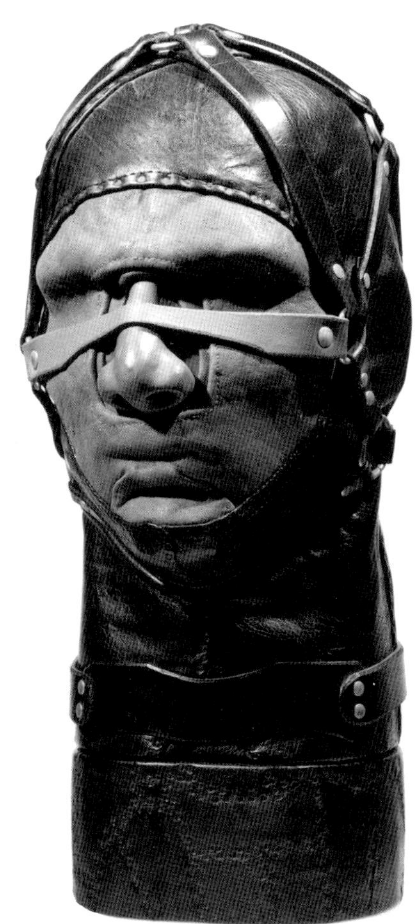

References
Barrette, Bill: *Eva Hesse Sculpture,* Timken Publishers, New York, 1989.
Johnson, Ellen H.: "Order and Chaos: From the Diaries of Eva Hesse," *Art in America,* Summer 1983, pp. 110–118.
Lippard, Lucy R.: *Eva Hesse,* New York University Press, New York, 1976.
Nemser, Cindy: "An Interview with Eva Hesse," *Artforum,* May 1970, pp. 59–63.

H & H, 1965
Mixed media on particle board
27 × 27½ × 4⅞
Lent by Jane M. Timken

Born in Hamburg in 1936, Eva Hesse emigrated to New York in 1939 with her parents and sister to escape the Nazi persecution of the Jews. She attended the High School of Industrial Design and Cooper Union before earning a Bachelor of Fine Arts Degree at the Yale School of Art and Architecture in 1959. Two years later she married the sculptor Tom Doyle and traveled with him to Germany, where they remained until the fall of 1965.

H & H was executed in June 1965 while the artist was still in Germany. During her stay, frustrated with her drawings and paintings, Hesse began to include sculptural elements in her work. Her assemblages from this period, which include such varied materials as papier-mâché and industrially fabricated objects, are transitional to her mature sculpture.

Although, like all her works, *H & H* reflects on one level a vestige of her personal life, it is not sealed-off experience. The title refers to the brand of pipe tobacco her husband smoked, and the white wooden element is actually a discarded piece from one of his sculptures. This work is not meant to be a portrait, however, but a reference to an experience, which Hesse allows us to enter by juxtaposing the sculptural and painted forms.

The surface of the work is broken up by the addition of wire and wood or built up by papier-mâché and painted with both glossy and matte finishes. The cord-bound wire projecting from the wood form connects with one of the pair of ovoid shapes, which in turn is joined to the other by a painted line. These ovoids are flat, uneven in shape, and enclosed by the raised surface and striped pattern. Although all the surfaces are treated differently, they are interconnected; thus no element of the painting is isolated, and the tensions set up by the different materials and paint harmonize rather than unbalance the work.

Tension of form and material were of deep interest to Hesse. She was also concerned with the permanence and impermanence of materials, which are represented in *H & H* by the fragility of the papier-mâché opposed to the hardness of the wood and the relatively short life of the wood compared with that of the wire.

Hesse's own life was short. Still a young artist whose importance was just being recognized, Hesse collapsed in April 1969 with a brain tumor. Despite her declining health, she continued to work. She died in May 1970 at the age of thirty-four, leaving behind her a startling artistic legacy.

AT

Eva Hesse

1936–1970

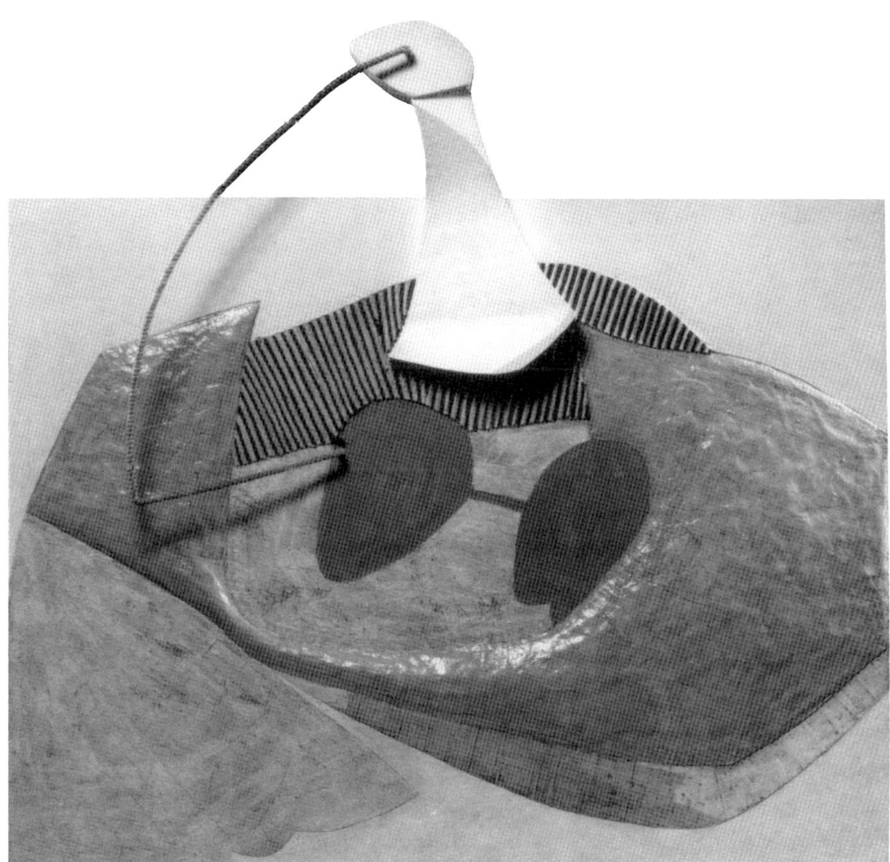

Jenny Holzer

Born 1953

Untitled Bench, 1988
Granite, 16 × 23 × 15¾
Edition of forty
Lent by Janet W. Ketcham

Jenny Holzer, one of the most prominent artists on the contemporary scene, was born in Gallipolis, Ohio, and began her career as an abstract painter while studying at the Rhode Island School of Design from 1974 to 1976. Eventually she became frustrated with the style she was working in, which she has characterized as "pretty good third generation stripe painting"[1] and as a departure began incorporating words in her pictures.

In 1977 Holzer moved to New York, where she not only continued to include words in her compositions but began placing messages on benches and in telephone booths for people to find. This interest in communication launched her into a Pure Writing phase.

From 1977 to 1979 Holzer created the Truisms, a series of political and social one-liners, often amusing and contradictory in their meaning. Her varied prose deals with a range of statements on art, politics, criticism, and the mundane, which she calls "mock clichés."[2] They have appeared in a variety of formats—initially on posters and T-shirts, more recently on benches and giant electric signboards. Holzer likes to tackle big cultural issues in a direct way to reach a large audience. Her message is the medium.

The granite bench shown here is from an edition of forty commissioned in 1988 to benefit the New Museum in New York. Although untitled, the bench displays selections from the Truisms. As with the original Truism posters, the prose is not narrative, presenting instead an array of disparate, impersonal statements with diverse and contradictory meanings.

A traditional and universal symbol of repose, the bench is one of Holzer's favorite supports for her texts. Carved into granite, the message seems permanent and monumental while inviting peaceful contemplation. The effect her benches have is completely different from that of her flashing signboards, which seize one's attention much more urgently.

Holzer is above all a master communicator with society at large. Her messages are accessible to all viewers by virtue of their simple and direct language and because they can be seen anywhere from museums to galleries to parks and the street itself. They reach out to people in an attempt to jar them into awareness. As she has said, "If you want to reach a general audience, it's not art issues that are going to compel them to stop on their way to lunch, but it has to be life issues."[3]

MYZ

1.
Interview with Diane Waldman, in *Jenny Holzer,* Solomon R. Guggenheim Museum and Harry N. Abrams, New York, 1989, p. 9.
2.
Ibid., p. 10.
3.
Ibid., p. 15.

Additional References
Holzer, Jenny: *Abuse of Power Comes as No Surprise,* Press of the Nova Scotia College of Art and Design, Halifax, 1983.
————: *Signs,* Des Moines Art Center, Des Moines, 1986.
Marincola, Paula: *Jenny Holzer,* University of Pennsylvania Institute of Contemporary Art, Philadelphia, June 11–July 31, 1983.

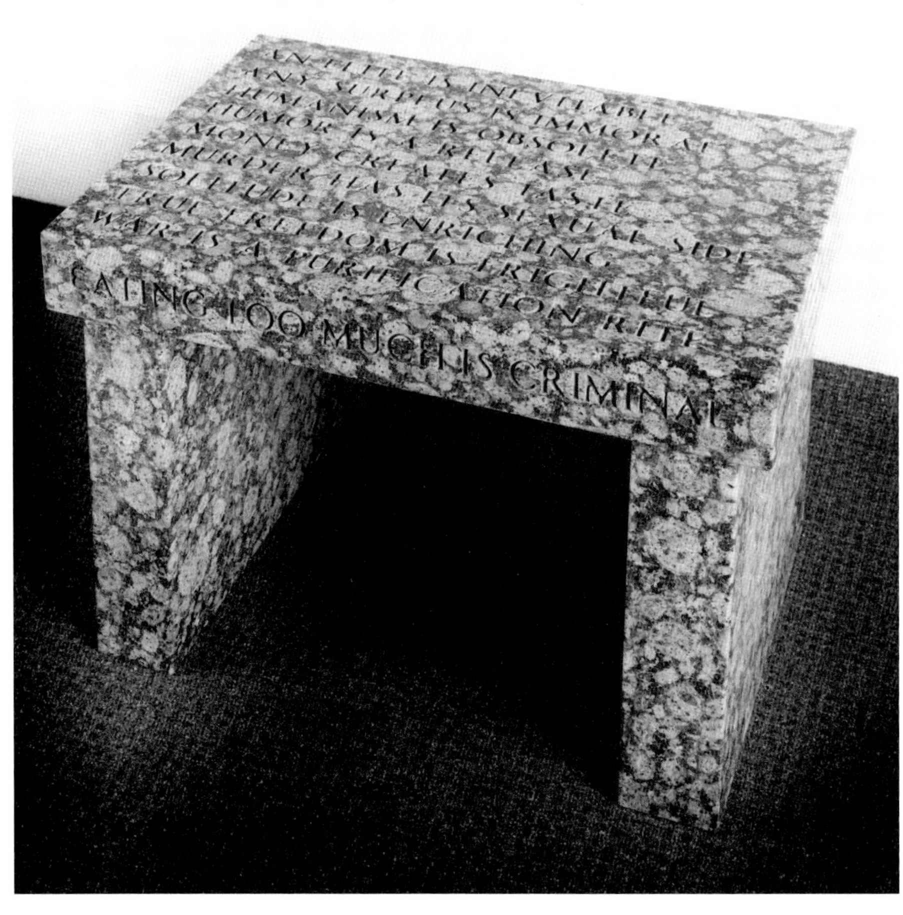

1.
Sol LeWitt, "Paragraphs on Conceptual Art," *Artforum,* June 1967, p. 80; reprinted in Alicia Legg (ed.), *Sol LeWitt,* The Museum of Modern Art, New York, 1978, p. 166.
2.
Sol LeWitt, "The Cube," *Art in America,* July–August 1967, p. 54; reprinted in Legg, p. 172.
3.
Lucy R. Lippard, "The Structures, . . . ," in Legg, pp. 24–25.

Additional References
Alloway, Lawrence: "Sol LeWitt: Modules, Walls, Books," *Artforum,* April 1975, pp. 38–45.
Kuspit, Donald: "Sol LeWitt: The Look of Thought," *Art in America,* September–October 1975, pp. 42–49.
Masheck, Joseph: "Kuspit's LeWitt: Has He Got Style?" *Art in America* November–December 1976, pp. 107–111.

Cube Structure Based on Nine Modules
1976–1977
Painted wood, 43 × 43 × 43
Made by Akira Hagihara
Smith College Museum of Art, purchased

In "Paragraphs on Conceptual Art" (1967) LeWitt wrote

> I will refer to the kind of art in which I am involved as conceptual art. In conceptual art the idea or concept is the most important aspect of the work. When an artist uses a conceptual form of art, it means that all of the planning and decisions are made beforehand and the execution is a perfunctory affair. The idea becomes a machine that makes the art.[1]

This article served as an apologia for conceptualism, a movement characterized by the creation of works that appeal to the mind rather than the viewer's eye or emotions.

"Paragraphs" came at an important point in LeWitt's artistic development. He was born in Hartford, Connecticut, and received his Bachelor of Fine Arts degree from Syracuse University in 1949. Four years later he was in New York. In the early 1960s LeWitt began making three-dimensional constructions; skeletal cubic modules in serial arrangements followed. The cube was selected in part because the artist found the form both basic and uninteresting.[2] When he deemed the original black too expressive in late 1965, LeWitt started painting the structures white instead. Two years later, the artist stopped making his own pieces in keeping

with his indifference to craftsmanship. In short, by the time he wrote "Paragraphs," LeWitt had established a modus operandi which called for some explanation.

Cube Structure Based on Nine Modules, a product of LeWitt's mature period, is one of eighteen variations on the subject. Like all his modular structures before and after this series, it has aesthetic ties to constructivism. LeWitt, who admires modular architecture, worked briefly with I.M. Pei in the 1950s, and the influence of the Homage to the Square series by Josef Albers* is apparent in the repetitious use of the cube.

Although *Cube Structure Based on Nine Modules* and its variations taken as a group seem mathematically logical in their methodical exploration of an idea, LeWitt would argue that the original concept was intuitive. He does not think of his work as rational. The decision to deal with that number of cubes on that number of modules was totally arbitrary, just like the establishment of the proportions of the basic form and the decision to paint the struts white. And like those decisions, once made, it stands.

Such formal decisions in LeWitt's work are comparable to the rules for a piece of twelve-tone music, which restrict compositional choices but not creativity. Within self-imposed limits, the artist conceives of his design like a composer,[3] and like a composer he puts the execution into other hands, in this case those of Akira Hagihara.
EJN

Sol LeWitt

Born 1928

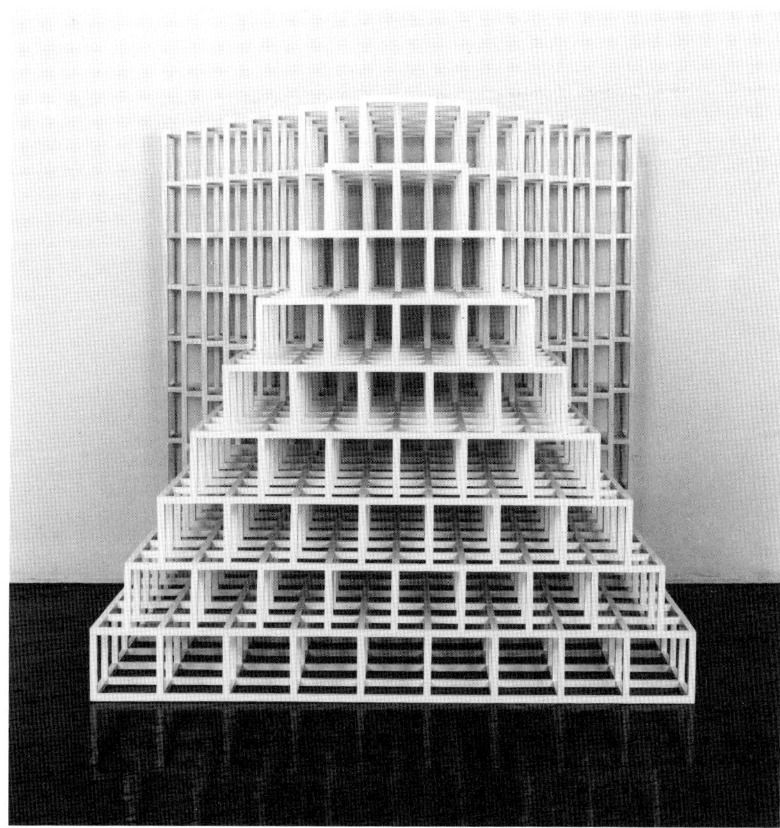

Clyde Lynds

Born 1936

Starbox, 1973
Mixed media, 6½ × 18¼ × 8¼
Lent by Mr. and Mrs. Frederick Morgan

Lynds was born in Jersey City and studied at the Art Students League and the Frank J. Reilly School in New York. He has always been inquisitive about different materials and how he might put them to use. His *Starbox* is the first of a series of luminous boxes made early in his career when he was doing a great deal of experimenting with forms and materials. Lynds says that "*Starbox* has the most poetry to it. As is often the case, the first piece has the germ of something that you get away from later."[1] These boxes were inspired by Joseph Cornell's assemblages. But if Cornell's boxes create a magical miniature world, Lynds's create a miniature magical universe.

Starbox is lit by fiber optics, a technology Lynds continues to explore. "By varying the length and placement of these [fiber-optical elements], Lynds achieves marvelous astral effects."[2] Polarized light reveals the internal stresses of a resin sphere, creating a delicate pink orb. Starry pinpoints of light cluster together. Lynds's more recent sculptures are "programmed (long burning bulbs and slowly spinning discs, some with colored lenses concealed in their bases) so that constellations and their colors slowly change."[3] They suggest seasonal cycles, changes from day to night, or the blinking of city lights.

Lynds had an early acquaintance with electronics. While studying at the Art Students League in New York from 1958 to 1963, he worked making neon signs. In the mid-1960s and 1970s he began to explore the possibilities offered by a fusion of electronics and art. Lynds distinguishes himself from many other "light" artists in that he designs and executes his electronic work himself. Furthermore, "Each work is marked by the artist's refusal to submit to the mechanistic seductions of his materials. . . . Each work is approached as a separate entity."[4]

This serenely designed box, midnight-colored, encloses a celestial assemblage. Although the graphic description of the lid evokes the rings of Saturn, Lynds warns against reading his art literally. "I like art that's richly associative, beyond the motivations that originally inform it," he has said.[5] The polished brass clock piece is presented like a precious object. Detached from its wind-up whole, it is nonfunctioning, suggesting time suspended. Before creating this assemblage Lynds visited a museum of ancient measuring instruments and was fascinated by the ability they had to locate an individual in time and space. He created paintings of geometric machine parts before he began incorporating them bodily into his works.

For the past eight years Lynds has been creating megaliths inscribed with enigmatic symbols inspired by ancient Mesoamerican sources. By embedding fiber-optic cables in the surface of sand-blasted concrete he suggests the dematerialization of stone through light. Recently his work has become larger and more public; he is presently working on a site-specific sculpture at Townsend Harris High School, commissioned by the City of New York.

SS

1.
Interview by SS with Clyde Lynds, January 25, 1991.
2.
Sol Littman, "Quieter Lights," *Toronto Star,* April 2, 1978.
3.
Paul Richards, "Stele Work at Wallace Wentworth," *The Washington Post,* November 21, 1985.
4.
Miriam Brumer, "Clyde Lynds," *Arts Magazine,* Summer 1969, p. 62.
5.
Patricia Malarcher, "Artist Creates 'Magical Objects' with Fiber Optics," *The New York Times,* August 12, 1990.

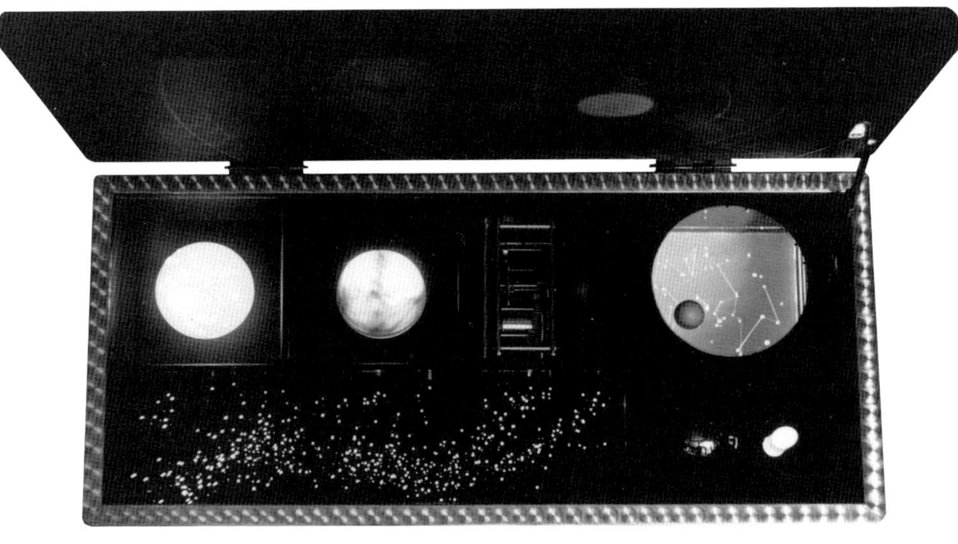

Four Piece Reclining Figure, 1972
Bronze, length 29
Edition of nine
Lent by Ryda and Robert H. Levi

Few would dispute the claim that Henry Moore is the most influential western sculptor of the twentieth century. He was born in Castleford, Yorkshire, in 1898, into a large, caring family. At Castleford Secondary School a strong influence was his art teacher Alice Gostick, who had family ties to the Continent and kept her students abreast of the latest developments in the arts. After graduation and teacher training Moore taught at Castleford until 1917. He enlisted at the age of eighteen, was gassed in the Battle of Cambrai, and spent two months in the hospital.

In 1921 at the Leeds College of Art he won a Royal Exhibition Scholarship and entered the Royal College of Art in London. After three years he received a traveling scholarship but stayed on for a year as an instructor before journeying through France and Italy, where he could see the work of Masaccio, Michelangelo, Giotto, and the Pisani at first hand.

In the late 1920s Moore emerged as one of the most innovative and creative of contemporary sculptors. His first one-man exhibition was held at the Warren Gallery in London in 1928. The next (Leicester Galleries, London, 1931) led to his first sale to a museum on the Continent, the Museum für Kunst und Gewerbe in Hamburg.

Although the critics of the 1930s did not always greet his work with enthusiasm, Moore's rise was now meteoric, with numerous one-man and group exhibitions, awards, and honors throughout Europe and North America. His first exhibition in the United States was held in 1943, and three years later a major retrospective of his work was mounted by the Museum of Modern Art in New York. In 1974 the Henry Moore Centre opened in Toronto, the gift of more than 200 sculptures, graphics, and original plasters making it one of the major repositories of Moore's work. In 1977 the Henry Moore Foundation was established in Much Haddam, Hertfordshire, to which the artist donated studios, grounds, and a collection of works. His death in 1986 at the age of eighty-eight ended a long, productive, and hugely creative life.

Moore's entire career was spent exploring the human figure. *Four Piece Reclining Figure* represents a late manifestation of a series begun in 1924 and continued throughout his life. All the early reclining figures are entire, recognizably human, and predominantly female; but the passage of time brought greater and greater abstraction, so that by the late 1950s some figures are in two pieces and in the 1970s three- and even four-piece figures are common. These divided sculptures have been called "figurative landscapes,"[1] in which the spaces become as crucial as the forms themselves.

MG

1.
Steven W. Rosen, in Budd Harris Bishop et al., *Henry Moore: The Reclining Figure,* Columbus Museum of Art, Columbus, Ohio, 1984, p. 14.

Additional References
Bowness, Alan (ed.): *Henry Moore: Sculpture and Drawings,* vol. 4, *Complete Sculpture 1964–73,* Lund Humphries, London, 1977.
Sylvester, David: *Henry Moore,* Frederick A. Praeger, New York, 1968.
Wight, Frederick S.: "Henry Moore: The Reclining Figure," *Journal of Aesthetics and Art Criticism,* December 1947, pp. 95–105.

Henry Moore

1898–1986

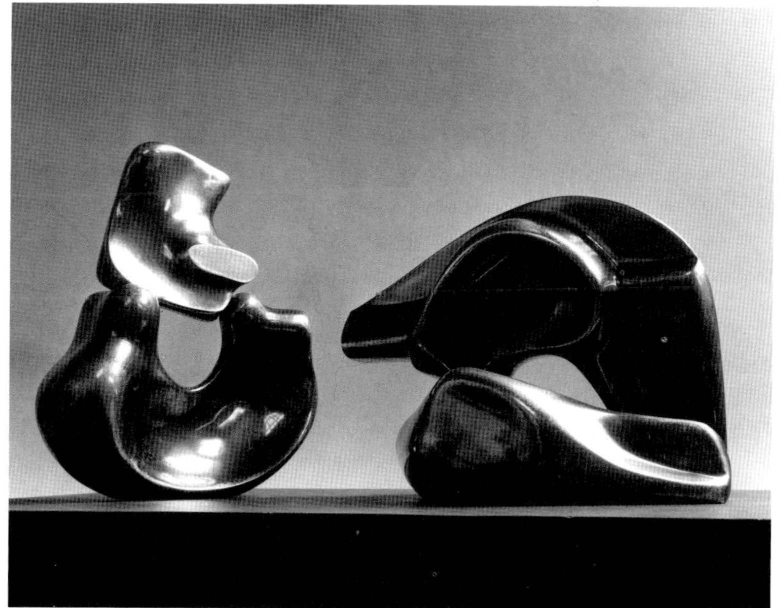

Robert Morris

Born 1931

Untitled, 1970
Seven strips of red felt, 102 × 146 × ⅜
Lent by Barbara Jakobson

A native of New York City, Robert Morris studied at the Kansas City Art Institute and the California School of Fine Arts before serving in the army during the Korean War. Upon his discharge he resumed his education at Reed College. Morris lived in San Francisco for several years before moving to New York in 1961. He received a Master's degree in Art History from Hunter College in 1963 and began teaching there in 1967.

Although Morris is frequently associated with minimalism, he has traversed a wide spectrum of media and styles. Starting out as an abstract painter, Morris also embraced dance and performance art, film, and the corpus of sculpture for which he is best known; he has recently returned to painting. Barbara Rose aptly describes his progression through these different artistic modes as an odyssey, writing that Morris's work "did not follow a path of stylistic evolution, but conformed instead to the journey of the hero, who, cursed by the gods, seeks salvation in miraculous escape."[1]

Like the work of other minimalist artists, Morris's sculptures tend to be reductive and made of nontraditional and industrial materials which are arranged or collected rather than constructed or carved. As ordinary forms and materials, they rely upon the perceptual and conceptual interaction of the viewer in order to become art.

Untitled displays all these traits. Consisting of seven strips of red industrial felt, the work acquires presence only when displayed. There is some theatricality in the work since although the content never changes, the arrangement of the strips may. Describing the work as "very elegant—almost baroque," Marti Mayo goes on to explain that for Morris

> the idea . . . in art is foremost and . . . the form it takes is a reflection of the behavior of the artist—or process—by which it is made. Art categories are not important or useful, and the materials of which art is made are irrelevant. What is important is the process and its origin in the artist's idea.[2]

Hence *Untitled* is a work that speaks not only of itself but of the process by which it came to be. In this vein Marcia Tucker points out that

> The mystery of "technique" has been eliminated, and the information about how it was made is available simply by looking at it. The process is as straightforward as the work. . . . Space and material are . . . crucial, so that the structure of the piece is indistinguishable from the space in which the piece exists. Nothing is hidden and nothing is contained; it is all *there*.[3]

AT

1.
Barbara Rose in Terrie Sultan, *Robert Morris: Inability to Endure or Deny the World,* The Corcoran Gallery of Art, Washington, D.C., 1990, pp. 7–8.
2.
Marti Mayo, *Robert Morris: Selected Works 1970–1980,* Contemporary Arts Museum, Houston, 1981, p. 6.
3.
Marcia Tucker, *Robert Morris,* Whitney Museum of American Art, New York, 1970, pp. 10, 38.

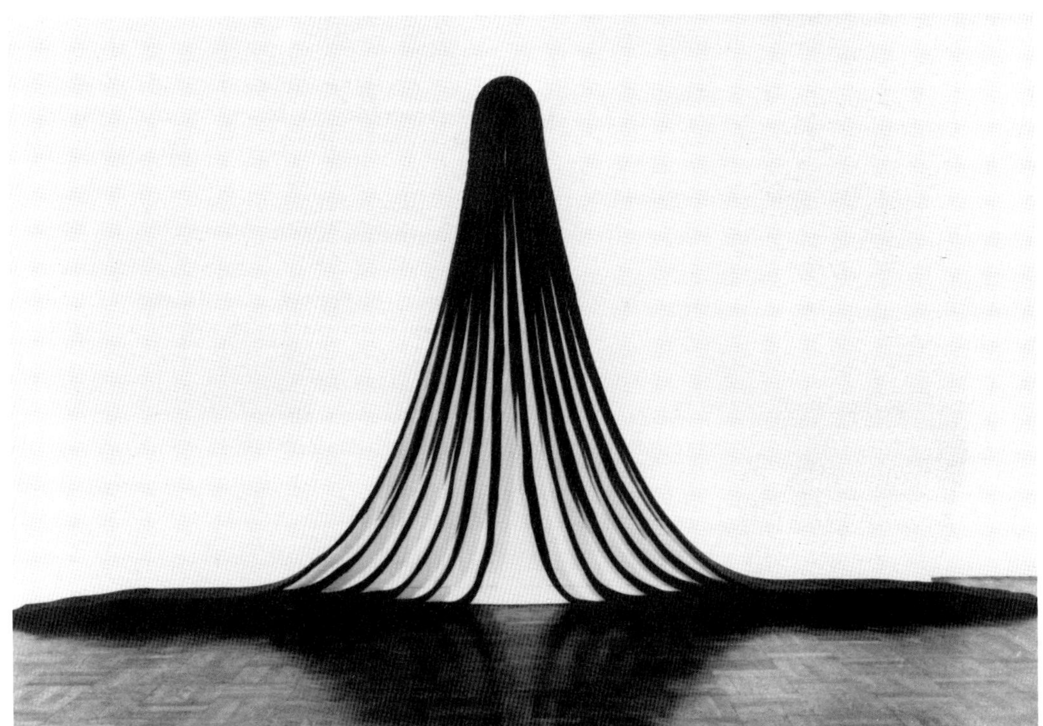

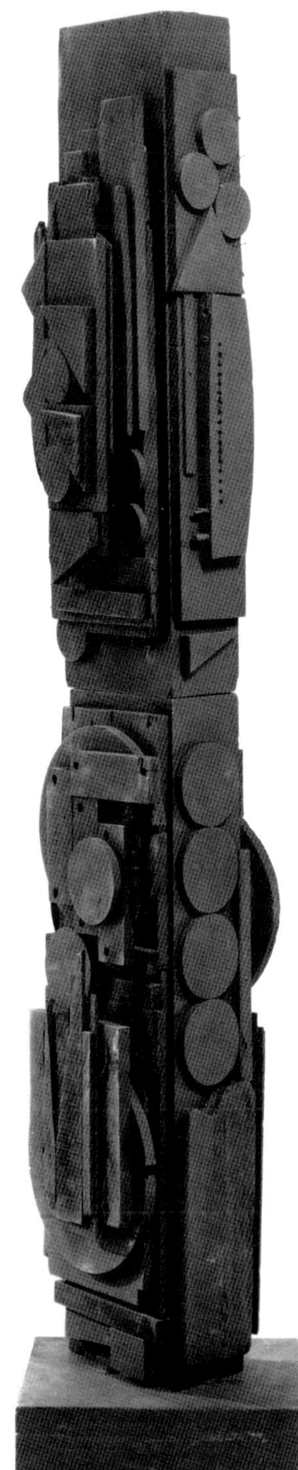

Distant Column, 1963
Painted wood, 80 × 15 × 12½
Smith College Museum of Art, purchased with funds given by Donald Millar in honor of his daughters Brenda M. Baldwin (Brenda Millar '49) and Mrs. John W. O'Boyle (Nancy Millar '52)

Louise Nevelson

1899–1987

Throughout her long and productive career as a sculptor Louise Nevelson maintained an uncompromising belief in the absolute power of the will. As Edward Albee says, "She sensed that she was special, and it was a conviction that stayed with her until finally she proved herself right."[1] After discovering that she could not find meaning in marriage, Nevelson devoted herself to fulfilling her life through art. She stated that the most important thing in her life was to claim herself totally. "I'm not looking for the truth. I'm looking to fulfill my life to its fullest capacity."[2]

Born in Russia and raised in Maine, Nevelson studied and worked in New York City for the rest of her life. True to her romantic individualism, she resisted the identification of conscious influences on her art. However, through her studies with Hans Hofmann in Munich in 1931 she became familiar with cubism and other early modernist movements. In 1945–1950 she made two trips to Mexico to see Mayan ruins, nurturing her lifelong interest in pre-Columbian art. She expanded her artistic vision by studying voice, dance, and drama.

Since creating *Black Majesty* in 1965, Nevelson has been best known for her monochrome wooden assemblages. Although she explored a variety of materials—stone, bronze, and terra cotta in the early 1940s; Plexiglas and welded aluminum in the late 1960s; and Cor-ten steel in her latter years—Nevelson always returned to wood. As in all Nevelson's constructions, the parts of *Distant Column* are as fascinating as the whole. A monumental presence, the column is composed of found wooden objects densely assembled in intricate geometries. The sculpture is unified by a repetition of circular and triangular forms and an austere layer of black paint (Nevelson painted some of her assemblages white or gold).

Beginning with *The Royal Voyage* of 1956, Nevelson created dramatic sculptural environments in which a spatial arrangement of column, box, and wall assemblages structured a physical and visual experience. After 1961, however, her sculptures were predominantly independent pieces like *Distant Column.* A monolith composed of compact, almost airless layers, *Distant Column* both compresses space and displays it. While the column is imposing, distancing us, the multiplicity of detail invites exploration.

With her characteristic passion for absolutes, Nevelson claimed that by covering her assemblages with monochrome paint she erased from them all previous associations.[3] In fact, in her transformations of both form and meaning Nevelson respects the rich histories of the wooden fragments she assembles. In *Distant Column* sections of a fruit crate, chair legs, and crown molding are disguised but not subsumed. Sawed, sanded, splintered, cracked, and drilled, studded with nails, and impaled by wooden pegs, the wood is textured with its past.

ss

1.
Edward Albee, *Louise Nevelson: Atmospheres and Environments,* Clarkson N. Potter, Inc., New York, 1980, p. 21.
2.
Obituary, *Daily Hampshire Gazette,* April 18, 1987.
3.
Diana Mackown, *Dawns and Dusks,* Charles Scribner & Son, New York, 1976, p. 83.

Additional References
Glimcher, Arnold B.: *Louise Nevelson,* E. P. Dutton & Co., New York, 1976.
Nemser, Cindy: "Louise Nevelson," in *Art Talk: Conversations with 12 Women Artists,* Charles Scribner & Son, New York, 1975.

Claes Oldenburg

Born 1929

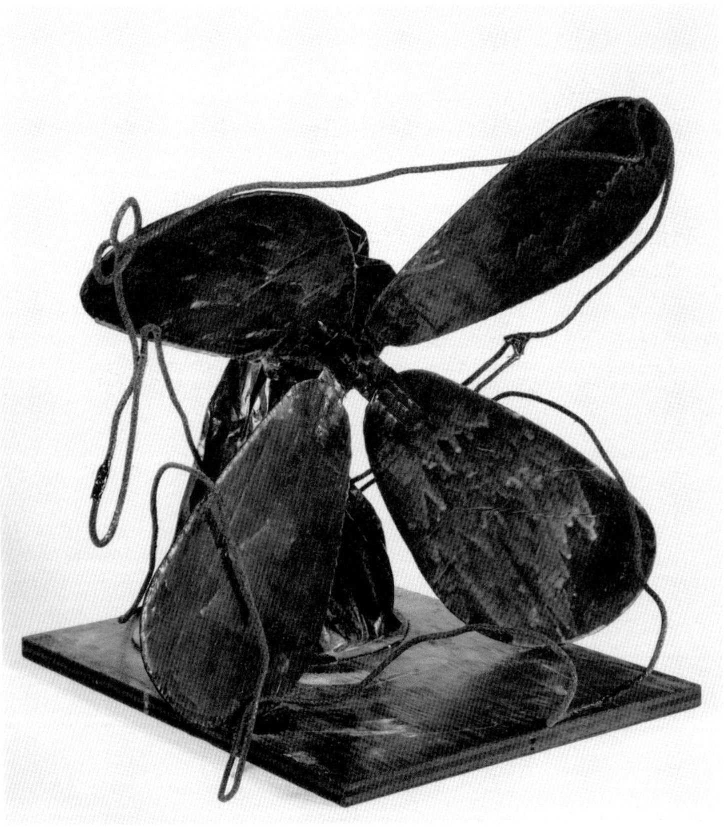

Soft Fan, 1965
Black enamel paint on wood, paper, and rope
$19^{5}/_{8} \times 22^{1}/_{8} \times 21^{3}/_{8}$
Smith College Museum of Art, purchased

Claes Oldenburg's works of the 1960s represent such commonplace objects as a fan, a toilet, a clothespin, or a lipstick. Although Oldenburg, like many pop artists of that period, strove to create an art related to human experience, he preferred to deal with objects people use in their everyday lives instead of focusing on the human form. He avoids realistic representation by using unexpected materials, disparate colors, unlikely textures, and absurd proportions to comment on human experience through humorous contradiction.

It was during his senior year at Yale that Oldenburg realized that he wanted to become an artist. He attributes his inventiveness not to his education but to his childhood experience: "Everything I created, I created as a child."[1] His years as a young boy in Sweden and his upbringing in America developed an acute awareness of his surroundings. A major early influence was the pictures (mainly of household items) which an aunt in Sweden cut out of popular magazines, mounted in scrapbooks, and sent to him in the United States.

At the outset of his career Oldenburg explored various painting styles, experimenting with abstract expressionism but painting mostly nudes and portraits. In 1959, when he shifted his attention to sculpture, *The Street* and *The Store* were among his first treatments of human environments. In these and subsequent works Oldenburg concentrated on ordinary objects of everyday life.

Around the time of *The Home,* in 1964, the artist also began to create his soft sculptures, which translate the hard surfaces of commonplace things into soft vinyl forms. In this series *Soft Fan* is the result of transforming a fan in the artist's studio from a rigid and inflexible object into a relaxed and pliant sculpture. The practice of divorcing the practical fan from its function makes it comical, belying our normal associations with mundane objects.

Soft Fan is the model for the *Giant Soft Fan,* constructed in 1967, which is both enormous and extreme in its physical contradiction. The model can only hint at the delightful absurdity of the finished work.
LHG

1.
Ellen H. Johnson, *Claes Oldenburg,* Penguin Books, Harmondsworth, Middlesex, England, 1971, pp. 22–23.

Additional References
Mayer, Hansjorg: *Claes Oldenburg: Press Log May 1974–August 1976,* H. Mayer, Stuttgart, for Leo Castelli Gallery, London, vol. 2, 1976.
Rose, Barbara: *Claes Oldenburg,* The Museum of Modern Art and New York Graphic Society, Greenwich, Conn., 1970.

Angry Father, 1984
Angry Mother, 1984
Bronze, each 16 × 27 × 3¼
Cast 1987, each second of an edition of three
Lent by Eliot and Wilson Nolen

A native of Wichita, Kansas, Tom Otterness came to New York when he was eighteen and studied at the Art Students League. A founding member of Collaborative Projects in 1977 and one of the prime forces behind the 1980 Times Square Show, Otterness frequently explores social issues in his seemingly playful art. Since the late 1970s he has been making small generic figures, first of Hydrocal or plaster but now usually cast in bronze. The present pieces share certain stylistic connections with the early forms in that the people are small, rounded, and generalized.

Although cast and issued as separate works of art, *Angry Father* and *Angry Mother* are pendants, variations on a related theme. They are also major elements of a large work, *The Gates*[1] (1984), in which parents nurture, chastise, and instruct their children only to be overthrown by them. As richly carved doors with a functional as well as aesthetic purpose, *The Gates* was produced shortly after Otterness visited Italy, where he would have seen comparable architectural elements on civic and religious buildings. The overall form, with its stylized figures carved in wood, recalls similar African objects. But *The Gates* also reflects Otterness's own interest in the decorative nature of the sculpture. In his first solo exhibition at Brooke Alexander in New York in 1983, his extensive architectural frieze dealing with man as a social and political being could be purchased and installed by the running foot. *Angry Father* and *Angry Mother* continue Otterness's practice of producing and marketing discrete elements from a larger work of art.

Complex multiple compositions such as the frieze, *The Gates,* and most recently *The Tables* (1986–1987) provide narratives on particular subjects or themes. The sequential images of *The Gates* deal with the instructive and destructive aspects of parenting and, by extension, with the abuse of power. The rounded and diminutive forms of Otterness's ur-people in *Angry Father* and *Angry Mother* make them seem at first glance like harmless descendants of the Pillsbury doughboy.[2] Divorced from the broad, narrative context of *The Gates,* the generalized father, mother, and children resemble characters in a domestic cartoon episode despite the emotionally charged situation. But Otterness's intention is not to entertain his viewers. Like the children of *The Gates,* who reverse the power structure of the adult world in the last two scenes of the door by shackling their parents and hanging them upside down, Otterness turns the tables on us. Initially amused by his engaging toy-like figures, we are ultimately confronted with the unspoken tyranny in social and political relationships.
EJN

1.
Discussed and illustrated in Walter Robinson, "Arcadian Hijinks," *Art in America,* December 1985, p. 94.
2.
Ibid., p. 96.

Additional References
Herrera, Hayden: *Tom Otterness,* James Corcoran Gallery, Santa Monica, October 27–November 24, 1990, and Brooke Alexander, New York, November 3–30, 1990.
Kirshner, Judith Russi: "Tom Otterness' Frieze," *Artforum,* October 1983, pp. 57–60.

Tom Otterness

Born 1952

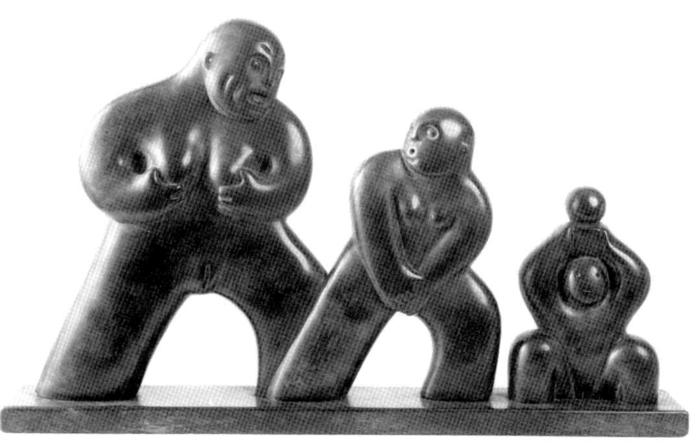

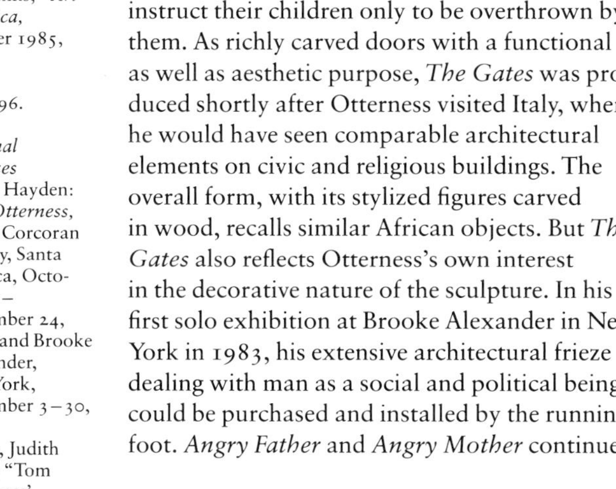

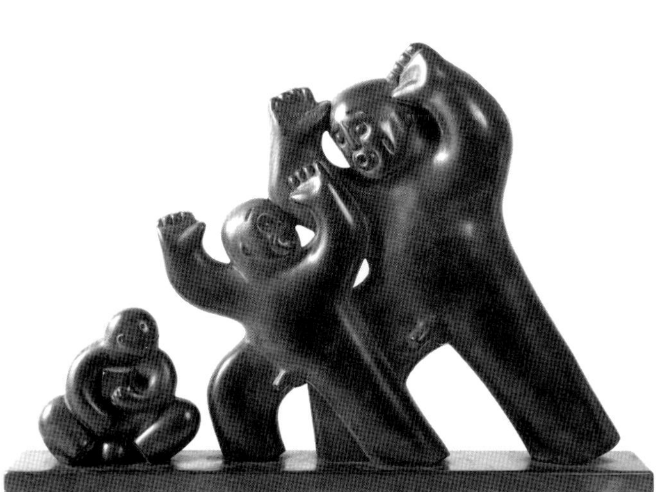

Lucas Samaras

Born 1936

Box #36, 1965
Mixed media, 6¾ × 13¼ × 9½
Lent by Ann and Richard Solomon

A survivor of the Second World War and the Civil War in Greece, Lucas Samaras emigrated from Macedonia to the United States at the age of eleven in 1948. A graduate of Rutgers University, where he studied with George Segal and Allan Kaprow, Samaras was given his first exhibition at the Reuben Gallery in New York in 1959 while he was still studying under Meyer Schapiro at Columbia University. With his involvement in Happenings and experimentation with materials, Samaras's early career reflects the transition from traditional media to new forms in the late 1950s and early 1960s. His insistently self-referential art resists categorization, however, and generally stands apart from the mainstream movements of the last three decades.

Samaras has explored a variety of forms, including room installations (the first, in 1964, recreated his own bedroom in New Jersey) and the recurrent object themes of books, boxes, and chairs. He has worked in virtually all media— oil, pastel, bronze, fabric, assemblage, film, and photography. Despite the diversity of his artistic production, the series of boxes Samaras has created since his first three-sided piece, *Prism with Face* (1960), can perhaps be seen as a paradigm of his art. Involving many different materials, two-dimensional surface, and three-dimensional forms, Samaras's boxes have been compared to modern reliquaries and metaphors for the body and for the artist himself.[1]

Photography plays a part in many of the boxes, including *Box #36*, which opens to reveal a black and white photograph of the artist's brooding eyes, repeated abstractly on the exterior of the box by bull's-eye concentric circles and referred to by the pair of broken glasses inside the box. Because this box takes the form of a velvet-lined jewel case, the viewer's encounter with the artist is startling: the photograph is placed in the lid, where one might expect to see one's own image reflected in a mirror.[2] The act of opening *Box #36* gives a sense of intrusion, of entering into another's privacy, a feeling that is certainly not accidental to the piece, which offers the additional unsettling discovery of fingers nested among the faceted crystals.

The visually seductive surfaces of *Box #36*, with its stripes of brightly colored yarns, enliven the exterior and engage the viewer; however, other Samaras boxes bristle with an armament of dangerous objects—pins, razor blades, nails, and knives—that carry a potential threat to the hand. In the 1970s Samaras's "stiff" boxes of Cor-ten steel and wire boxes flirt with minimalism, but the artist has also continued to make assemblage boxes, expanding on the simpler drawer boxes of the 1960s to more elaborate proscenium-stage boxes encrusted with jewel-like pebbles and stones. Later boxes often incorporate narrative elements.[3] "Palms, pocketbooks, packets of energy, conversations, rooms," Samaras's boxes are "intimate but quite lethal things"[4] that offer the viewer both invitation and dare.

LM

1.
Thomas McEvilley, "Intimate but Lethal Things: The Art of Lucas Samaras," in *Lucas Samaras Objects and Subjects 1969–1986*, Denver Art Museum and Abbeville Press, New York, 1988, pp. 18–23.
2.
John C. Siegfried, "On Peering into Lucas Samaras' Boxes," in *Lucas Samaras Boxes*, Museum of Contemporary Art, Chicago, 1971, n.p.
3.
Roberta Smith, "Repeated Exposures: Lucas Samaras in Three Dimensions," in *Lucas Samaras Objects and Subjects*, pp. 57–60.
4.
"On Boxes," in *Lucas Samaras*, Whitney Museum of American Art, New York, 1972, n.p.

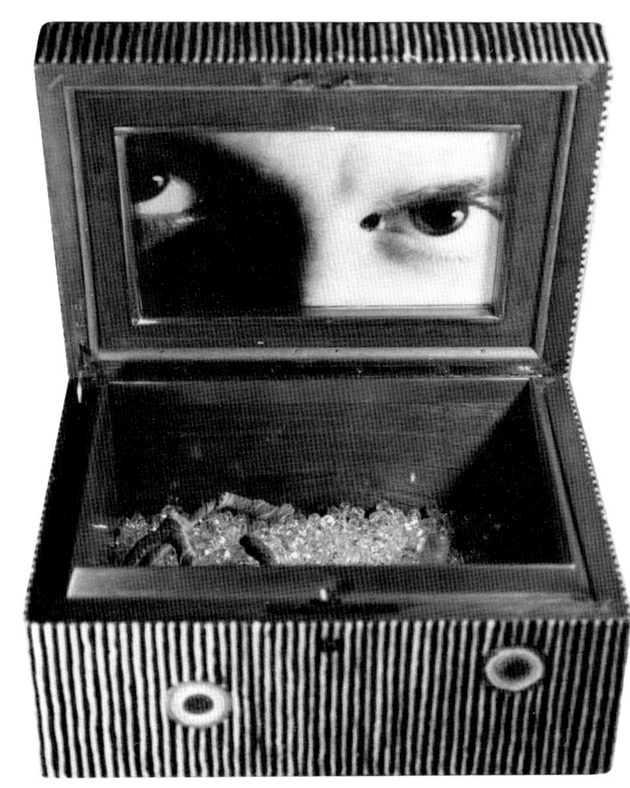

Agricola XXI, 1959
Steel, 40 × 32 × 11
Lent by Mr. and Mrs. Frederick Morgan

Although Smith died an untimely death at the height of his career, he had already created a body of work that established him as one of the most important sculptors of the postwar years. Born in Decatur, Indiana, Smith had little contact with art as he grew up in the Middle West. After deciding to become an artist at Ohio University in the mid-1920s, he attended the Art Students League in New York.

In 1929 when studying with the Czech constructivist painter Jan Matulka, Smith came to know the work of the Spanish artist Julio Gonzalez, one of the pioneers of abstract metal sculpture. Smith began making sculptures of found metal objects or soldered metal and started welding only in 1932.[1] Throughout his career Smith also produced drawings and paintings—frequently to help develop his ideas for sculptures.

Smith's first series of metal sculptures, called Medals for Dishonor, consisted of fifteen bronze medallions; the idea for these antiwar medals was inspired by the collection of war medals he had seen in the British Museum in 1936.[2] With his progression to large-scale works came his recognition as a metal sculptor.

In 1950 he started a series of sculptures with overall themes; the first of these was Agricola, from the Latin word for farmer, begun in 1951 in homage to agriculture. The series was created over nine years and consists of seventeen pieces, each incorporating tools or parts of farm machinery (the artist later added earlier works containing farm implements,[3] which explains the anomalous numbering). The sculptures were concerned with line and space but also alluded to the human form.

The Agricola series reflects as well Smith's admiration for classical art. Not only is the title of the series in Latin but Smith's signature on most of the pieces is inscribed in Greek. *Agricola XXI,* the next to last, was executed eight years later than most of the others in the series. Constructed of found steel farm machinery, the work plays with space in its compositional orchestration of forms: shapes inside the large circles repeat projections outside the circle. The work also suggests motion by the way different forms are interconnected.

BH

1.
Jorn Merkert (ed.), *David Smith: Sculpture and Drawings,* Prestel-Verlag, Munich, 1986, p. 14.
2.
David Smith, "Works by David Smith," *Artforum,* December 1979, p. 28.
3.
Merkert, p. 40.

Additional References
Gray, Cleve (ed.): *Sculpture and Writings by David Smith,* Thames and Hudson, London, 1968.
Marcus, Stanley E.: *David Smith: The Sculptor and His Work,* Cornell University Press, Ithaca, N.Y., and London, 1983.

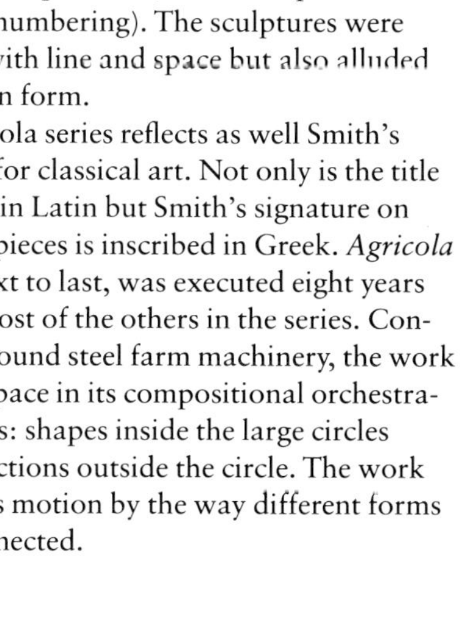

David Smith

1906–1965

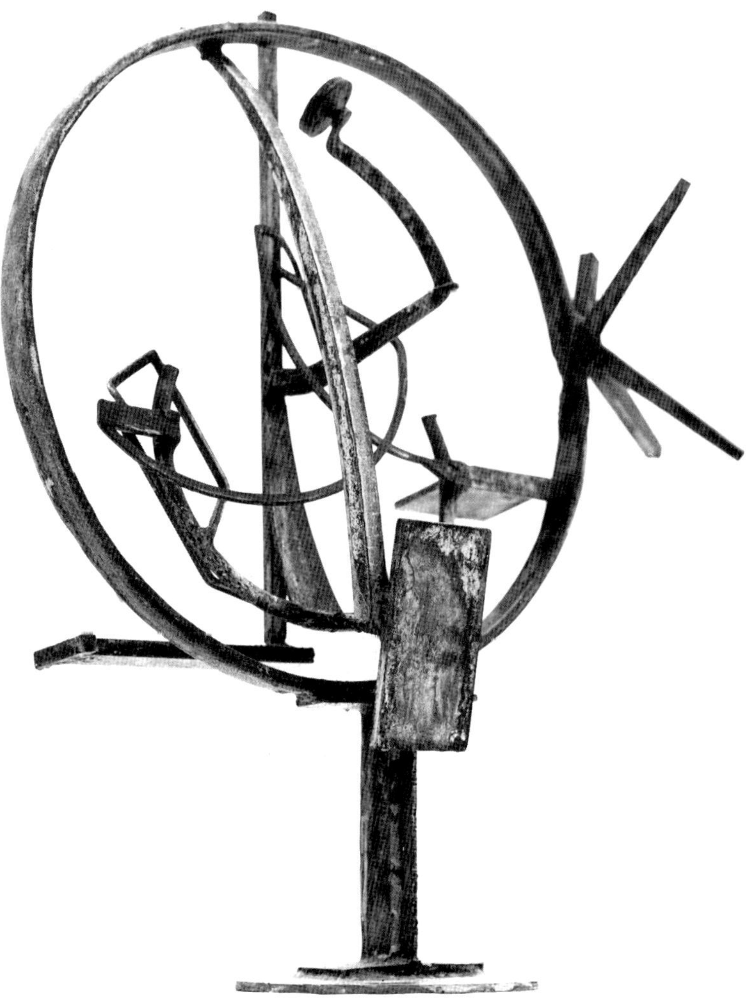

Ruth Vollmer

1903–1982

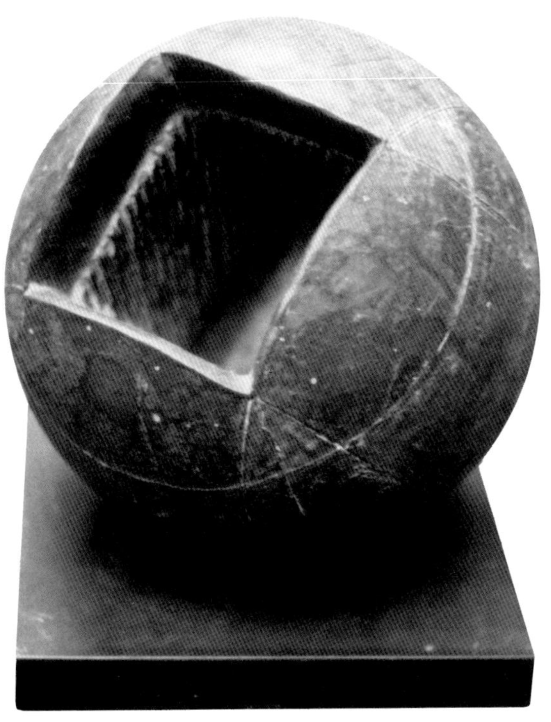

Sphere with Small Square, 1963
Bronze, 9½ diameter
Lent by Jane M. Timken

Ruth Vollmer grew up in Munich, the cultural center of Germany in the early 1900s. Since her family traveled extensively pursuing musical careers, her education was an informal one. In 1930 she married Hermann Vollmer, a pediatrician, and five years later they emigrated to the United States.

Vollmer played a key role in the New York art scene of the 1950s, and her home was a gathering place for young artists. Although she was older than the minimalists with whom she associated— Dan Flavin, Donald Judd, Carl Andre,* and Sol LeWitt*—she was often inspired by them.

Most of Vollmer's work is on a small scale and takes its cue from geometry. *Sphere with Small Square* is no exception. Vollmer describes her fascination with the sphere:

> ...the exploration of the sphere...leads me, in the process of working, deeper and deeper into myself; into my loves and idiosyncrasies in relation to this form. After I have made many pieces, in pursuit of exploring the sphere, I come out not understanding an iota more about this mysterious form than when I first started.[1]

The bronze sphere rests on an indentation of the base, so that it can be turned or removed. A square shaft with grooved sides offers entry into the core. Despite the powerful reduction of the form and the heaviness of the metal, the ball strikes the viewer as organic, with a spirit of its own. Its ability to move and be moved reinforces this quality and invites viewer involvement.

"Celebratory" and "romantic" are unusual words to find applied to the work of a minimalist, but they do in fact describe *Sphere with Small Square* with its rich patina and delicately textured surface. The small size of the work is belied by its geometric grandeur and sensual surface as it seems to address the issue of opposites and complements—convex and concave, male and female, active and passive. For the artist the shape of the sphere had an inherent mystery which she explored in numerous variations. Vollmer once said

> I can vaguely perceive a variety of manifestations: cosmic and earthly, biological and crystalline. But my concern while exploring the sphere is to maintain, not destroy the mystery.[2]

Sphere with Small Square helps us understand her fascination with this endlessly changing form.

VCK

1.
B.H. Friedman, "The Quiet World of Ruth Vollmer," *Art International,* July 1965, p. 29.
2.
Stephen Westfall, "Preserving the Mystery: The Art of Ruth Vollmer," *Arts Magazine,* February 1984, pp. 74–76.

Additional Reference
Storr, Robert: "Ruth Vollmer," *Art in America,* January 1984, pp. 128–129.

1.
Uncommon Ground: Virginia Artists 1990, Museum of Fine Arts, Richmond, October 23– December 16, 1990, p. 114.
2.
See David Kidd's description of a teahouse in Suzanne Slesin, Stafford Cliff, and Daniel Rozensztroch, *Japanese Style,* Clarkson N. Potter, Inc., New York, 1987, p. XI.

Additional References
Barbiero, Daniel: "Reviews," *New Art Examiner,* June 1987, p. 49.
Borum, Jenifer P.: "Yuriko Yamaguchi: Penine Hart Gallery," *Artforum,* January 1990, p. 142.
Laget, Mokha: "Reviews," *New Art Examiner,* Summer 1989, p. 44.

Origin #1, 1989
Wood, wire, and glass jars, 64 × 84 × 9½
Smith College Museum of Art, purchased with funds from the National Endowment for the Arts and Museum Members

Yuriko Yamaguchi's wall assemblage of polychromed wood, glass jars, and wire is a delight to contemplate and a challenge to understand. Presented with the artist's personal language, the viewer is invited to decode this mixture of universal symbols (plus and minus signs) and familiar shapes whose significance seems just out of reach, as if they had once been part of a common human vocabulary now forgotten.

Many of the symbols in *Origin #1* (bean-shaped objects in the upper part, for example) speak of life and, judging by their presentation, life's preciousness. These forms have been lovingly shaped of wood; like a baby's skin, their smooth surfaces invite a caress. As our eyes move from left to right, the creations are transformed but remain cradled in unchanging supports while the metamorphosis continues. Below, the objects in the glass jars seem to be alive or waiting to come to life, protected and nourished in a warm safe place. Here, too, the theme of renewal is foremost.

Much of this work addresses the question of opposites; plus and minus, life and death, light and dark, rest and activity. The shapes of the objects themselves reflect these differences, and their arrangement suggests an orderly world: everything has its place; each object relates to its neighbors. These relationships give the separate objects their identities. *Origin #1* is part of a large body of Yamaguchi's ongoing work which she calls Shapes as the Integral Parts of Proving My Physical and Spiritual Existence.

> My work is a transposition of my intense feeling for nature and the universe, and an expression of both its mystery and its immutable laws. My sculpture is about the divine nature that is behind the myth of life and the psychological tension I experience in my life. I want my sculpture to be both a visual poem and a meditation evoking universal themes.[1]

Yamaguchi was born in Japan, where she spent her childhood. Interested in western art, she studied design at Osaka Junior College. When she came to the United States in 1971, she took up painting in the belief that sculpture would be physically impossible to manage. In graduate school at the University of Maryland, however, when she began to add pieces of rope and fabric to her canvases, her teacher encouraged her to explore three-dimensional work. She took up woodcarving, which has been her main interest ever since.

Although familiar with western cultural history, Yamaguchi still retains a Japanese sensibility. The stark, simple beauty of her work recalls the perfection of traditional Japanese interiors.[2] Yamaguchi's work displays a reverence for order and cleanliness and a sensitivity to the use of the perfect object for a particular occasion. A spirituality pervades her work, a respect for solitude and quiet. In a meditative state of mind Yamaguchi creates the forms and puts them together to express her feelings about her origins. So too the viewer attempts to put together the pieces of the puzzle to understand the essence of *Origin #1.*
VCK

Yuriko Yamaguchi

Born 1948

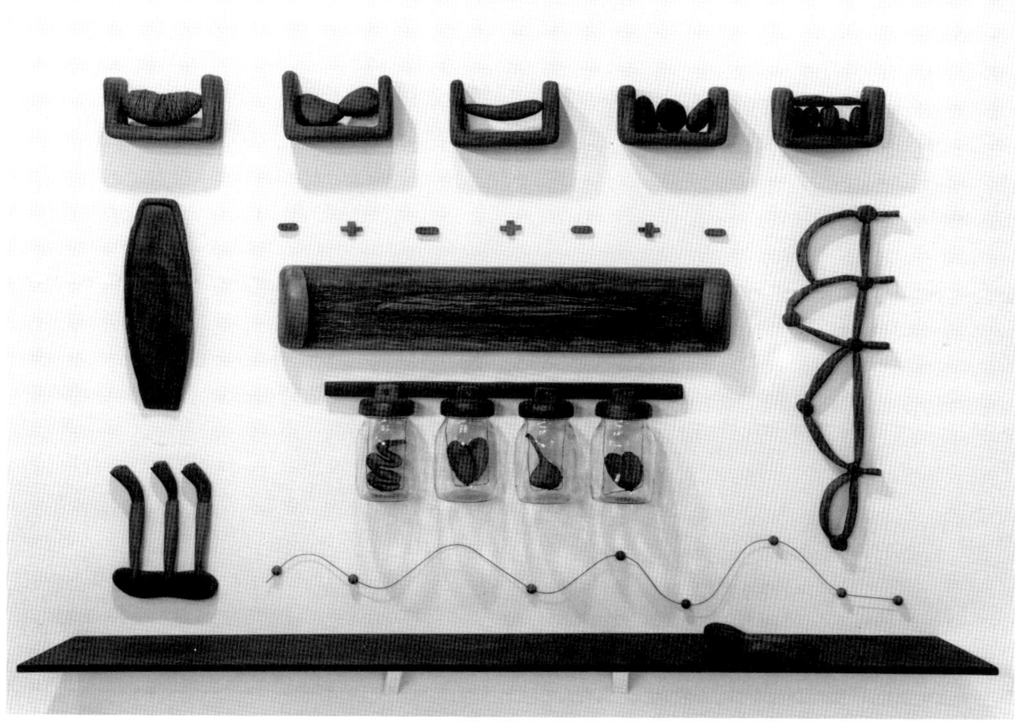

Index of Artists

SMITH COLLECTS CONTEMPORARY

was designed by Gilbert Associates and
printed by Garamond Pridemark Press on
Gleneagle paper.

The principal type is Sabon, designed by Jan
Tschichold, with Hans Meyer's Syntax bold.

1500 copies for the Smith College
Museum of Art.

May 1991